Communications
in Computer and Information Science 1816

Rationale

The CCIS series is devoted to the publication of proceedings of computer science conferences. Its aim is to efficiently disseminate original research results in informatics in printed and electronic form. While the focus is on publication of peer-reviewed full papers presenting mature work, inclusion of reviewed short papers reporting on work in progress is welcome, too. Besides globally relevant meetings with internationally representative program committees guaranteeing a strict peer-reviewing and paper selection process, conferences run by societies or of high regional or national relevance are also considered for publication.

Topics

The topical scope of CCIS spans the entire spectrum of informatics ranging from foundational topics in the theory of computing to information and communications science and technology and a broad variety of interdisciplinary application fields.

Information for Volume Editors and Authors

Publication in CCIS is free of charge. No royalties are paid, however, we offer registered conference participants temporary free access to the online version of the conference proceedings on SpringerLink (http://link.springer.com) by means of an http referrer from the conference website and/or a number of complimentary printed copies, as specified in the official acceptance email of the event.

CCIS proceedings can be published in time for distribution at conferences or as post-proceedings, and delivered in the form of printed books and/or electronically as USBs and/or e-content licenses for accessing proceedings at SpringerLink. Furthermore, CCIS proceedings are included in the CCIS electronic book series hosted in the SpringerLink digital library at http://link.springer.com/bookseries/7899. Conferences publishing in CCIS are allowed to use Online Conference Service (OCS) for managing the whole proceedings lifecycle (from submission and reviewing to preparing for publication) free of charge.

Publication process

The language of publication is exclusively English. Authors publishing in CCIS have to sign the Springer CCIS copyright transfer form, however, they are free to use their material published in CCIS for substantially changed, more elaborate subsequent publications elsewhere. For the preparation of the camera-ready papers/files, authors have to strictly adhere to the Springer CCIS Authors' Instructions and are strongly encouraged to use the CCIS LaTeX style files or templates.

Abstracting/Indexing

CCIS is abstracted/indexed in DBLP, Google Scholar, EI-Compendex, Mathematical Reviews, SCImago, Scopus. CCIS volumes are also submitted for the inclusion in ISI Proceedings.

How to start

To start the evaluation of your proposal for inclusion in the CCIS series, please send an e-mail to ccis@springer.com.

Anita Bartulović · Linda Mijić · Max Silberztein
Editors

Formalizing Natural Languages: Applications to Natural Language Processing and Digital Humanities

17th International Conference, NooJ 2023
Zadar, Croatia, May 31 – June 2, 2023
Revised Selected Papers

Springer

Editors
Anita Bartulović
University of Zadar
Zadar, Croatia

Linda Mijić
University of Zadar
Zadar, Croatia

Max Silberztein ⓘ
Université de Franche-Comté
Besançon, France

ISSN 1865-0929   ISSN 1865-0937 (electronic)
Communications in Computer and Information Science
ISBN 978-3-031-56645-5   ISBN 978-3-031-56646-2 (eBook)
https://doi.org/10.1007/978-3-031-56646-2

This Springer imprint is published by the registered company Springer Nature Switzerland AG
The registered company address is: Gewerbestrasse 11, 6330 Cham, Switzerland

Paper in this product is recyclable.

In Honor of Peter Machonis

The alumni of Maurice Gross's LADL laboratory and the international NooJ teams around Max Silberztein are deeply saddened to announce the death at the age of 71 of our colleague and friend Professor Peter Aloysius Machonis of the Department of French and Linguistics at Florida International University, who passed away on March 8, 2023, after an eleven-year battle with a long and painful illness.

Peter, who obtained his PhD in 1982 from the University of Pennsylvania, joined Florida International University in 1983. Since 2005, he was Director of French and Francophone Studies.

His research focused on two areas. In the fields of "history of the French language" and "varieties of French outside France", he published over thirty articles and book chapters, as well as two books: *Histoire de la langue : du latin à l'ancien français* (1990, University Press), *Le Moyen Français : évolution de la langue* (2005, Presses Universitaires du Nouveau Monde) and an important book chapter in *Les variétés du français parlé dans l'espace francophone : ressources pour l'enseignement* about "French in North America" (2010, Ophrys Editions). The first two are remarkable summations of the evolution of French (first phonological and morphological, then syntactic in the case of the second, extending to the history of grammar), an interest that Peter retained from his youth at the Catho d'Angers. His contribution in the third book is the result of fieldwork, which he also encouraged his students to undertake. His second line of research began in the early 1980s, when Peter joined Maurice Gross's LADL laboratory, which directed him towards syntactic research on English and the development of the English lexicon-grammar. His work in this field also led him to be interested in the problem of "neutral" or ergative verbs, for which he built the corresponding tables, which contain 500 verbal entries (compared with 400 for French).

More recently, Peter turned his attention to the problem of phrasal verbs (which has recently again aroused a great deal of interest throughout the linguistic and computational-linguistic community): he produced a set of 1,200 verb entries formalized with the linguistic platform NooJ, which enabled him to identify around 300 compositional phrasal verbs, where the particle appears to bring an aspectual element (completeness/intensity/directionality) to the simple verb.

Professor Peter A. Machonis was the only representative of the lexicon-grammar approach in North America: he always tackled problems that are difficult to analyze linguistically (hence the many applications of his research in Natural Language Processing) and that present difficulty for non-English speakers. In this respect, he won international recognition at the scientific conferences in which he has taken part, including the *NooJ* and the *Lexiques-Grammaires comparés* conferences. At the same time, his work demonstrates a definite mastery of major linguistic issues, including the latest and those that have occupied linguists from time immemorial.

Peter was always appreciated by all his colleagues and students, whom he loved to teach. His absence is and will be deeply felt by the entire academic community in the United States, France and the world.

Mireille Piot

Editors' Preface

NooJ is a linguistic development environment that provides tools for linguists to develop linguistic resources that formalize a large gamut of linguistic phenomena: typography, orthography, lexicons for simple words, multiword units and discontinuous expressions, inflectional, derivational and agglutinative morphology, local, phrase-structure and dependency grammars, as well as transformational and semantic grammars.

To describe each type of linguistic phenomenon, NooJ offers formalisms that cover the extent of Chomsky-Schützenberger's hierarchy: regular grammars, context-free grammars, context-sensitive grammars and unrestricted grammars. Grammars can then be applied to texts automatically by NooJ's parsers, which range from very efficient finite-state automata and transducers to very powerful Turing Machines. This makes NooJ's approach different from most other computational linguistic tools that offer a unique formalism to their users and are not compatible with each other. NooJ contains a rich toolbox that allows linguists to construct, test, debug, maintain, accumulate and share large linguistic resources.

NooJ parsers can apply any set of linguistic resources to any corpus of texts, to extract examples or counterexamples, annotate matching sequences, perform statistical analyses and so on. Because NooJ's linguistic resources are neutral, they can also be used by NooJ to generate texts automatically. By combining NooJ's parsers and generators, one can construct sophisticated software applications, such as automatic machine translation, semantic analysis and paraphrasing software.

Since its first release in 2002, several private companies have used NooJ's linguistic engine to construct business applications in several domains, from Business Intelligence to Opinion Analysis. To date, there are NooJ modules available for over 50 languages. In 2013, an open-source version for NooJ was released, based on the Java technology and available to all as a GPL project and supported and distributed by the European Metashare platform. The NooJ platform is in constant evolution:

(1) NooJ has been recently enhanced with new features to respond to the needs of researchers who analyze texts in various domains of Human and Social Sciences (history, literature and political studies, psychology, sociology, etc.), and more generally of all the professionals who need to explore their corpus of texts and perform some discourse analyses. An interface specifically designed for the Digital Humanities has been implemented in the ATISHS software, see: https://atishs.univ-fcomte.fr.

(2) The new linguistic engine for NooJ "RA" was presented to the participants of the NooJ 2022 conference. It is open-source, written in the Swift programming language, is available on the Gitlab platform and is compatible with the LINUX, macOS and Windows platforms. It can be downloaded from: https://www.nooj4nlp.org/downloads.html.

(3) Using the linguistic engine "RA", a new Web interface for NooJ, specifically developed for teaching Corpus linguistics and Text Analysis, is now available at: http://webnooj.univ-fcomte.fr.

This volume contains 19 articles selected from the 38 papers that were selected by the conference scientific committee and presented at the NooJ International Conference 2023, organized at the *University of Zadar* in Croatia, May 31st – June 2nd.

The following articles are organized in four parts: "Morphological and Lexical Resources", "Syntactic and Semantic Resources", "Corpus Linguistics and Discourse Analysis" and "Natural Language Processing Applications".

The four articles in the first part involve the construction of electronic dictionaries and morphological grammars to formalize various linguistic phenomena in several languages.

In "NooJ Dictionary for Rromani: Importing of an Editorial Dictionary to the NooJ System", Masako Watabe shows how she used an existing editorial dictionary for Rromani, i.e., a dictionary meant to be used by people, to construct an electronic dictionary, i.e., a database that contains formalized linguistic properties and can thus be processed by automatic linguistic software. The process mainly involved making some information explicit and consistent; the new available electronic dictionary covers the four dialects of Rromani.

In "Latin Pronouns, Numerals and Prepositions in the NooJ Tool", Anita Bartulović and Linda Mijić present a new set of linguistic resources for Medieval Latin, which consists of an electronic dictionary as well a set of morphological grammars to formalize the inflection of pronouns and numerals. The authors showed how they used syntactic grammars to extract prepositional phrases from a corpus of Medieval Latin.

In "Towards a Linguistic Annotation of Arabic Legal Texts: A Multilingual Electronic Dictionary for Arabic", Khadija Ait ElFqih, Maria Pia Di Buono and Johanna Monti show that the lack of terminological data in the legal domain makes most machine translation systems fail to produce correct translations. The authors show that by using syntactic grammars, they were able to extract terms from legal texts and construct an electronic dictionary associated with some morphological information. They then added the translation of each entry. The resulting dictionary can be used to annotate legal texts in Arabic automatically.

In "Recognition of Frozen Expressions in Belarusian NooJ Module", Yauheniya Zianouka, David Latyshevich, Mikita Suprunchuk and Yuras Hetsevich present a new electronic dictionary of phraseological units in Belarusian. They show how this dictionary can be used to perform various computations automatically, including to improve applications related to speech delimitation and production.

The six articles in the second part involve the construction of syntactic and transformational grammars.

In "A Proposal for the Processing of the Nucleus Verb Phrase of Pronominal (SVNPr) Verbs in Spanish", Andrea Fernanda Rodrigo, Rodolfo Bonino and Silvia Susana Reyes address the problem of formalizing adjectives, adverbs and verbs in the context of pedagogical applications that aim at teaching Argentinian Rioplatense Spanish as a second language; in particular, they had to develop a specific set of morphological resources to formalize pronominal verbs. To test the new linguistic resources, they constructed a corpus of Rioplatense Spanish.

In "German *selbst*-Compounds: Towards a NooJ Grammar", Marco Angster presents a new grammar that can be used to analyze German *selbst*-compounds. He evaluated the grammars by applying them to a large Web-based corpus of German.

In "Disambiguation Grammars for the Ukrainian Module", Olena Saint-Joanis proposes a classification of grammatical homonyms in Ukrainian and presents a corresponding set of syntactic grammars that can be used to automatically perform some morpho-syntactic disambiguation of Ukrainian words.

In "Automatic Disambiguation of the Belarusian-Russian Legal Parallel Corpus in NooJ", Valery Varanovich, Mikita Suprunchuk, Yauheniya Zianouka and Yuras Hetsevich address the problems of the massive ambiguity of many terms in Belarusian legal codes. As Russian and Belarusian are the two official languages in Belarus, all law codes must be translated from Russian to Belarusian. A first automatic process produces results that contain ambiguities, which need to be solved by professional translators, linguists and legal experts. However, some ambiguities can be solved automatically using syntactic grammars: the authors present these grammars.

In "Syntactic-Semantic Analysis of Perception Verbs in the Croatian Language", Daša Farkaš and Kristina Kocijan study the verbs of perception in Croatian using a corpus-based approach. They selected 86 verbs and classified them into five semantic classes. They described these verbs, their class and their properties in an electronic dictionary. Then, they automatically applied the dictionary to various texts, recognizing and annotating over 200,000 verbal forms of perception, which they validated.

In "NooJ Grammars for Morphophonemic Continuity and Semantic Discontinuity", Mario Monteleone studies the phenomenon of Morphophonemic Continuity (MC) which connects pairs of support verb + predicative noun/adjective with the corresponding simple sentences, e.g., *Max ha adorazione per Maria = Max adora Maria*. He then presents a set of syntactic grammars to describe (support verb – predicative noun) associations and produce the corresponding simple sentences automatically.

The three articles in the third part, "Corpus Linguistics and Discourse Analysis", discuss the construction and the exploration of large corpora of texts as well as the implementation of various discourse analyses.

In "Explicit Language in English Song Lyrics: Should We Be Concerned?", Mila Bikić and Valerija Bočkaj have collected a corpus of 300 English song lyrics from six genres of music (pop, rock, etc.), artists' gender and dates (from the 1950s to the 2000s). They developed a set of linguistic resources and syntactic grammar to identify profane words and phrases, applied these resources to the corpus of lyrics, and then studied the distribution of profanity in songs, across genres of music, gender of artists and decades.

In "Immigrant in the Light of Language Production", Barbara Vodanović studies the semantic usage of the term "immigrant" in the Croatian newspaper *Jutrarnji list* from 30 August 2015 to 17 January 2023. She developed a set of syntactic grammars to characterize this term and its partial synonyms and collocates and applied them to the corpus to perform a statistical analysis of its occurrences.

In "Semantic Analysis of Migrants' Self-Entrepreneurship Ecosystem Narratives", Cecilia Olivieri, Lorenzo Maggio Laquidara and Agathe Semlali show how NooJ can be used as a powerful tool in socio-linguistic studies. By analyzing a corpus consisting of semi-structured interviews, they conducted a series of operations to identify congruence patterns, overlapping expressions, divergence patterns and low occurrences and showed that NooJ-powered discourse analysis makes it possible to aid qualitative methods with quantitative assessments, heralding promising developments in computational sociolinguistics.

The last section, dedicated to the presentation of various Natural Language Processing Applications, contains the following six articles.

In "Deciphering the Nomenclature of Chemical Compounds in NooJ", Kristina Kocijan, Krešimir Šojat and Tomislav Portada present an algorithm for the automatic recognition of chemical compound names in Croatian. The algorithm uses three levels of linguistic resources: a dictionary, a morphological grammar and a syntactic grammar. The algorithm recognizes various variations of chemical names.

In his article "SANTI-Network Prototype of an Indonesian Multi-Level Tagger", Prihantoro presents the prototype of a multi-level tagger for Indonesian capable of performing morphological, morpho-syntactic and semantic annotations in a single pass. NooJ users can now apply morphological-POS-semantic searches on texts previously parsed with this tagger.

In "NooJ Linguistic Resources for Paraphrase Generation of Italian Support Verb Construction", Nicola Cirillo proposes a formal strategy to produce paraphrases of support verb constructions, based on the notion of *lexical function*. He developed an Italian dictionary and a transformational grammar that can perform automatic paraphrase generation of Italian support-verb sentences.

In "Spelling Error Detection and Correction for Arabic Using NooJ", Rafik Kassmi, Samir Mbarki and Abdelaziz Mouloudi present an implementation of a spell checker for Arabic. After classifying the various types of spelling errors, they present the spell checker prototype (Al Mudaqiq), the grammars they developed to detect spelling errors, as well as the grammar that produces the corresponding potential corrections. Finally, they present an improved algorithm to rank these correction candidates. Then, they present a Web interface of their prototype and perform some tests and evaluations.

In "Automatic Translation of Continuous and Fixed Arabic Frozen Expressions Using the NooJ Platform", Asmaa Kourtin and Samir Mbarki address the problem of translating frozen expressions from Arabic to English and French. They enhanced the existing lexicon-grammar tables of Arabic frozen expressions by adding their French and English translations; then, they converted these lexicon-grammar tables into NooJ, which makes it possible for NooJ to recognize these frozen expressions in Arabic texts and then translate them automatically. Finally, they evaluate the translator through various testing on diverse texts.

In "The Automatic Translation of Arabic Psychological Verbs Using the NooJ Platform", Asmaa Amzali and Mohammed Mourchid study psychological verbs in English and Arabic, highlighting the points of convergence and divergence between the two languages and developing a dictionary of about 400 psychological verbs. Then, they propose a methodology to develop an automatic translator for Arabic psychological verbs. Finally, they evaluate the translator by applying it to several texts.

This volume should be of interest to all users of the NooJ software because it presents the latest development of its linguistic resources, as well as a large variety of new applications, both in the Digital Humanities and in Natural Language Processing.

Linguists, as well as Computational Linguists who work on Arabic, Belarusian, Croatian, English, Latin, Indonesian, Italian or Spanish, will find advanced, up-to-the-minute linguistic studies for these languages.

We think that the reader will appreciate the importance of this volume, both for the intrinsic value of each linguistic formalization and the underlying methodology, as well as for the potential for developing NLP applications along with linguistic-based corpus processors in the Social Sciences.

The Editors

Organization

Scientific Committee

Max Silberztein (Chair)   Université de Bourgogne Franche-Comté, France
Marco Angster   University of Zadar, Croatia
Farida Aoughlis   Mouloud Mammeri University, Algeria
Anabela Barreiro   INESC-ID, Portugal
Anita Bartulović   University of Zadar, Croatia
Magali Bigey   Université de Franche-Comté, France
Xavier Blanco   Autonomous University of Barcelona, Spain
Krzysztof Bogacki   University of Warsaw, Poland
Christian Boitet   Université Joseph Fourier, France
Héla Fehri   University of Sfax, Tunisia
Zoe Gavriilidou   Democritus University of Thrace, Greece
Yuras Hetsevich   National Academy of Sciences, Belarus
Kristina Kocijan   University of Zagreb, Croatia
Walter Koza   National University of General Sarmiento, Argentina
Philippe Lambert   Université de Lorraine, France
Laetitia Leonarduzzi   Université d'Aix-Marseille, France
Peter Machonis   Florida International University, USA
Ignazio Mauro Mirto   University of Palermo, Italy
Samir Mbarki   Ibn Tofail University, Morocco
Slim Mesfar   University of Manouba, Tunisia
Elisabeth Métais   Conservatoire National des Arts et Métiers, France
Linda Mijić   University of Zadar, Croatia
Michelangelo Misuraca   University of Calabria, Italy
Mario Monteleone   University of Salerno, Italy
Johanna Monti   University of Naples "L'Orientale", Italy
Thierry Poibeau   Laboratoire Lattice, CNRS, France
Jan Radimský   University of South Bohemia, Czech Republic
Andrea Rodrigo   University of Rosario, Argentina
Marko Tadić   University of Zagreb, Croatia
Izabella Thomas   Université de Franche-Comté, France
Marijana Tomić   University of Zadar, Croatia

François Trouilleux   Université Clermont Auvergne, France
Agnès Tutin   Université Grenoble Alpes, France
Agata Jackiewicz   Université Paul Valéry Montpellier, France

Organizing Committee

Linda Mijić   University of Zadar, Croatia
Anita Bartulović   University of Zadar, Croatia
Marijana Tomić   University of Zadar, Croatia
Laura Grzunov   University of Zadar, Croatia
Kristina Kocijan   University of Zagreb, Croatia
Max Silberztein   Université de Bourgogne Franche-Comté, France

Contents

Corpus Linguistics and Discourse Analysis

Natural Language Processing Applications

Contributors

Asmaa Amzali Science Research Laboratory, Faculty of Science, Ibn Tofail University, Kenitra, Morocco

Marco Angster University of Zadar, Zadar, Croatia

Anita Bartulović Department of Classical Philology, University of Zadar, Zadar, Croatia

Mila Bikić Faculty of Humanities and Social Sciences, University of Zagreb, Zagreb, Croatia

Rodolfo Bonino CETEHIPL, IES "Olga Cossettini", Rosario, Argentina

Valerija Bočkaj Faculty of Humanities and Social Sciences, University of Zagreb, Zagreb, Croatia

Maria Pia Di Buono UNIOR NLP Research Group, University of Naples 'L'Orientale', Naples, Italy

Nicola Cirillo University of Salerno, Fisciano, SA, Italy

Khadija Ait ElFqih UNIOR NLP Research Group, University of Naples 'L'Orientale', Naples, Italy

Daša Farkaš Department of Linguistics, Faculty of Humanities and Social Sciences, University of Zagreb, Zagreb, Croatia

Yuras Hetsevich United Institute of Informatics Problems of the National Academy of Sciences of Belarus, Minsk, Belarus

Rafik Kassmi EDPAGS Laboratory, Department of Computer Science, Faculty of Science, Ibn Tofail University, Kénitra, Morocco

Kristina Kocijan Department of Information and Communication Sciences, Faculty of Humanities and Social Sciences, University of Zagreb, Zagreb, Croatia

Asmaa Kourtin Computer Science Research Laboratory, Faculty of Science, Ibn Tofail University, Kenitra, Morocco

Lorenzo Maggio Laquidara X23 – Science in Society, Treviglio, Italy

David Latyshevich United Institute of Informatics Problems of the National Academy of Sciences of Belarus, Minsk, Belarus

Samir Mbarki EDPAGS Laboratory, Department of Computer Science, Faculty of Science, Ibn Tofail University, Kénitra, Morocco;
EDPAGS Laboratory, Faculty of Science, Ibn Tofail University, Kenitra, Morocco

Linda Mijić Department of Classical Philology, University of Zadar, Zadar, Croatia

Mario Monteleone Università degli Studi di Salerno, Fisciano, SA, Italy

Johanna Monti UNIOR NLP Research Group, University of Naples 'L'Orientale', Naples, Italy

Abdelaziz Mouloudi EDPAGS Laboratory, Department of Computer Science, Faculty of Science, Ibn Tofail University, Kénitra, Morocco

Mohammed Mourchid Science Research Laboratory, Faculty of Science, Ibn Tofail University, Kenitra, Morocco

Cecilia Olivieri X23 – Science in Society, Treviglio, Italy

Tomislav Portada Ruđer Bošković Institute, Zagreb, Croatia

Prihantoro Universitas Diponegoro, Semarang, Indonesia

Silvia Susana Reyes Facultad de Humanidades y Artes, CETEHIPL, Universidad Nacional de Rosario, Rosario, Argentina

Andrea Fernanda Rodrigo Facultad de Humanidades y Artes, CETEHIPL, Universidad Nacional de Rosario, Rosario, Argentina

Olena Saint-Joanis University Bourgogne Franche-Comté, Besançon, France; CREE, INALCO, Paris, France

Agathe Semlali X23 – Science in Society, Treviglio, Italy

Krešimir Šojat Department of Linguistics, Faculty of Humanities and Social Sciences, University of Zagreb, Zagreb, Croatia

Mikita Suprunchuk Minsk State Linguistic University, Minsk, Belarus; United Institute of Informatics Problems of the National Academy of Sciences of Belarus, Minsk, Belarus

Valery Varanovich Belarusian State University, Minsk, Belarus

Barbara Vodanović University of Zadar, Zadar, Croatia

Masako Watabe University of Franche-Comté, C.R.I.T., Besançon, France

Yauheniya Zianouka United Institute of Informatics Problems of the National Academy of Sciences of Belarus, Minsk, Belarus

Morphological and Lexical Resources

SANTI-Network Prototype of an Indonesian Multi-level Tagger

Prihantoro(⊠)

Universitas Diponegoro, Semarang, Indonesia
prihantoro@live.undip.ac.id

Abstract. A multi-level tagger (MLT) to annotate Indonesian texts is crucial for corpus-based analyses. Prior to implementing the creation of such an MLT, a prototype is required as a model. The primary objective of this project is to develop a prototype of an Indonesian MLT that enables users to perform morphological, morphosyntactic (POS) and semantic annotation in a single pass using NooJ [1]. Currently, two NooJ-based Indonesian taggers are available: SANTI-morf (morphology) and SANTI-POS (morphosyntax). Note that no automatic semantic tagger is available for the Indonesian language; thus, semantic annotation functionality needs to be created and evaluated; these are subsidiary aims. Even though NooJ-based Indonesian morphological and POS (and later semantic) analysis systems are available, users cannot apply multiple tagging in one pass. The prototype is expected to demonstrate how to perform morphology-POS-semantic annotation in one pass. To fulfill the aims of this study, I implemented the following methodological procedure. I initially augmented selected SANTI-POS lexical entries (more than 400) with semantic analysis labels (using the USAS tagset). For this prototype, only the first semantic analysis label was considered. Then, the lexicon was included in NooJ resources, alongside SANTI-POS and SANTI-morf resources. A prototype was successfully created. The average precision, coverage and ambiguity rates of the prototype are 85%, 86% and 15%, respectively. Users can now tag a corpus with this MLT prototype and perform morphological-POS-semantic searches.

Keywords: Indonesian · Annotation · Morphology · POS · Semantic · Corpus · NooJ

1 Introduction

This study was motivated by the need for a multi-level tagger (MLT) capable of performing not just one but multiple forms of linguistic annotation on Indonesian texts. Such a tool ideally allows users to perform various linguistic annotation forms in a single system and in one pass, such as NooJ [1], Stanza [2] and Stanford Core NLP [3], among many others.

There are at least two main challenges to creating such a system: interoperability and availability. Several studies have shown that some taggers for Indonesian are available for use, but they only offer annotation for one type of linguistic analysis. TLM-Ina

© The Author(s), under exclusive license to Springer Nature Switzerland AG 2024
A. Bartulović et al. (Eds.): NooJ 2023, CCIS 1816, pp. 3–15, 2024.
https://doi.org/10.1007/978-3-031-56646-2_1

[4] and SANTI-morf [5–8] are systems that offer automatic morphological annotation. Other systems, namely IPOSTagger [9], TreeTagger [10] and SANTI-POS,[1] offer morphosyntactic analyses. An exception is MorphInd [11], which offers both morphological and morphosyntactic annotation but not semantic. As both SANTI-morf and SANTI-POS are built on the same platform, NooJ, they are potentially interoperable from an interoperability standpoint. However, to date, there is no best practice on how to merge two analytic systems in NooJ.

If one wishes to combine systems that were developed on distinct platforms, it is necessary to execute a number of thorough integration procedures. Integrating two systems on the same platform poses methodological challenges, as well. Even though SANTI-morf and SANTI-POS are built on NooJ, users cannot utilize both systems simultaneously. Two analyses cannot be performed in one pass.

In terms of availability, we can only merge what we have. Note that none of the systems listed above offer meaning or semantic annotation. Even if sophisticated tools and procedures to combine existing systems were available, they would never be able to offer semantic annotation. This is true as there are several well-known MLTs for the Indonesian, such as Stanza [2] and Aksara [12], but none include semantic analysis. In addition, morphological analyses in two systems are provided at the word level, as opposed to the morpheme level, as in SANTI-morf.

The current state implies at least three gaps. First, no system currently offers semantic annotation for the Indonesian. Saelan and Purwarianti [13] generated a Mind Map Generator, which includes the "semantic" analysis. The analysis provided, however, is predicate-argument semantics, which includes syntactic analysis. This is in contrast to the semantic analysis targeted in this project (see Sect. 3), which is unrelated to syntax. Second, for Indonesian, no system can perform morphological, POS/morphosyntactic and semantic annotation in a single pass. Thirdly, morphological and morphosyntactic analyses (and semantic, when available) for Indonesian in NooJ have not yet been merged.

These circumstances translate into the three aims of this study. First, it aims to make the semantic annotation for Indonesian available as a prototype using NooJ. Note that none of the current tools has the capability to do so.

The second objective of this study is to propose a method for combining morphological, morphosyntactic and semantic analyses in NooJ for Indonesian. While other MLTs exist, such as Stanza, Stanford Core NLP and Aksara, semantic annotation capabilities have never been implemented for the Indonesian language. In addition, no project in the NooJ community has ever incorporated these three functionalities.

Attainment of the first two objectives is required to accomplish the third one: to create a SANTI-network, a prototype MLT that can provide morphological, morphosyntactic and semantic annotation in a single pass using the NooJ platform and to evaluate its performance. Such an MLT has never been created in NooJ before, and so the prototype can potentially serve as best practice within the NooJ community.

This study has a number of important implications and makes several valuable contributions. First, the prototype will demonstrate how users can annotate Indonesian texts with the MLT prototype and conduct morphological, morphosyntactic and semantic

---

[1] Available at: https://nooj.univ-fcomte.fr/resources.html (last accessed 2023/08/28).

searches or any combination thereof, simultaneously. Second, it helps to advance Indonesian NLP research by allowing the prototype to be developed into a fully operational system that can be used in downstream applications for information retrieval, text profiling and sentiment analysis, among many others. Third, it is a significant methodological approach for the NooJ community because it provides a previously unseen procedure for integrating multiple systems.

2 Methods

To fulfill the first aim, I first enhanced the SANTI-POS lexicon with semantic analyses. The SANTI-POS lexicon was selected because it focuses its analyses at the word token level, which is the token level at which semantic analyses will be incorporated. Of all the entries, I purposively selected high-frequency entries to be enhanced. The selection criterion is based on the analysis of the frequency lists in three Indonesian corpora in CQPweb Lancaster[2] (LCC Indonesian 2023,[3] BPPT-PAN Indonesian[4] and UI-1M[5]). Only words with a relative frequency of more than 50.00 PMW (per million words) were selected (proper nouns were excluded).

The preference for the USAS tagset over other tagsets is due to the fact that the USAS tagset has been implemented to create a semantic annotation system for not only Indonesian.[6] But also numerous other languages, including English, Spanish, Portuguese and Urdu. See Rayson's W-Matrix [14].

The lexicon was subsequently transformed into a NooJ POS+ semantic dictionary for Indonesian. In addition, several NooJ grammars were created. By combining resources, a system for the automatic semantic annotation of Indonesian was developed. This accomplishes the underlying aim of this project.

In order to accomplish the second and third objectives, a number of resource-merging strategies were tested to enable the completion of all forms of annotation in a single pass. This was accomplished by modifying and remodifying NooJ's resource configuration until the objectives were met with the greatest efficiency (fewest resources and steps). Once the prototype was fully functional, it was applied to a testbed corpus (10k+ tokens, randomly selected sentences from LCC Indonesian 2023), and its precision, coverage and ambiguity rate were evaluated.

---

[2] https://cqpweb.lancs.ac.uk/usr/index.php?ui=welcome (last accessed 2023/08/28).

[3] Available at: https://cqpweb.lancs.ac.uk/lccindonesianv3/ (last accessed 2023/08/28).

[4] Available at: https://cqpweb.lancs.ac.uk/bpptpanid/ (last accessed 2023/08/28).

[5] Available at: https://cqpweb.lancs.ac.uk/ui1m/ (last accessed 2023/08/28).

[6] In parallel, I am working closely with Prof. Paul Rayson to create a statistical semantic tagger for the Indonesian using the USAS tagset.

3   Findings and Discussions

3.1   Semantic Annotation

The semantic annotation scheme adhered to in this project is USAS, as used in W-Matrix [14], whose tagset is available online in the USAS repository.[7] As stated in Sect. 2, more than 400 entries were chosen for inclusion in the semantic lexicon prototype. Each lexical item is followed by a tab and a semantic lexicon analysis label, encoded explicitly, as shown in Table 1.

Table 1. Semantic lexicon of Indonesian for the USAS semantic tagger (sample).

Word	POS Tag	Headword	Semantic Tag
absis	NN	Absis	N2
absolut	JJ	Absolut	A5.1+
absolutism	NN	Absolutism	G1.2
absorpsi	NN	Absorpsi	O4.1
absorptive	JJ	Absorptif	O4.1
abstain	VB	Abstain	S1.1.3
abstrak	JJ	Abstrak	A1.6
absurd	JJ	Absurd	S1.2.6
absurdisme	NN	Absurd	Q4.1
abu	NN	Abu	O1.1

For this semantic annotation system prototype, some elements of the USAS tagset have not been adopted: neuter, male and female distinction, antecedent, idiom, rarity and multiword unit. The extent to which these USAS tagset elements are adopted will be discussed once the prototype has been developed into a full-capacity semantic annotation system.

The tagset has also been adapted to comply with NooJ's tagging format. For instance, polarity analysis in the USAS tagset is originally indicated by plus (+) or minus (−) characters, representing (respectively) positive and negative polarities. These two characters are used in the tag-final position in the USAS tag format. For instance, a minus character is appended to A15−, the semantic tag for 'danger'.

However, in the NooJ tagging format [1], these characters are technically different in terms of their functions. First, the plus or minus characters are given before a value, not after, such as +HUM, which means human (it may be given to word tokens such as man, king, thief, among many others). For example, if HUM refers to 'human', then changing plus to minus negates the value and therefore non-human. To deal with this, I used +POS and +NEG for positive and negative polarities.

---

[7] https://ucrel.lancs.ac.uk/usas/USASSemanticTagset.pdf (last accessed 2023/08/28).

There were two SANTI systems available: SANTI-morf (morphology) and SANTI-POS (part-of-speech/morphosyntax). Semantic annotation was incorporated into the dictionaries in both systems.

The incorporation of explicit semantic labels into POS tags adheres to best practices in a number of language resources[8] present in NooJ, such as English and French. A small number of semantic tags have been added to the POS tags of particular entries in the resources of these two languages. Note that the coverage of the dictionaries created for this project is not like SANTI-morf or SANTI-POS, as it is limited to those entries where semantic labels incorporated into the dictionaries are used. However, in the future, all entries will have semantic tags; thus, a significantly broader coverage is expected.

The incorporation of semantic tags into SANTI-POS (see Table 2) is limited to the root because the root carries the core semantic meaning. Incorporating semantic tags into the SANTI-POS root dictionary seems to suggest redundancy because the same semantic tags have been incorporated into POS tags. However, as I will show later in 3.2, I argue that incorporation will make the disambiguation process easier.

Table 2. Incorporation of semantic analysis labels into root and full-form entries (sample).

Dictionary	Entry
POS + Semantic dictionary	absurdisme,absurd,NN + Q4.1
SANTI-morf + semantic	absurdisme,ROOT + NOUN + Q4.1

3.2 Morphology, Morphosyntax and Semantic Annotation Combined

Prior to the completion of the prototype, SANTI-morf and SANTI-POS cannot be used simultaneously. To combine the three annotations form, the content of NooJ POS dictionaries was added to the SANTI-morf dictionary, with the highest priority (after compilation: EN-v4-DykaA1.nod; see Fig. 1) for a variety of reasons. In terms of a preference for SANTI-morf over SANTI-POS, incorporating morpheme annotation into SANTI-POS is more difficult due to the complexity of SANTI-morf configuration in comparison to SANTI-POS. For prototyping purposes, only the content of the main SANTI-POS dictionary is incorporated.

Second, incorporating SANTI-morf resources into SANTI-POS necessitates a fundamental shift in methodology. The dictionary-grammar combinations in SANTI-morf must be translated into fully analyzed morphological entries. A project to accomplish this is currently underway but still in its earliest stages; therefore, this option is not yet feasible.

Third, and for this very reason, SANTI-morf dictionaries include a small number of word-level entries, termed full-form entries in SANTI-morf, which have been morphologically analyzed. These entries are prioritized (using the +UNAMB operator) to limit the productivity of NooJ grammar. Morphological grammars will only function when

---

[8] Available at: https://nooj.univ-fcomte.fr/resources.html (last accessed 2023/08/28).

Priority	Resource
H9	EN-v4-DykaA1.nod
H8	EN-v4-DykaA2.nod
H7	EN-v4-DykaA3.nod
H6	EN-v4-YumiA1.nom
H5	EN-v4-YumiA2.nom
H4	EN-v4-YumiA3.nom
H3	EN-v4-YumiA4.nom
H2	EN-v4-YumiG1.nom
H1	EN-v4-YumiG2.nom
L1	EN-v4-YumiG3.nom

Fig. 1. Incorporation of semantic tags with the highest priority.

there is no match in prioritized entries. As for full-form entries from SANTI-POS, they must have the same priority as the root so that both morphosyntax-semantic and morphological annotation can coexist (ambiguous). The enhancement of dictionary entries is equivalent to the enhancement of SANTI-morf [7] and SANTI-POS dictionaries. See Table 3.

Table 3. Dictionary entries, their type and prioritization (sample).

Entry Type	Prioritization	Entry[a]
Full-form entries from SANTI-POS	Yes	terpidana, <ter,PFX + R_NOU + PAT + teR> <pidana,ROOT + NOU + G2.1 + NEG> +UNAMB
Full-form entries from SANTI-POS	Yes	terpidana,pidana,NN + G2.1 + NEG <ter,PFX + R_NOU + PAT + teR> <pidana,ROOT + NOU> + UNAMB
Root-form entries from SANTI-POS	No	absurd,ROOT + FULL + ADJ + Q4.1
Full-form entries from SANTI-POS	No	absurdisme,absurd,NN + Q4.1

[a]The version presented here is simplified. For instance, the simplified version for *terpidana* is: terpidana,<ter,PFX+R_NOU+PAT+teR><pida na,ROOT+NOU>+UNAMB, whereas the original version is terpdana,<ter,PFX+R_NOU+PAT+teR+DykaA1+ID=teR%PFX%R_NOU %PAT%DykaA1><pidana,ROOT+NOU+DykaA1+ID=pidana%ROOT%NOU%DykaA1>+UNAMB.

The entry line *terpidana* 'a convict' is prioritized (+UNAMB). Thus, when NooJ recognizes *terpidana* as a word that has been indexed in NooJ text, the system will apply the entry line and stop. In this way, the grammar that recognizes *ter-* as an accidental passive will not be applied. Nonetheless, because the corresponding full-form entry (POS) is also prioritized (+UNAMB), both forms may surface. Therefore, semantic, morphology and POS/morphosyntactic annotation forms are all obtained from the dictionary.

This approach differs for the word *absurdisme* 'absurdism'. POS and semantic annotation are derived from dictionary entries, whereas morphological annotation is derived from a combination of root entry in the dictionary and a rule in the morphological grammar. This can happen because the grammar and the corresponding dictionary entries (root or full forms) are not prioritized; they are at the same level.

Although the approaches differ slightly, the annotation results are not significantly different. Figure 2 shows the annotation of *terpidana* and *absurdisme*. In this annotation, semantic labels are encoded explicitly, unlike the Saelan and Purwarianti's [13] tool, which only connects words that are instance arguments of a node. The incorporation of these explicit semantic analysis labels is also considered an improvement of the early SANTI-morf, as compared to Saelan and Purwarianti's [13] tool.

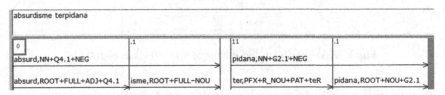

Fig. 2. Analysis of *absurdisme terpidana* using the prototype.

The annotation demonstrated in Fig. 2 is ambiguous in one way but unambiguous in another. If we refer to a very strict definition that 'ambiguous' refers to multiple analyses, then the annotation is indeed ambiguous. However, if we define ambiguity as multiple analyses at the same level, then the annotation is not ambiguous because the word receives both morphological and POS+ semantic annotation. None of the annotations is ambiguous at the morphological, POS/morphosyntactic or semantic level.

Now, we will turn to cases in which annotation is ambiguous at one or multiple levels (see Fig. 3). The figure shows annotation for a 3-word sentence, namely, *keuangan bisa ambruk*. Of these three words, only the first one is polymorphemic; the others are monomorphemic. In terms of these three words, only *bisa* is ambiguously annotated. We can see that the word *bisa* receives four annotations. The correct annotations are marked with checkmarks (two upper annotations).

The ambiguity lies not only in the semantic tags but also in the grammatical tags. We can see that *bisa* may function as a noun 'venom' (NN in POS tag and NOUN in morphological tag) or an adverb of modality (MD in POS tag and ADV in morphological tag). In this context, the correct use is the latter. Thus, the annotations of *bisa* as a noun word or noun root must be removed.

It necessitates a disambiguation grammar capable of removing the two incorrect annotations while retaining the two correct ones. By defining a correct label in the disambiguation grammar (1), the NooJ disambiguation grammar preserves correct annotations. Figure 4 shows a disambiguation grammar that keeps the first annotation but removes the other three. Annotations that have been removed are denoted by (x). The grammar employs a contextual disambiguation technique by examining the morphological annotation of right-adjacent tokens.

(1) `<bisa>/<ROOT+ADV+A7> <ROOT+VERB>`

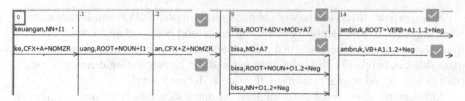

Fig. 3. An ambiguous analysis of *keuangan bisa ambruk* with correct analyses checkmarked.

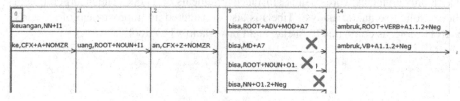

Fig. 4. First disambiguation attempt of *bisa* (50% successful).

This, however, is not the desired outcome, as the second annotation is also eliminated. Conversely, the following disambiguation grammar (2) preserves the second annotations but removes the first, third and fourth ones. Observe Fig. 5. This is an issue because the first annotation is actually correct. Either way, only one annotation can be retained.

(2) `<bisa>/<MD+A7> <VB>`

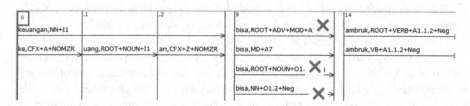

Fig. 5. Second disambiguation attempt of *bisa* (50% successful).

From a NooJ perspective, there is nothing wrong with the two annotations. This is because NooJ refers to the first definition of ambiguity discussed earlier. However, from the perspective of the SANTI-network, this is incorrect. We need to preserve the two annotations even though, for NooJ, this means that ambiguity is still retained.

The nature of NooJ disambiguation grammar is the removal of incorrect tags, and the preservation of correct tags earlier was considered a disadvantage. However, we can turn this challenge into an opportunity. The aforementioned grammar had a flaw in that it could not preserve two annotations with different labels.

For the grammar to function as desired, the two correct annotations must have identical labels. Note that the semantic analysis label has been incorporated into the morphological tags. Therefore, this should be used. Previously, I focused on resolving grammatical ambiguity through the application of grammatical tags in the disambiguation grammar. However, I overlooked the actual use of semantic tags. The first two annotations (correct ones) include the semantic label A7, whereas the lower two annotations use a different semantic tag, as shown in Fig. 5. The semantic label, whose tags are desired to be removed for venom, is O1.2+ Neg.

Actually, there is a technical issue. The first tag in the POS+ semantic and morphological annotations are distinct. We will encounter the same issue whether we use <ROOT + A7 > or <MD + A7>. The first option is to add a label to the beginning of each dictionary entry, as demonstrated in examples (3) and (4). This tag is PSM (POS-semantic-morpheme). The corresponding grammar for disambiguation is shown in (5).

(3) `bisa,PSM+ROOT+A7`
(4) `bisa,PSM+MD+A7`
(5) `<bisa>/<PSM+A7> <ambruk>`

The second alternative is to move A7 to the beginning of the tag. See examples (6) and (7). At this point, the creation of annotation labels, as expressed earlier, is unnecessary. The label A7 can instantly be used, and there is no need to specify anything. See the disambiguation grammar in (8)

(6) `A7+ROOT+NOUN a`
(7) `A7+MD a`
(8) `<bisa>/<A7><ambruk>`

However, NooJ offers a more effective solution. The wildcard label in NooJ can be combined with any other label in a tag. This wildcard is frequently used for corpus searches, but it could also be utilized in a disambiguation grammar. DIC was the NooJ wildcard label in the past, but as of now, ALU is the correct label. Thus, the disambiguation grammar is `<bisa>/<ALU+A7> <ambruk>`, as shown in (9).

(9) `<bisa>/<ALU+A7><ambruk>`

Compared to the previous two alternatives, the third alternative is the most effective. This is due to the fact that there is no need to alter the dictionary entries. Even though the disambiguation results of these three options are comparable, I prefer the third option. Figure 6 demonstrates the application of this grammar and the retention of two correct annotations (POS+ semantic and morphology).

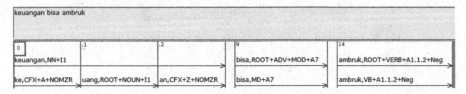

Fig. 6. Third disambiguation attempt of *bisa* (100% successful).

Disambiguation using the aforementioned disambiguation technique perfectly removes annotations at the grammatical level as well as at the semantic level. There might be a question of how to resolve ambiguity at the level of semantics only. In principle, it is very similar; the same approach is adopted. For instance, *coklat* in Indonesian may be interpreted as a color, 'brown', or a food, 'chocolate'. Observe the annotations in Fig. 7, where *coklat* in *kue coklat* has four annotations. In this context, *coklat* is not food but the color of a car *mobil*.

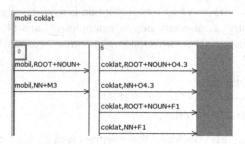

Fig. 7. Ambiguous analyses of *coklat* 'chocolate' or 'brown'.

Visualized annotations can be further described as follows. The first and third annotations are caused by semantic ambiguities but present at the morpheme level of annotation. As for the second and fourth, they are ambiguities at the POS+ Semantic level of annotation. My objective was to eliminate annotations containing the term F1 (food). For this, I employed a slightly different method. Instead of requesting that NooJ preserve annotations whose tags contained the semantic label M3, I requested that NooJ preserve annotations that lacked the F1 label. See the disambiguation grammar shown in (10) and its corresponding output in Fig. 8. The success of incorporating semantic analysis labels means that the current SANTI-morf performs better as compared to its earlier versions [5–8].

(10) `<ALU-F1>coklat/<ALU-F1>`

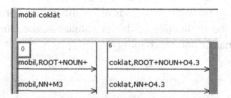

Fig. 8. Successful disambiguation of *coklat* 'chocolate' or 'brown'.

3.3 Evaluation

The prototype's performance was evaluated against a testbed corpus, whose creation is concisely described as follows. I randomly extracted 10K+ words from the LCC Indonesian Corpus in CQPweb (500 M+ tokens). A frequency list was then created. From the top-ten word items,[9] concordance lines were extracted. One thousand sentences from the concordance lines for each word were selected. Three evaluative measures are shown in Table 4.

The prototype scores 99% precision on morphological analysis, 95% on morphosyntactic analysis and only 63% on semantic analysis. The precision of morphological analysis is similar to SANTI-morf's precision [8] despite different testbed corpora. The precision of morphosyntactic analysis is slightly less than SANTI-POS but still at a relatively tolerable level. This demonstrates that SANTI-morf performs more consistently than SANTI-POS; therefore, SANTI-POS consistency must be enhanced. As for semantic annotation, the expected low precision results from the limited dictionary entries and grammars used in the prototype (a semantic lexicon containing only 400+ entries and a small number of grammars). The average level of accuracy is 85%.

Table 4. Performance evaluation.

	Precision (%)	Ambiguity (%)	Coverage (%)
Morphology	99	1	100
Morphosyntax	95	7	100
Semantic	63	38	58
Average	**85**	**15**	**86**

Morphological, POS/morphosyntactic and semantic annotation were found to have ambiguity rates of 1%, 7% and 38%, respectively. In Prihantoro [8], the ambiguity rates for morphological and POS/morphosyntactic annotation were determined to be 1% and 5%, respectively. The high ambiguity rates for semantic annotation indicate that disambiguation methods must be improved. Currently, only disambiguation grammars are employed. The prioritization system still follows SANTI-POS, and thus may further be improved to meet the needs of semantic disambiguation. In total, the mean of ambiguity rate was found to be 15%.

The discrepancy in coverage rates between morphology-morphosyntax and semantic annotation is extremely high. The morphology and morphosyntax coverage rates are 100%. As for semantic annotation, the system can only cover 63% (6,300+ tokens) of the testbed, meaning that 37% (3,700+) is left unanalyzed. The reasons for this are: (1) the paucity of resources, both quantity and quality, particularly dictionary entries, and (2) the absence of a guessing mechanism. Note that SANTI-morf and SANTI-POS are equipped with a Guesser module (see [8]). Thus, even if the primary resources (dictionaries and grammars) fail to inform proper annotation labels, the system will guess, and 100% coverage can virtually be achieved.

---

[9] In LCC Indonesian CQPweb, punctuations are considered tokens, thus excluded from the top-ten count as these are not word items.

4 Conclusion

In this paper, I argue that all the aforementioned objectives have been accomplished. Semantic analysis labels in SANTI-morf and SANTI-POS tags have been incorporated, which were previously absent. The performance of semantic annotation has also been tested in terms of precision coverage and ambiguity rates. No evaluation was ever conducted before the completion of this project. This demonstrates the accomplishment of the subsidiary aims. A SANTI-network prototype has also been developed, and its performance on morphological, POS/morphosyntax and semantic annotation has also been measured. This shows that the main aim, creating a SANTI-network (an MLT for morphology-POS/morphosyntax-semantics), which was absent previously, has been completed.

As for further studies, at least two areas can be improved. First, this prototype is developed based on 400+ selected entries, and only the first semantic labels were considered. In terms of numbers, the coverage can be expanded to include all entries in SANTI-morf and SANTI-POS, as well as secondary or tertiary semantic labels. In this project, the incorporation of semantic analysis labels was carried out by a single annotator. In the future, I expect more annotators to annotate the same data. In this way, an inter-rater agreement can be formulated (amplified with focus-group discussions), hoping to improve the accuracy of the semantic analysis.

The next aspect I would like to enhance is evaluation. Evaluation of the SANTI-network prototype was performed on a 10K-token testbed. This size can be expanded to, for instance, 100K or more. Further evaluation can suggest more improvements in terms of resources (dictionaries and grammars) or system configuration.

References

1. Silberztein, M.: Formalizing Natural Languages: The NooJ Approach. Wiley-ISTE, London (2016)
2. Qi, P., Zhang, Y., Zhang, Y., Bolton, J., Manning, C.D.: Stanza: a python natural language processing toolkit for many human languages. In: Celikyilmaz, A., Wen, T.H. (eds.) Proceedings of the 58th Annual Meeting of the Association for Computational Linguistics: System Demonstrations, pp. 101–108. ACL, Online (2020)
3. Manning, C., et al.: The Stanford CoreNLP Natural Language Processing Toolkit. In: Bontcheva, K., Zhu J. (eds.) Proceedings of 52nd Annual Meeting of the Association for Computational Linguistics: System Demonstrations, pp. 55–60. ACL, Baltimore (2014)
4. Pisceldo, F., Mahendra, R., Manurung, R., Arka, I.W.: A two-level morphological analyser for the indonesian language. In: Stokes, N., Powers, D. (eds.) Australasian Language Technology Association Workshop, pp. 142–150. Hobart, Australia (2008)
5. Prihantoro: Current Implementation and Future Prospects of SANTI-Morf V.1.0. Ranah: Jurnal Kajian Bahasa **10**(2), 411 (2021)
6. Prihantoro: The Morphological Annotation of Reduplication-Circumfix Intersection in Indonesian. In: Bekavac, B., Kocijan, K., Silberztein, M., Šojat, K. (eds.) Formalising Natural Languages: Applications to Natural Language Processing and Digital Humanities. 14th International Conference, NooJ 2020, Zagreb, Croatia, June 5–7, 2020, Revised Selected Papers, pp. 37–48. Springer, Cham (2021)
7. Prihantoro: SANTI-Morf Dictionaries. Lexicography **9**(2), 175–191 (2022)

8. Prihantoro: An Automatic Morphological Analysis System for Indonesian. PhD thesis. Lancaster University, Lancaster (2021)
9. Wicaksono, A.F., Purwarianti, A.: HMM Based Part-of-Speech Tagger for Bahasa Indonesia. In: Fourth International MALINDO Workshop. Jakarta (2010)
10. Schmid, H.: Improvements in part-of-speech tagging with an application to german. In: Armstrong, S., Church, K., Isabelle, P., Manzi, S., Tzoukermann, E., Yarowsky, D. (eds.) Natural Language Processing Using Very Large Corpora. Text, Speech and Language Technology, pp. 13–25. Springer, Dordrecht (1999)
11. Larasati, S.D., Kuboň, V., Zeman, D.: Indonesian Morphology Tool (MorphInd): Towards an Indonesian Corpus. In: Mahlow, C., Piotrowski, M. (eds.) Systems and Frameworks for Computational Morphology, pp. 119–129. Springer, Berlin, Heidelberg (2011)
12. Hanifmuti, M.Y., Alfina, I.: Aksara: An Indonesian Morphological Analyzer That Conforms to the UD v2 Annotation Guidelines. In: Lu, Y., Dong, M., Soon, L.-K., Hoon Gan, K. (eds.) 2020 International Conference on Asian Language Processing (IALP), pp. 86–91. Institute of Electrical and Electronics Engineers Inc. (2020)
13. Saelan, A., Purwarianti, A.: Generating mind map from indonesian text using natural language processing tools. Procedia Technol. **11**, 1163–1169 (2013)
14. Rayson, P.: From Key Words to Key Semantic Domains. Int. J. Corpus Linguist. **13**(4), 519–549 (2008)

Deciphering the Nomenclature of Chemical Compounds in NooJ

Kristina Kocijan[1]([✉]) [iD], Krešimir Šojat[2] [iD], and Tomislav Portada[3] [iD]

[1] Department of Information and Communication Sciences, Faculty of Humanities and Social Sciences, University of Zagreb, Zagreb, Croatia
`krkocijan@ffzg.unizg.hr`
[2] Department of Linguistics, Faculty of Humanities and Social Sciences, University of Zagreb, Zagreb, Croatia
`ksojat@ffzg.unizg.hr`
[3] Ruđer Bošković Institute, Zagreb, Croatia
`tomislav.portada@irb.hr`

Abstract. This paper proposes a multifaceted approach to the design of an algorithm for the automatic recognition of chemical compounds in Croatian written as multiword expressions. The algorithm, which we have named the Croatian Chemical Compounds Module, consists of three layers: it uses (1) the NooJ dictionary as the basis for (2) a morphological grammar, and both (1) and (2) are used for (3) a syntactic grammar. This module supports not only single-unit words and homoatomic entities but also variations of chemical names recognized through a variety of suffixes, multiplicative prefixes, hyphens, Roman and Latin numerals, Greek letters, and round, square and curly brackets. Terminological diversity and inconsistency in writing style are discussed as they present a great problem for any such endeavor.

Keyword: Chemical Compounds · Nomenclature · Morphology · Syntactic Grammar · Multiword Expressions · Croatian · NooJ

1 Introduction

Names of chemical compounds are found in a myriad of texts from different domains, and thus pose an important language element that, due to its complexity, needs a layered approach within natural language processing (NLP).

What we propose in this study is a multifaceted approach to the design of an algorithm which is well supported by NooJ [1]. This algorithm, named the Croatian Chemical Compounds Module (CroChem), consists of three layers: it uses (1) the NooJ dictionary as the basis for (2) a morphological grammar, and both (1, 2) are used for (3) the design of a syntactic grammar.

We start with a dictionary of 118 basic chemical elements [2], extracted from the periodic table of elements. This dictionary also includes the derivational grammar that helps us produce and recognize all the (possessive and/or compositional) adjective forms

A. Bartulović et al. (Eds.): NooJ 2023, CCIS 1816, pp. 16–27, 2024.
https://doi.org/10.1007/978-3-031-56646-2_2

derived from the nouns denoting chemical elements, as is the case with 'calcium' in *calcium oxide* or 'sodium' in *sodium oxide* (e.g., *kalcij*, N -> *kalcijev*, A [calcium, N -> calcium, A]; *natrij*, N -> *natrijev*, A [sodium, N -> sodium, A]), as well as from the names of common cations (e.g., *amonij*, N -> *amonijev*, A [ammonium, N -> ammonium, A]). In the following step, the morphological grammar is designed to recognize single-unit words, denoting different variations of chemical names through a variety of suffixes (e.g., *sumpor*, N -> *sumporast*, A, masculine I *sumporna*, A, feminine [sulfur, N -> sulfurous, A I sulfuric, A]; *klor*, N -> *klorid*, A I *klorovodičan*, A [chlorine, N -> chloric, A I hydrochloric, A]), but also multiplicative prefixes (*di-*, *tri-*, *tetra-*, *bis-*, *tris-*, *tetrakis-*) used for simple and complex entities (e.g., *dioxygen*, *trichloride*).

The algorithm that we use for the detection of multiword expressions (MWEs), at this stage mainly binary compounds [3, 4], is designed within the NooJ syntax grammar. This grammar uses both the main dictionary and the morphological grammar to recognize complex chemical compounds (e.g., *aluminijev oksid* 'aluminium oxide'; *kalcijev karbonat* 'calcium carbonate'; *sumporna kiselina* 'sulfuric acid'; *željezov(III) hidroksid* 'iron(III) hydroxide', *željezov(II) sulfat* 'iron(II) sulfate') but also to recognize even the most complex of compounds [5] where digits, words, hyphens, brackets, and even commas are used (e.g., *(6E,13E)-18-brom-12-butil-11-klor-4,8-dietil-5-hidroksi-15-metoksitrikosa-6,13-dien-19-in-3,9-dion*).

Our main goal is to recognize a full compound. However, while recognizing an entire multiword expression, we want to be able to detect smaller units (elements) that make the compound lay the ground for the augmented grammar design that will be able to produce the chemical formula as well. This information could be used in search queries and in machine translations. The results would also be valuable in the building of specialized lexica and the systematization of scientific nomenclature.

In the remaining sections, we display some relevant previous work that served as inspiration and as an introduction to the practical part of the algorithm's design. This is followed by a detailed description of the rules for naming chemical elements which served as the basis for the proposed algorithm. We conclude the paper with a short discussion of the study's results and possible future paths.

2 Previous Research on Chemical Nomenclature

Most of the research and discussion so far in the area where chemistry and linguistics overlap, both in English and in Croatian, have mainly dealt with the etymological and historical aspects of chemical terminology [6–8], the standardization of terminology and spellings [9], the meaning and context of the use of certain names [10, 11] or proposals, reviews, controversies and disputes relating to general or specific issues in the field of chemical terminology [6–8].

As far as the Croatian chemical nomenclature is concerned, a good historical overview of its development from the very beginning until the early 1990s was given by Vladimir Simeon in the preface to the Croatian translation of the IUPAC Inorganic compounds Nomenclature [17]. This review shows that the historical development and present state of the Croatian chemical nomenclature are not only conditioned by the development of chemistry as a science and profession, but mainly by the influence of two opposing linguistic political currents: (1) the Unitarian (Yugoslav) approach, which acted from the point of view that all South Slavic nations should develop a unique and standard chemical nomenclature and (2) the national (Croatian) approach, which felt that Croats should develop their national chemical names regardless of the names used by other South Slavic peoples. This situation is further complicated by individual initiatives such as the so-called Strohal proposal for the anion Nomenclature of acids [18].

Such a combination of circumstances had the consequence that for many terms in the Croatian chemical nomenclature there are (or there were) two and often even three names – Croatian, Serbian and "Yugoslav" or in fact (neo)Latin names (e.g., respectively, *dušik* vs. *azot* vs. *nitrogen* for 'nitrogen'; or *dušična kiselina* vs. *azotna kiselina* vs. *nitratna kiselina* for 'nitric acid').

In recent years, a lot of work has been done on harmonizing chemical nomenclature in Croatia. Two projects dedicated to this aim are the KENA (Chemical terminology) and KELANA (Chemical and Laboratory terminology) projects. They were both executed within the larger, general terminological coordination program STRUNA at the Institute for Croatian Language and Linguistics. Another important project is *Croatian Terminology in Analytical Chemistry,* conducted at the Faculty of Chemical Engineering and Technology at the University of Zagreb [19], as well as several smaller individual initiatives in this area that also include some work within a computational linguistics framework.

In parallel with these, there were also approaches based on the idea that Croatian chemical nomenclature should be developed as part of the nomenclature of some other discipline (most often pharmacy), rather than chemistry [20]. Unfortunately, the results of such efforts have led to the development of double rules, causing additional confusion in an area that is quite complex in itself, even without this influence.

On the other hand, research on the development of computer algorithms that would derive a chemical structure from a given chemical name, and vice versa, of algorithms that would assign an appropriate name to a given chemical structure, are of a more recent date. On top of that, these models are created almost exclusively for English. Such approaches are, at the same time, both complex and interdisciplinary, and they require researchers to be experts not only in chemistry but in computational linguistics as well. An excellent example of one such approach is the open-source algorithm OPSIN, developed at Cambridge University [21], which transforms a given chemical name with exceptional accuracy and reliability into a diagram of the appropriate chemical structure.

In addition to the OPSIN algorithm, there are numerous commercial algorithms that operate in both directions – i.e., not only do they convert a given chemical name into a chemical structure, but they also generate a systematic chemical name from a given chemical structure. These algorithms are usually part of larger software packages for drawing and processing chemical structures. Examples include *ChemDraw, ChemDoodle, ChemSketch, Marvin* and others. Such examples illustrate and confirm the need and usefulness of research linking chemistry and computational linguistics, but also in languages other than English. With this study, we hope to make a small contribution in that direction, bringing less-resourced languages a bit closer to the bigger players in the NLP arena.

3 About Chemical Compound Nomenclature

IUPAC or the International Union of Pure and Applied Chemistry, is an international organization responsible for preparing rules or conventions for naming chemical compounds. These rules tell us which word fragment can be placed in what position in the name of a chemical compound and are more or less applicable across different languages. However, the rules within a language are a different domain and are fertile ground for diversity, which gives us language-specific variances of the rules.

Concerning the Croatian language in particular, these variances are further emphasized due to differences in the rules used by chemists versus those that are used by pharmacists, as well as the linguistic currents to which the two are more inclined. At this stage of our research project, the differences were mainly realized through different word categories. If we consider, for example, the multiword expression for the chemical compound 'sodium chloride', we will find different realizations, since it can be written in three ways:

a. [adjective + noun] *natrijev klorid* (or, very rarely, *natrijski klorid*),
b. half-compound word *natrij-klorid*,
c. [noun + noun] *natrij klorid* (although orthographically incorrect, it is used and occurs in the corpora).

In some cases, the compounds are written either as (orthographically incorrect) one word (e.g., *acetilklorid,* the correct form being half-compound *acetil-klorid*), a multiword expression (e.g., *cinkov klorid*) or as multiple words connected with a hyphen (e.g., *amonij-klorid*) and/or brackets embracing numerals denoting the oxidation state of the cation in cases in which multiple oxidation states are possible (e.g., *željezov(II) klorid*). In cases where brackets are used, they should be written with no space between the previous word and an opening bracket but with a space between the closing bracket and the following word. However, examples in the corpora show different variations ranging from no spaces at all (e.g., *željezov(II)klorid*) to space used before and after the brackets (e.g., *željezov (II) klorid*) or space before but not after the bracket (e.g., *željezov (II)klorid*).

Prescribed language syntax for chemical nomenclature introduces (1) elements that can be found in this sublanguage and (2) the position where each element can be found. Within elements, we can recognize different sets:

- **words** (e.g., sodium, calcium, acid),
- **affixes**, i.e., either only prefix or suffix or both (e.g., *prop-, pent-, -an, -en, -in, -ol*, as in examples like *propan, propen, pentan, penten,* etc.),
- **hyphens**,
- **numerals**, either Roman or Arabic, but with different meanings and positions

  o Roman numerals used as single values like in carbon(**II**) oxide,
  o multiple Arabic numerals can be found separated with a comma, as in **2,3,3**-trimetilpentan),

- **letters** from the Greek alphabet,
- **brackets**: round (), square [] and curly { }.

Additional rules that we have taken into account include one stipulating that numerals and Greek alphabet letters cannot be found at the end of a compound name. Further, a hyphen can occur neither at the beginning nor the end of a compound name. However, we have come across frequent typographical errors in the texts, in which an extra space appears before or after a hyphen. This fact, unfortunately, further complicates the situation.

Due to such a large number of elements that need to be taken into consideration, we had to approach the design of the morphological and syntactic grammar wisely in order for the algorithm to successfully recognize as many combinations of compounds as possible. The steps we have taken are explained in the following chapter on methodology.

4 Methodology

The design of the Croatian NooJ module for Chemistry can be divided into four basic stages: (1) preparation of the dictionary, (2) designing the morphological grammar, (3) designing the syntactic grammar and (4) corpus annotation. We will unfold the first three stages in more detail in the following subsections.

4.1 Data Collection – Building the Dictionary

Our NooJ dictionary for chemistry with 118 chemical elements was designed from scratch, and it mirrors the elements found in the periodic table. Each dictionary entry includes the name of an element followed by its grammatical description (all the elements are **m**-masculine **c**-common **N**-nouns) and the names of the paradigms used for the inflection [+FLX] and derivation [+DRV], as in the following examples:

- **bakar**,N+c+m+Domena=KEM+DomenaType=KemElement+Symbol=Cu
  +FLX=METAR+DRV=OV_B:ORAHOV
- **brom**,N+c+m+Domena=KEM+DomenaType=KemElement+Symbol=Br
  +FLX=BAT+DRV=OV:ORAHOV**+DRV=IDNI:MUZIČKI**
  +DRV=OVODIČNI:MUZIČKI
- **dušik**,N+c+m+Domena=KEM+DomenaType=KemElement+Symbol=N
  +FLX=OTOK+DRV=OV:ORAHOV**+DRV=ČNI:MUZIČKI**
  +DRV=ASTI:MUZIČKI
- **fosfor**,N+c+m+Domena=KEM+DomenaType=KemElement+Symbol=P
  +FLX=ALAT+DRV=OV:ORAHOV**+DRV=NI:MUZIČKI**
- **sumpor**,N+c+m+Domena=KEM+DomenaType=KemElement+Symbol=S
  +FLX=ALAT+DRV=OV:ORAHOV**+DRV=NI:MUZIČKI**
  +DRV=ASTI:MUZIČKI
- **olovo**,N+c+m+Domena=KEM+DomenaType=KemElement+Symbol=Pb
  +FLX=BLAGO+DRV=V:ORAHOV**+DRV=LJEV:ORAHOV**
- **zlato**,N+c+m+Domena=KEM+DomenaType=KemElement+Symbol=Au
  +FLX=OTOK+DRV=V:ORAHOV.

Entries are further augmented with the annotations for the chemical **domain** [+Domena = KEM]; the type with which we indicated that it is a basic chemical element (and not, for example, a chemical compound) [+DomenaType = KemElement]; and the chemical symbol used for each element – e.g., for bromine [+Symbol = Br]. The inclusion of the chemical symbol was important for subsequent stages of the project in which the generation of the chemical formula of the compounds is planned but also for the search engine to detect any occurrences of an element, whether it is a single entity or part of a multiword expression.

The purpose of storing derivational attributes in the dictionary was to facilitate the recognition of proper and/or compositional adjectives derived from the nouns and related to them. This is particularly important since those derivations represent electropositive parts of chemical compounds that will have to be recognized in the text as parts of multiword expressions.

Generally, adjectives in Croatian can be formed via numerous types of word-formation processes. Some of these processes encompass suffixation, prefixation, combinations of suffixation and prefixation, and compounding, as well as various combinations of compounding and affixation (either suffixation and/or prefixation). The most productive and frequent process in the derivation of adjectives is suffixation. The stems that are used for adjectival derivation are predominantly nouns. There are a variety of suffixes used for the derivation of adjectives. Babić [22] lists 160 suffixes used for the derivation of adjectives in the Croatian language.[1] In this study, we were dealing mostly with highly productive derivational suffixes like -ov, -ev and -in, which are used for the formation of possessive and proper adjectives in Croatian. In this domain, we came across some less productive suffixes (e.g., -ast), as well. Whereas it is not common to use a variety of suffixes with the same stem in general language, in a domain-specific type of language like the language of chemistry, it is a rather frequent phenomenon. Each of these suffixes is used to denote a different type of chemical compound and, therefore, has a distinctive role in this domain.

So, for example, the recognition of (derived) proper adjectives was crucial for the recognition of multiword expressions such as *kalcijev klorid* 'calcium chloride' or *amonijev fosfat* 'ammonium phosphate'. However, the examples from the corpus showed the need for compositional adjectives, as well, but only for some chemical elements, such as lead (*olovo – olovljev* [A+ compositional]), while elements like gold and copper do not take this form. Therefore, in the second iteration of the dictionary, it was necessary to add derivational descriptions for compositional adjectives, as well, like for phosphorus *fosfor* and nitrogen *dušik*:

- *fosfor* [N] -> *fosforov* [A+proper] -> *fosforni* [A+compositional]
- *dušik* [N] -> *dušikov* [A+proper] -> *dušični* [A+compositional].

In some cases, two additional derivational descriptions were needed, since the double formation of adjectives is possible in the Croatian language, as for sulfur *sumpor*:

- *sumpor* [N] -> *sumporov* [A+possessive] -> *sumporni* [A+compositional] -> *sumporasti* [A+compositional].

---

[1] Generally, suffixation is the most productive derivational process in Croatian. Babić [22] provides a list of 771 suffixes used for the derivation of all parts of speech (526 suffixes for nouns, 160 suffixes for adjectives, 61 suffixes for verbs and 24 suffixes for adverbs). On the other hand, there are only 77 prefixes used in the derivation of all major parts of speech.

Nevertheless, knowing only the basic chemical elements and their adjectival derivations was not enough, because elements like numerals and brackets may be included as well, and taking all those varieties into account would make the number of dictionary elements too large. Additionally, it was also important for us to mark the type of compound that is formed, which in some cases is achieved by prefixes or suffixes, and in some cases, with both. Putting these combinations directly into the dictionary would put an additional burden on the size and maintenance of the dictionary. Thus, to recognize such forms, we opted for morphological grammar.

4.2 Morphological Grammar

The morphological grammar is designed to recognize single units denoting different variations of chemical forms through a variety of suffixes. For instance, if we consider the example *didušikov trioksid* 'dinitrogen trioxide', the existing NooJ dictionary resource allows us only to recognize the substrings *dušik,N -> dušikov,A* and *oksid,N*. Prefixes, in this case *di-* and *tri-*, denoting two and three atoms of nitrogen and oxygen, respectively, are recognized by means of the morphological grammar (Fig. 1).

If we are to follow the bold (orange) path in Fig. 1, we will first recognize the prefix, defined in the subgraph "Locants" (Fig. 1 – marker 1), after which the remainder of the word will be recognized (Fig. 1 – marker 2), and if validated as either an adjective or a noun found in the dictionary and having a feature domain defined as +Domena = KEM (Fig. 1 – marker 3), it will be accepted as a valid string inheriting the word category and all inflectional and semantic properties of the adjective or a noun that was recognized from (Fig. 1 – marker 4). Thus, for the given example, the first word, *didušikov*, will be recognized as an adjective, and the second word, *trioksid*, as a noun.

The second example, *etan-1,2-diol*, does not use any data from the main dictionary, and both words (*etan, diol*) are entirely recognized by the morphological grammar. In this particular case, we would need to use the subgraph "UGLJIKOVODIK" where 'et' will be recognized as a part denoting the number of carbon atoms and 'an' as a suffix for alkane. This word will be annotated as a noun from the chemical domain with corresponding markers for case and number that are defined within the sub-graph "CaseEndings" (Fig. 1). And finally, to recognize the word 'diol', subgraph "Locants" is used where we recognize the parts *di + ol*. Since neither is defined in the main dictionary, we are directed toward the "CaseEndings" subgraph, where additional information is collected about the case and number.

Although all of the individual elements are recognized by this grammar (Fig. 1), still, we see them only as separate entities. In order to join them into one concept or a multiword expression, we will need to use the syntactic grammar, which is further explained in the next section.

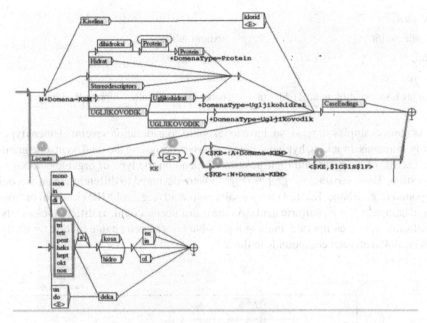

Fig. 1. Morphological grammar for recognizing simple chemical units.

4.3 Syntactic Grammar

The algorithm for the detection of MWEs is designed within the NooJ syntax grammar. It uses data from the previously described (1) main dictionary and (2) the morphological grammar to recognize complex chemical compounds, complex both in their nature and in their word formation. Some examples:

• aluminijev oksid	'aluminium oxide'
• didušikov trioksid	'dinitrogen trioxide'
• etan-1,2-diol	'ethane-1,2-diol'
• bakrov(II) klorid	'copper(II) chloride'
• kositrov(II) klorid	'tin(II) chloride'
• zlatov(III) klorid	'gold(III) chloride'
• sumporna kiselina	'sulfuric acid'
• natrijev hidroksid	'sodium hydroxide'
• željezov(III) hidroksid	'iron(III) hydroxide'
• magnezijev karbonat	'magnesium carbonate'
• magnezijev sulfat	'magnesium sulfate'
• željezov(II) sulfat	'iron(II) sulfate'
• bakrov(II) sulfat pentahidrat	'copper(II) sulfate pentahydrate'

(*continued*)

(*continued*)

• natrijev sulfit	'sodium sulfite'
• barijev nitrat	'barium nitrate'
• olovov acetat	'lead acetate'
• kalijev bis(oksalato)kuprat(II) dihidrat	'potassium bis(oxalato)cuprate(II) dihydrate'

As these examples suggest, we have to take into consideration several element types (words, numerals, brackets, hyphens, commas) when designing the final, syntactic grammar. The list of elements and their positions depend on the type of organic compound in question. Thus, separate subgraphs (Fig. 2) were designed to differentiate an alcohol compound (e.g., ethane-1,2-diol) from a salt compound (e.g., gold(III) chloride) or from an acid compound (e.g., sulfuric acid). As the transducer recognizes different elements, it marks the type of compound, making it possible for a search engine to look for all the acids or all the alcohol compounds in the text.

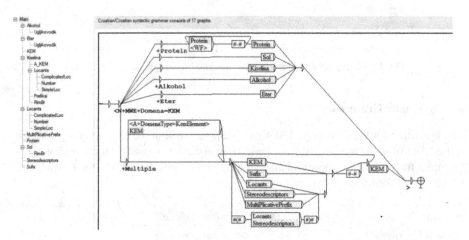

Fig. 2. A syntactic grammar that recognizes MWEs from the Chemistry domain.

5 Discussion and Conclusion

The results presented in this article provide a good basis for any further work in the domain of chemistry-related NLP. We are aware, however, that, although needed, these are just the initial steps.

The design of the Croatian NooJ module for Chemistry – CroChem allows us to recognize strings that have a chemical element in any position within a single word (e.g., **brom**butil) and also expressions with two words where the first one is an adjective derived from a noun of a chemical element and the second one is a noun from the chemical domain (e.g., *aluminijev oksid*). We can expand this basic list with examples in which numbers, hyphens, commas and brackets are also present, as well as any valid combination of single chemical elements. Our goal was to recognize multiword expressions with at least two components. Applying the proposed model, we have so far succeeded in recognizing various complex expressions, such as a compound made out of 32 carbon atoms, named: *(6E,13E)-18-brom-12-butil-11-klor-4,8-dietil-5-hidroksi-15-metoksitrikosa-6,13-dien-19-in-3,9-dion* (Fig. 3).

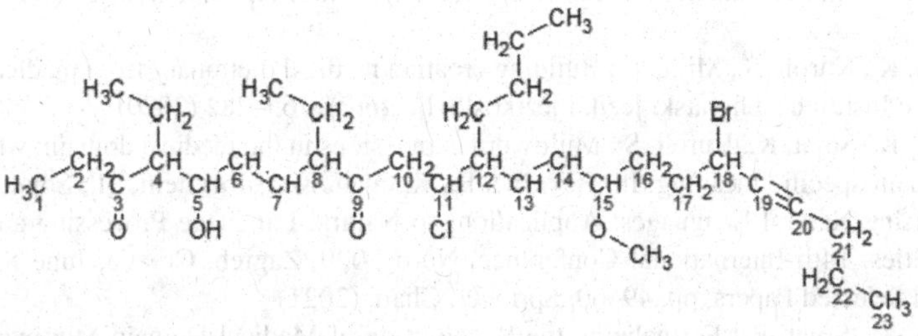

Fig. 3. Molecule with a hydrocarbon chain consisting of 23 carbons – its name is recognized by the Croatian NooJ module for chemistry.

Nevertheless, additional challenges arose, such as recognizing names that cannot be obtained by dissecting their parts, such as the ozone molecule, which consists of 3 oxygen atoms or the water molecule, which consists of two hydrogen and one oxygen atoms. These are similar to minerals whose chemical ingredients we recognize, but which are not visible in the name of the compound itself, for example, the mineral pyrite, which consists of iron and sulfur.

An additional challenge is represented by concepts that appear in the chemical domain but are already present in the general language, such as the word *bakar* in the meaning of a chemical compound 'copper' but also a city in Croatia (Bakar) or the word *bor*, which has three meanings, a chemical element 'boron', a tree ('pine', *Pinus sylvestris*) and a city in Serbia (Bor). Some adjectives derived from nouns already exist in the general language, such as an adjective in the feminine gender of the noun mercury (*živina*, from *živa*), which stands for a chemical element in the chemical domain, while in the general language, this word defines poultry or some domestic animal. Challenges defined in this section remain to be solved in the future steps of the project.

A very big problem in the computational processing of Croatian texts in which chemical names appear is terminological diversity as well as inconsistency by a great number of authors. In the computational processing of general language texts, such errors and inconsistencies can often be identified automatically and corrected based on context, but this is significantly more difficult and is often impossible with chemical terminology. This is because, in chemical terms, there are many sets of words in which two adjacent words differ by just one letter, spacing, or even by just one non-alphabetic character – e.g., *N,N-dimetiloksamid* versus *N,N'-dimetiloksamid*.

In our opinion, further work in this area could also be oriented towards the automatic translation of chemical names from Croatian into English (and vice versa) and linking the thus translated text with existing state-of-the-art algorithms for the interpretation of chemical names in English, such as OPSIN. This would shift the focus of the work from the problem of analysis and processing of Croatian chemical names to the problem of translating Croatian names into English, in which there are already good and satisfactory solutions for further processing such generated chemical names.

References

1. Silberztein, M.: Formalizing Natural Languages: The NooJ Approach. Wiley-ISTE, London (2016)
2. Kocijan, K., Kurolt, S., Mijić, L.: Building croatian medical dictionary from medical corpus. Rasprave Instituta za hrvatski jezik i jezikoslovlje **46**(2), 765–782 (2020)
3. Kocijan, K., Šojat, K., Kurolt, S.: Multiword expressions in the medical domain: who carries the domain-specific meaning. In: Bekavac, B., Kocijan, K., Silberztein, M., Šojat, K. (eds.) Formalising Natural Languages: Applications to Natural Language Processing and Digital Humanities. 14th International Conference, NooJ 2020, Zagreb, Croatia, June 5–7, 2020, Revised Selected Papers, pp. 49–60. Springer, Cham (2021)
4. Kocijan, K., Šojat, K.: Formalizing the Recognition of Medical Domain Multiword Units. In: Dash, S., Parida, S., Tello, E., Acharya, B., Bojar, O. (eds.) Natural Language Processing in Healthcare: A Special Focus on Low Resource Languages, pp. 89–120. CRC Press, Boca Raton (2022)
5. Portada, T., Stilinović, V.: Što treba znati o hrvatskoj kemijskoj nomenklaturi? Kem. Ind. **56**(4), 209–215 (2007)
6. Ball, D.W.: Elemental Etymology: What's in a Name? J. Chem. Educ. **62**, 787–788 (1985)
7. Ringnes, V.: Origin of the names of chemical elements. J. Chem. Educ. **66**, 731–738 (1989)
8. Raos, N., Portada, T., Stilinović, V.: Anionic names of acids: an experiment in chemical nomenclature. Bull. Hist. Chem. **38**, 61–66 (2013)
9. Dijskstra, A.J., Hellwich, K.-H., Hartshorn, R.M., Reedijk, J., Szabo, E.: End-of-Line Hyphenation of Chemical Names (IUPAC Recommendations 2020). Pure Appl. Chem. **93**(1), 47–68 (2021)
10. Raos, N.: Kako definirati organsku kemiju? Kem. Ind. **71**(7–8), 507–512 (2022)
11. Gotkova, T., Chepurnykh, N.: Public perception and usage of the term carbon: linguistic analysis in an environmental social media corpus. Psychol. Lang. Commun. **26**(1), 297–312 (2022)
12. Giomini, C., Cardinali, M.E., Cardellini, L.: Simples and compounds: a proposal. Chem. Int. **27**(1), 18 (2005)
13. Portada, T., Stilinović, V.: Simples and compounds: another opinion. Chem. Int. **27**(5), 20 (2005)
14. Portada, T., Stilinović, V.: Prijedlog pridjevske funkcijsko-razredne nomenklature. Kem. Ind. **58**(10), 461–464 (2009)
15. Portada, T.: Kako na hrvatskom jeziku reći entacapone? Kem. Ind. **61**(3), 177–178 (2012)
16. Ingrosso, F., Polguère, A.: How terms meet in small-world lexical networks: the case of chemistry terminology. In: Poibeau, T., Faber, P. (eds.) Proceedings of the 11th International Conference on Terminology and Artificial Intelligence, pp. 167–171. Granada (2015)
17. Simeon, V.: Proslov hrvatskomu izdanju. In: Međunarodna unija za čistu i primijenjenu kemiju, Hrvatska nomenklatura anorganske kemije, preporuke HKD 1995, pp. IX–XVI. Školska knjiga, Zagreb (1996)
18. Strohal, D.: Prijedlog za izmjenu kemijskog nazivlja kiselina. Kemijski vjestnik **15**(16), 126 (1941/1942)
19. Stojanov, T., Lewis, K., Portada, T.: Rad na Struni na primjeru hrvatskoga kemijskog nazivlja. In: Ledinek, N., Žagar Karer, M., Humar, M. (eds.) Terminologija in sodobna terminografija, pp. 181–194 (2009)

20. Grdinić, V.: Farmaceutski naslovi u Hrvatskoj farmakopeji. Farm. Glas. **63**(1), 37–55 (2007)
21. Lowe, D.M., Corbett, P.T., Murray-Rust, P., Glen, R.C.: Chemical name to structure: OPSIN, an open source solution. J. Chem. Inf. Model. **51**(3), 739–753 (2011)
22. Babić, S.: Tvorba riječi u hrvatskome književnome jeziku. HAZU i Nakladni zavod Globus, Zagreb (2002)

NooJ Dictionary for Rromani: Importing of an Editorial Dictionary to the NooJ System

Masako Watabe[(✉)] [iD]

University of Franche-Comté, C.R.I.T., Besançon, France
masakowatabe@free.fr

Abstract. This article presents the process of importing an editorial dictionary [1] into the NooJ system. The current module for Rromani contains only 640 dictionary entries. However, we have written the central inflectional grammars of nouns, verbs, adjectives and grammatical words using the NooJ environment. Now, we import the editorial dictionary to complete the NooJ dictionary. Rromani language has a complex dialect structure, yet its dialectal equivalents show systematic correspondences between them [2]. This fact encourages us to develop a single and joint module for the entire Rromani language. The editorial dictionary mentioned above includes variants of the four Rromani dialects. The problem is that the information related to part of speech (POS) categories is absent or not precise enough to be processed by the NooJ parser. We have made implicit information explicit and identified 2,559 nouns, 830 adjectives and 686 verbs among 4,524 entries. However, we still have to identify the categories of other 448 words by referring to additional dictionaries [3–5]. We would first complete importing the entire editorial dictionary and then examine each entry to perfect the inflectional morphology and formalize the derivational morphology in the NooJ module for Rromani.

Keywords: Diasystem · Electronic Dictionary · NooJ · Polylectal · Rromani Language

1 A Single Module for the Four Dialects of Rromani

Rromani is the language of the Rromani people, one of Europe's most significant minorities in terms of population.[1] However, schools rarely teach Rromani, except in Romania.[2] Only two universities (INALCO in Paris and the University of Bucharest) offer specialized courses in Rromani studies adopting the standardized Rromani alphabet.[3]

The characteristic feature of Rromani dialectology is that geographical distance does not correspond to linguistic distance. The two main isoglosses are not areal. Each of these isoglosses systematically concerns a set of dialectal variants at various levels:

---

[1] The population is estimated from 10 to 12 million in Europe and 3 million in the Americas [6].

[2] The Romanian government recognizes the teaching of the Rromani language and culture from elementary school through to university.

[3] The graphic standard was defined at the IRU (International Rromani Union) Congress 1990.

© The Author(s), under exclusive license to Springer Nature Switzerland AG 2024
A. Bartulović et al. (Eds.): NooJ 2023, CCIS 1816, pp. 28–38, 2024.
https://doi.org/10.1007/978-3-031-56646-2_3

morphological, phonological, lexical and syntactic. This fact represents a diasystem, i.e., systematic correspondences between interdialectal variants (Tables 1 and 2).

Table 1. Dialectal variants between the two superdialects: O and E.

	O superdialect	E superdialect	Translation
Morphology	*dikhlŏm*	*dikhlem*	'(I) saw'
	som	*Sem*	'(I) am'
	o Rromnă	*e Rromnă*	'the Rromani women'
	asàndilăs	*asàjas*	'(he/she) laughed'
Phonology	*khoni*	*khoj*	'grease'
	daj	*Dej*	'mother'
Lexicon	*puzgal*	*istral*	'to slip'[4]
	ćulal	*pităl*	'to drip'
Syntax	*phureder po phuro*	*maj phuro*	'older' (about age)

Table 2. Dialectal variants between the two dialect subgroups: with or without mutation.

	Without mutation	With mutation	Translation
Phonology	*ćhavo* [ʧʰavo]	*ćhavo* [çavo]	'Rromani boy, son'
	ʒukel [ʤukel]	*ʒukel* [ʐukel]	'dog'
	tiro, to, klo, ko	*tĭro, tŏ*	'your'
Lexicon	*Men*	*korr*	'neck'
Syntax	*po, piro*	*pesqo*	'one's own'

The first isogloss forms the two superdialects: O and E. The second isogloss comprises the two dialect subgroups according to phonetic mutation:[5] with or without mutation. The two isoglosses crossing each other form the four dialects of Rromani: O-bi, O-mu, E-bi and E-mu[6] [7].

The current NooJ module for Rromani contains only 640 dictionary entries. However, we have already developed central inflectional grammars for nouns, adjectives, verbs and grammatical words, such as personal pronouns and determiners.

•

---

[4] There is no infinitive in Rromani. The form of the third person singular in the present tense substitutes for an entry word in dictionaries.

[5] Two alveolar affricates [ʧʰ] and [ʤ] turn into alveolo-palatal fricatives [ç] and [ʐ].

[6] "bi" means 'without' in Rromani, and "mu" is the initial of the word *mutàcia* [*mutation*].

2 An Editorial Dictionary

We decided to use an editorial dictionary, *Morri angluni rromane ćhibăqi evroputni lavustik* [1], to complement the NooJ dictionary for Rromani.

It is the only polylectal and multilingual dictionary that exists. It includes numerous lexical and morphological variants of all four dialects of Rromani. The entry words are translated into ten target languages: Croatian, English, French, German, Greek, Hungarian, Romanian, Slovak, Spanish and Ukrainian. This dictionary adopts the standardized Rromani alphabet.

We will describe the conversion process of the information associated with each entry of this editorial dictionary into formalized property codes to construct the electronic NooJ dictionary.

2.1 Absence of POS Category

The content of an entry of the initial editorial dictionary consists of two or three sections: an entry word in Rromani, its translation and potential synonyms.

The entry section begins with a lemma. If it is a variable word, its inflectional endings follow the lemma. If it is a dialectal variant, its dialectal properties also follow the lemma.

The translation section consists of words translated into ten target languages.

The synonym section consists of potential synonyms related or not related to dialects. If it is a dialectal variant, its dialectal properties follow it.

It is a valuable dictionary from a didactic and dialectological point of view, as it includes inflectional morphology and dialectal variants. On the other hand, categories of part of speech (POS) are implicit or absent. However, there is some information to help identify three categories: nouns, adjectives and verbs. There is no clue related to other categories.

2.2 Nouns

There are two genders in Rromani: masculine and feminine (e.g., *bakro* 'sheep' and *kher* 'house' are masculine, *bakri* 'ewe' and *phuv* 'earth' are feminine).

There are two numbers in Rromani: singular and plural (e.g., *kher* 'house' and *bakri* 'ewe' are singular, *khera* 'houses' and *bakră* 'ewes' are plural). Some nouns are only used in the plural (e.g., *love* 'money', *gada* 'clothes', *śośa* 'mustache').

Among masculine nouns, there are abstract nouns with the suffix *-pen* (e.g., *sastipen* 'health', *kidipen* 'meeting').

Masculine Nouns. In the editorial dictionary, if it is a noun, a definite article precedes the lemma, and its gender is indicated.

- *o* **dad**, **-es** *m.* **-a**, **-en**
  MA atya, apa; EN father; FR père; ES padre; DE Vater; UKR тато, батько; RO tată; HR otac; SLK otec; GK πατέρας.

For example, the entry word *dad* 'father' follows a definite article *o* 'the' in the direct masculine singular. The basic form, i.e., the direct singular form of the noun *dad,* has no inflectional ending. The inflectional endings of the other three forms follow the basic form: *-es* in the oblique[7] singular, *-a* in the direct plural and *-en* in the oblique plural. The forms of the word *dad* are:

- *dad* 'father' in the direct singular,
- *dades* 'father' in the oblique singular,
- *dada* 'fathers' in the direct plural,
- *daden* 'fathers' in the oblique plural.

There is an initial *m.* of the adjective *muršikano* 'masculine' between the singular and plural endings. Thanks to this information, users could understand that the entry *dad* is a masculine noun.

dad,N + hum + m + EN = "father" + FLX = rrom + DRV = rromorro:ćhavo.

In the NooJ dictionary, each line begins with a lemma followed by its category, potential lexical properties and the translation in the target language. Then, "FLX" precedes an inflectional paradigm, and "DRV"[8] precedes a derivational paradigm. One needs to indicate the inflectional paradigm of the derivative after a colon if it is different from the inflectional paradigm of the lemma.

For example, the entry *dad* precedes its category and lexical properties "N + hum + m" (masculine human noun), its translation in English (EN) is 'father', its inflectional paradigm (FLX) is named "rrom," its derivational paradigm (DRV) is called "rromorro", the inflectional paradigm of its derivative is named "ćhavo".

We named each paradigm with a representative word in Rromani. Users could thus understand the link between the lemma and its paradigms more concretely. For example, the noun *rrom* 'married man, husband' is used as an inflectional paradigm name to represent consonantal and oxytonic[9] masculine human nouns. In contrast, the noun *ćhavo* 'son, Rromani boy' is used as an inflectional paradigm name to represent vocalic and oxytonic masculine human nouns. The entry *dad* is an oxytonic and consonantal masculine human noun such as *rrom*. Its inflectional paradigm name is, therefore, "rrom". On the other hand, its diminutive *dadorro* 'little father' (in the affectionate sense) is vocalic such as *chavo*. Its inflectional paradigm name is, therefore, "ćhavo".

There are three semantic values of nouns: human, animal and inanimate object. Each of these has a specific morphosyntax. We need to add this lexical information to the NooJ dictionary manually.

Feminine Nouns. In the editorial dictionary, we have the following noun:

- *i* **daj**[1], -a ʒ. -a, -en
    = *i* **d/aj**[1], -ia ʒ. -ia, -ien
    MA anya; **EN** mother; **FR** mère; **ES** madre; **DE** Mutter; **UKR** мати; **RO** mamă; **HR** majka; **SLK** matka; **GK** μητέρα.
    [☞vi **dej**[23]]

---

[7] There are two cases in Rromani: direct and oblique.

[8] The diminutive is the only derivation developed in the current Rromani module.

[9] In Rromani, most words are oxytonic, whereas the borrowings are not oxytonic.

The entry *daj* 'mother' includes two inflectional paradigms: according to a long stem *daj* and a short one *d-*. The long stem *daj* has no inflectional ending as the basic form. The three other inflectional endings are: *-a* in the oblique singular and the direct plural, *-en* in the oblique plural. On the other hand, the short stem *d-* has an inflectional ending *-aj* to compose the basic form. The three other inflectional endings are: *-ia* in the oblique singular and the direct plural, *-ien* in the oblique plural.

- *daj* 'mother' in the direct singular,
- *daja/dia* 'mother' in the oblique singular,
- *daja/dia* 'mothers' in the direct plural,
- *dajen/dien* 'mothers' in the oblique plural.

There is an initial ʒ. of the adjective *ʒuvlikano* 'feminine' between the singular and plural endings. Thanks to this information, users could understand that the entry *daj* is a feminine noun.

Moreover, the noun meaning 'mother' has two dialectal variants: *daj* in the O super-dialect and *dej* in the E superdialect. For example, a superscript "1" following the entry *daj* is its dialectal value, i.e., the entry *daj* is a variant used in the O superdialect (the stratum 1^{10}). Then, there is a variant in another superdialect in the synonym section, i.e., *dej* is a variant used in the E superdialect (the strata 2 and 3). The word *vi* following an arrow in the synonym section means 'also' in Rromani. In the editorial dictionary, *daj* and *dej* are two different entries because of their different inflectional paradigms.

daj,N+hum+f+rro+EN="mother"+RRE="dej"+FLX=ćhaj+DRV=ćhajorri:rromni

The entry *daj* in the NooJ dictionary precedes its category and lexical values "N + hum + f" (feminine human noun), its translation in English (EN) is 'mother', its inflectional paradigm (FLX) is named "ćhaj" 'daughter, Rromani girl' (the paradigm specific to some oxytonic human feminine nouns ending in a semi-vowel "j"), its derivational paradigm (DRV) of the diminutive is named "ćhajorri" 'little girl', the inflectional paradigm of its derivative is named "rromni" 'married lady, wife' (the paradigm of vocalic and oxytonic human feminine nouns).

In addition, there is a lower-case tag, "rro", and an upper-case tag, "RRE", for this entry. Each of these tags corresponds to a superdialect, i.e., "rro" to the O superdialect and "RRE" to the E superdialect, while "rro" in lower-case is a dialect value of the entry *daj* and "RRE" in upper-case precedes the variant in the E superdialect *dej*.

When one applies a NooJ dictionary to a text including a dialectal variant, NooJ will annotate the dialectal affiliation of the variant and its equivalents used in other dialects (Fig. 1).

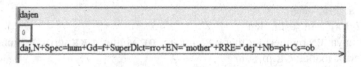

Fig. 1. Annotation of a variant *dajen* 'mothers'.

---

[10] The O-bi, O-mu, E-bi and E-mu dialects are named "strata 1, 1#, 2 and 3" in the editorial dictionary.

Nouns Only Used in the Plural. Some nouns exist only in the plural in Rromani. In this case, the basic form is the direct plural form. In the editorial dictionary, the basic form of this type of noun follows two variants of the definite article: *o* 'the' in the O superdialect and *e* 'the' in the E superdialect, and precedes the oblique plural ending and the abbreviation *sad pl.* 'only plural'.

- *o/e* **lov/e, -en-** (*sad pl.*)

    MA pénz; EN money; FR argent, mon-naie; ES dinero, moneda; DE Geld; UKR гроші; RO bani; HR novac; SLK peniaze; GK χρήματα, παράδες.

For example, the entry *love* 'money' is a noun used only in the plural, and its oblique form is *loven-*[11] 'money'.

love,N + ina + m + pl + EN = "money" + FLX = love.

The entry *love* in the NooJ dictionary precedes its category and lexical values "N + ina" (inanimate object nouns), its translation in English (EN) is 'money', and its inflectional paradigm (FLX) is also named "love". There is an additional lexical value, "pl" (plural), as this noun is used only in the plural. There is no derivational paradigm for this noun.[12]

Abstract Nouns. There are abstract nouns with the suffix *-Pen* in Rromani. This suffix has several dialectal variants, such as *-pe*, *-po*, *-ben*, *-mo* and *-mos*. The nouns with this suffix are oxytonic masculine but associated with a specific inflectional paradigm. There is a chapter in which the editorial dictionary explains the inflectional paradigm of this type of noun. Its inflectional endings are, therefore, absent in the entry section.

- *o* **sasti**$_{mo|s}^{pe|n}$

    MA egészség; EN health; FR santé; ES salud; DE Gesundheit; UKR здоров'я; RO sănătate; HR zdravlje; SLK zdravie; GK υγεία.

For example, the entry *sastipen*[13] consists of a lexeme *sasti-* and a set of suffix variants. It follows a definite article *o* 'the' in the direct masculine singular. This entry includes six variants: *sastipen*, *sastipe*, *sastipo*, *sastiben*, *sastimo* and *sastimos*, all of which mean 'health'.

sastipen,N+ina+m+EN="health"+FLX=sastipen

The entry *sastipen* in the NooJ dictionary precedes its category and lexical values "N + ina + m" (inanimate object masculine noun), its translation in English (EN) is 'health', its inflectional paradigm (FLX) is also named "sastipen". All nouns with the suffix *-pen* are associated with the same inflectional paradigm.

Number of Nouns. We have identified and counted masculine, feminine, plural and abstract nouns according to their specific information implicitly indicated in the editorial dictionary. There are 2,559 noun entries in total, i.e.,

---

[11] The oblique case of inanimate object nouns does not exist without a postposition in Rromani.

[12] In fact, the diminutive *lovorre* 'small coins' exists, but it is the plural diminutive form of the noun *lovo* 'coin', i.e., the singular form of *love* 'money'. *Lovo* and *love* are two different entries in the editorial dictionary because of their different meanings.

[13] This entry is a set of six variants. However, we call it *sastipen* expediently as its basic form.

- masculine nouns: 950 entries,
- feminine nouns: 1,124 entries,
- plural nouns: 55 entries,
- abstract nouns with -*pen*: 430 entries,
- = > all nouns: 2,559 entries.

2.3 Adjectives

There are two types of adjectives in Rromani: "large" and "narrow". "Large" adjectives (e.g., *buxlo* 'large', *barvalo* 'rich') are vocalic, while "narrow" adjectives (e.g., *tang* 'narrow', *godăver* 'intelligent') are consonantal. Adjectives agree in the number, gender and case of its determined noun.

"Large" Adjectives. The "large" adjectives are vocalic and have three inflectional endings: -*o* in the direct masculine singular, -*i* in the direct feminine singular, -*e* in the direct plural of both genders and the oblique of both numbers and genders. In the editorial dictionary, an abbreviation *pl.* (plural) is inserted between the endings -*i* and -*e* of the "large" adjectives.

- **barval/o**, -**i** *pl.* -**e**
    MA gazdag; **EN** rich; **FR** riche; **ES** rico; **DE** reich; **UKR** багатий; **RO** bogat; **HR** bogat; **SLK** bohatý; **GK** πλούσιος.

For example, the entry *barvalo* 'rich' is a vocalic and oxytonic adjective, i.e., a "large" adjective. Its basic form (i.e., direct masculine singular) consists of a stem *barval*- and an inflectional ending -*o*. Two other inflected forms are *barvali* with the ending -*i* in the direct feminine singular and *barvale* with the ending -*e* in the plural and oblique.

   barvalo,ADJ+EN="rich"+FLX=buxlo

The entry *barvalo* in the NooJ dictionary precedes its category "ADJ" (adjective), its translation in English (EN) is 'rich', and its inflectional paradigm (FLX) is named "buxlo" 'large'.

"Narrow" Adjectives. The "narrow" adjectives are consonantal, i.e., the basic form has no ending. In the direct singular, the basic form is used in both genders, while the inflectional ending -*e* is used in the oblique.

   In Rromani terminology, the oblique case is also named "B-ćham" 'B case'. The term "B-ćham" precedes the basic form of "narrow" adjectives in the editorial dictionary.

- **godăver** *B-ćham*: -**e**
    MA okos; **EN** intelligent, clever; **FR** intelligent; **ES** inteligente; **DE** klug, intelligent; **UKR** розумний; **RO** priceput, înțe-lept; **HR** pametan; **SLK** dôvtipný, inteligentný; **GK** έξυπνος.

For example, the entry *godăver* is a consonantal and oxytonic adjective, i.e., a "narrow" adjective. The basic form (i.e., direct singular) has no ending. Another inflected form is *godăvere* with the ending -*e* in the oblique.

   godăver,ADJ+EN= "intelligent, clever "+FLX=tang

The entry *godăver* in the NooJ dictionary precedes its category "ADJ" (adjective), its translation in English (EN) is 'intelligent, clever', and its inflectional paradigm (FLX) is named "tang" 'narrow'.

Number of Adjectives. We have identified and counted "large" and "narrow" adjectives according to their specific information implicitly indicated in the editorial dictionary. There are 830 adjective entries in total, i.e.,

- "large" adjectives: 682 entries,
- "narrow" adjectives: 148 entries,
- = > all adjectives: 830 entries.

2.4 Verbs

There are two verbal groups in Rromani according to their endings: *-el* and *-al* (e.g., *ćhinel* 'to cut' and *naśel* 'to run away' are "-el" verbs, *asal* 'to laugh' and *xal* 'to eat' are "-al" verbs).

We need to list other endings to find all the verbs in the editorial dictionary. Admittedly, all verbs end in *-el* or *-al* in basic form, i.e., present-tense third-person singular form, but there are subgroups of these endings. Some of the "-el" verbs end in *-sarel*, and are not associated with the inflectional paradigm of the "-el" verbs. Some of the "-al" verbs have a stem ending in *-a*, and consequently, their ending is *-l*. These verbs are not associated with the inflectional paradigm of "-al" verbs.

The editorial dictionary includes even inflected forms as verb entries, i.e., the mediopassive lexicalized, and thus treated as dictionary entries. The basic form of the mediopassive ends in *-ŏl* or *-ol*.

Verbs with -el. In the editorial dictionary, the entry section of a verb consists of the basic form and the endings in the past tense.

- **ćhin/el, -dăs**

    MA vág; EN to cut; FR couper; ES cortar, talar; DE (ab)schneiden; UKR (від)різа-ти; RO a tăia; HR rezati; SLK rezať, krájať; GK κόβει.
- **naś/el, -lo ÷ -lăs**

    MA (el)szökik, elfut; EN to flee, to run away; FR fuir, se sauver; ES huir, fugarse, escapar; DE (ent)fliehen; UKR втекти, тікати; RO a fugi, a scăpa; HR pobjeći, izbjeći; SLK pobehnúť, utekať; GK (απο)φεύγει, δραπετεύει.

For example, the entry *ćhinel* 'to cut' consists of the lexeme *ćhin-* and the present-tense ending *-el*. The basic form precedes the past-tense ending *-dăs*. The past-tense third-person singular form is *ćhindăs* '(he/she) cuts'.

The ending *-dăs* consists of two morphemes: a past-tense morpheme *-d-* and a third-person singular morpheme *-ăs*. There are two past-tense morphemes in Rromani: *-d-* and *-l-*. These morphemes depend on the final consonants of the lexeme. For example, *ćhinel* is associated with a morpheme *-d-* because of the final consonant *-n* of its lexeme *ćhin-*, on the other hand, *naśel* is associated with a morpheme *-l-* because of the final consonant *-ś* of its lexeme *naś-*.

The entry *naśel* 'to run away' has two types of past-tense ending: *-lo* and *-lăs*. The past-tense third-person singular form is *naślo* '(he) ran', *naśli* '(she) ran away', and *naślăs* '(he/she) ran'. The ending *-lo* is a variant used in the South of the Danube that concerns some intransitive verbs, and agrees with the gender of the subject, whereas other endings *-dăs* and *-lăs* are common to both genders.

ćhinel,V+tr+EN="to cut"+FLX=kerel
naśel,V+itr+EN="to run away"+FLX=beśel

For example, the entry *ćhinel* in the NooJ dictionary precedes its category and semantic value "V + tr" (transitive verb), its translation in English (EN) is 'to cut', its inflectional paradigm (FLX) is named "kerel" 'to do, to make'.

In the NooJ module for Rromani, we have written ten verbal inflectional grammars according to the tenses, the modalities, the aspects and the voices: present, past, future, imperfect, plus-perfect,[14] imperative, gerund, past passive participle, mediopassive present and mediopassive past. The last three do not concern intransitive verbs. The "Main" grammar of a transitive verb (e.g., "kerel") contains ten inflectional grammars, whereas the "Main" grammar of an intransitive verb (e.g., "beśel") contains seven inflectional grammars.

All verbs with *-el* inflect in the same way in the present tense: *-av* in the first person singular, *-es* in the second person singular, *-el* in the third person singular, *-as* in the first person plural and *-en* in the second and third person plural.

ćhinav '(I) cut', *ćhines* '(you) cut', *ćhinel* '(he/she) cuts', *ćhinas* '(we) cut', *ćhinen* '(you) cut', *ćhinen* '(they) cut'.

All verbs with *-el* inflect in the same way also in the past tense: *-ŏm/-em* in the first person singular, *-ăn* in the second person singular, *-ăs* in the third person singular, *-ăm* in the first person plural, *-en* in the second person plural and *-e* in the third person plural.

ćhindŏm/ćhindem '(I) cut', *ćhindăn* '(you) cut', *ćhindăs* '(he/she) cuts', *ćhindăm* '(we) cut', *ćhinden* '(you) cut', *ćhinde* '(they) cut'.

However, *ćhinel* and *naśel* are associated with their specific inflectional paradigms according to transitivity and the past-tense morphemes in the Rromani module. The paradigm "**kerel**" 'to do, to make' is associated with transitive verbs with a past-tense morpheme *-d-* such as *ćhinel* 'to cut'. The paradigm "**beśel**" 'to dwell, to be sitting down' is associated with intransitive verbs with a past-tense morpheme *-l-* such as *naśel* 'to run away'.

There are variants in the past tense first person singular (e.g., *ćhindŏm* '(I) cut' in the O superdialect, *ćhindem* '(I) cut' in the E superdialect). We have developed these variants in the inflectional morphology of the Rromani module. When applying the NooJ dictionary to a text including these variants, NooJ will annotate their dialectal properties (Fig. 2).

---

[14] There are analytic and synthetic forms in the future, the imperfect and the plus-perfect according to dialects of Rromani.

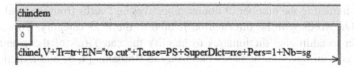

Fig. 2. Annotation of a variant *ćhindem* '(I) cut'.

Verbs with "-al".

- **as/al, -àndilo**[1] ÷ **-àndilăs**[1] ≈ **-àjas**[23]

  MA nevet; **EN** to laugh; **FR** rire; **ES** reir, reírse; **DE** lachen; **UKR** сміятися; **RO** a râde; **HR** smijati se; **SLK** smiať sa; **GK** γελάει.

The entry *asal* '*to laugh*' in the editorial dictionary consists of the lexeme *as-* and the present-tense ending *-al*. The basic form precedes three dialectal variants of past-tense endings *-àndilo* and *-àndilăs* used in the O superdialect (stratum 1) and *-àjas* used in the E superdialect (strata 2 and 3). The past-tense third-person singular forms are *asàndilo*[15] '(he) laughed', *asàndilăs* '(he/she) laughed' and *asàjas* '(he/she) laughed'.

asal,V+itr+EN="to laugh"+FLX=daral

The entry *asal* in the NooJ dictionary precedes its category and semantic value "V + itr" (intransitive verb), its translation in English (EN) is 'to laugh', its inflectional paradigm (FLX) is named "daral" 'to be afraid'.

Number of Verbs. We have identified and counted the verbs of the above six types according to their inflectional endings. There are 686 verb entries in total, i.e.,

- "-el" verbs: 476 entries,
- "-al" verbs: 39 entries,
- "-sarel" verbs: 77 entries,
- "-l" verbs: 23 entries,
- "-ŏl" verbs: 65 entries,
- "-ol" verbs: 6 entries,
- = > all verbs: 686 entries.

Number of Entry Words. We counted 4,525 entry words in the editorial dictionary, i.e.,

- nouns: 2559 entries,
- adjectives: 830 entries,
- verbs: 686 entries,
- others: 448 entries,
- = > all entry words: 4524 entries.

---

[15] This ending agrees with the genders of the subject: e.g., *asàndilo* '(he) laughed', *asàndili* '(she) laughed'.

After subtracting the number of nouns, adjectives and verbs from the total number, there are 448 words with no information related to the POS category. Therefore, we should refer to additional dictionaries to identify the categories of these entries. We would use two bilingual dictionaries published in Romania [4, 5] and a dictionary of structuring words published in France [3]. These dictionaries adopting the standardized Rromani alphabet would help determine the categories absent in the editorial dictionary and enrich the contents of the NooJ dictionary.

3 Conclusion and Perspective

We have identified 2,559 nouns, 830 adjectives and 686 verbs among 4,524 entries in the initial editorial dictionary and converted the information associated with each of these entries into formalized property codes to construct the electronic NooJ dictionary. We still have to identify the categories of 448 invariable words, such as adverbs, conjunctions and appositions.

We would first complete importing the entire editorial dictionary and then examine each entry to perfect the inflectional morphology and formalize the derivational morphology in the NooJ module for Rromani.

References

1. Courthiade, M., et al.: Morri angluni rromane ćhibǎqi evroputni lavustik. Romano Kher, Budapest (2009)
2. Courthiade, M.: Structure dialectale de la langue rromani. Études tsiganes **22**, 11–26 (2005)
3. Courthiade, M.: Lava-laćhǎrne an-i khetani rromani ćhib. INALCO, Paris (2007)
4. Sarǎu, G.: Dicţionar Romǎn-Rrom. SIGMA, Bucarest (2012)
5. Sarǎu, G.: Dicţionar Rrom-Romǎn. SIGMA, Bucarest (2012)
6. Gurbetovski, M. et al.: Guide de conversation rromani de poche. ASSIMIL, Chennevières-sur-Marne (2010)
7. Courthiade, M.: The Nominal Flexion in Rromani. In: Professor Gheorghe Sarǎu: A Life Devoted to the Rromani Language, pp. 157–211. Editura Universitǎţii din Bucureşti, Bucharest (2016)

Latin Pronouns, Numerals and Prepositions in the NooJ Tool

Anita Bartulović[(✉)] [ID] and Linda Mijić [ID]

Department of Classical Philology, University of Zadar, Zadar, Croatia
{abartulo,lmijic}@unizd.hr

Abstract. This paper is a contribution to the building of a NooJ module for medieval Latin. It presents a dictionary and grammars for the formalization of inflectional forms of pronouns and numerals. Furthermore, after expanding the dictionary with prepositions and conjunctions, we created a syntactic grammar for the extraction of prepositional phrases, which can include a varied number and types of inflectional words linked with one or more conjunctions. The compiled grammars were applied to a corpus of last wills and testaments written in medieval Latin in the Zadar commune. The results show a very high level of extraction of prepositional phrases, except for prepositional phrases containing full names, due to the complex and non-fixed structure of medieval full names.

Keywords: Medieval Latin · Last Wills and Testaments · Morphological Grammars · Latin Language · NooJ

1 Introduction

Since its first release in 2002, the NooJ software [1] has been widely used by researchers. NooJ modules for more than 50 languages are freely available online.[1] Most of these are for contemporary languages, which are well documented in databases, and as for classical languages, research has been conducted on ancient Greek participles [2]. The benefit of formalizing the language of notarial documents written in medieval Latin is the availability and processing of large amounts of different types of data essential for medieval studies.

This paper is a continuation of the work on building of a NooJ module for medieval Latin. Due to the fact that source texts are partially damaged (all documents are autographs), and that the language of that time was not uniform, i.e., standardized in the modern sense of the term, there are many challenges in preparing the corpus as well as creating algorithms for automatic recognition of these texts. Since NooJ resources for nouns, adjectives and adverbs [3–5] have already been created, the emphasis is now on other nominal forms (pronouns and numerals) and uninflected word classes (prepositions and conjunctions) and problems related to obtaining reliable results in the automatic recognition of these elements.

---

[1] Available at: www.nooj4nlp.net.

© The Author(s), under exclusive license to Springer Nature Switzerland AG 2024
A. Bartulović et al. (Eds.): NooJ 2023, CCIS 1816, pp. 39–50, 2024.
https://doi.org/10.1007/978-3-031-56646-2_4

This paper presents a dictionary and inflectional grammars for the recognition of all forms of pronouns (personal, possessive, reflexive, demonstrative, relative, interrogative, indefinite) and numerals (cardinal, ordinal), as well as morphological grammars for the recognition of compound (indefinite) pronouns (*aliqui* 'some', *quidam* 'someone, something', etc.). As the dictionary has been expanded with prepositions and conjunctions, we propose a syntactic grammar for the case government (rection) of prepositions, i.e., extraction of prepositional phrases, which can include a varied number and types of inflectional words linked with conjunctions and/or separated by commas. Special attention was paid to the local peculiarities of medieval Latin, considering the various changes and varieties in the formation of pronouns and numerals [6]. The compiled grammars have been applied to a corpus of 385 last wills and testaments (MedTest) written in the Zadar commune in the period from 1285 to 1409. Of these, 301 last wills and testaments were published in two Croatian editions of historical sources (*Codex diplomaticus regni Croatiae, Dalmatiae et Slavoniae* and *Notarilia Jadertina*), and 84 are manuscripts from notary records kept in the State Archives in Zadar [see more in 4]. The corpora consist of almost 250,000 tokens.

The paper is divided into the following sections: Sect. 2 presents the Properties' definition and Dictionary; Sect. 3 features an elaboration of the grammars for pronouns, numerals and prepositions; and in Sect. 4, the conclusion and planned future work are presented.

2   Properties' Definition and Dictionary

In the Properties' definition (see Table 1), we listed the types of pronouns as personal, possessive, reflexive, demonstrative, relative, interrogative and indefinite; numerals as cardinal, ordinal, distributives and adverbial, and finally conjunctions as coordinating and subordinating. Pronouns and numerals have additional features for case, gender and number. For prepositions, no definition was added.

Part of speech tag (POS), subtype and inflectional paradigm (if existing) was added to each lemma so that the dictionary entries look like the following examples:

```
ego,PRON+per+FLX=EGO
unus,NUM+card+FLX=UNUS
ante,PREP
antequam,C+subord.
```

Orthographic and morphological variants of a lemma are described by a superlemma, for example:

```
etiam,C+coord
ecciam,etiam,C+coord
eciam,etiam,C+coord
vicesimus,NUM+ord+FLX=CERTUS0
vigesimus,vicesimus,NUM+ord+FLX=CERTUS0
```

Table 1. Properties' definition for pronouns, numerals and conjunctions.

POS	Properties defined	Meanings of abbreviations
Pronouns	PRON_**Type** = per I ref I poss I posref I dem I rel I inter I indef I def;	# personal I reflexive I possessive I possessive-reflexive I demonstrative I relative I interrogative I indefinite I defective
	PRON_**Case** = Nom I G I D I Acc I Voc I Ab;	# nominative I genitive I dative I accusative I vocative I ablative
	PRON_**Gender** = m I f I n;	# masculine I feminine I neutral
	PRON_**Number** = s I p;	# singular I plural
Numerals	NUM_**Type** = card I ord I dis I ad;	# cardinal I ordinal I distributive I adverbial
	NUM_**Case** = Nom I G I D I Acc I Voc I Ab;	# nominative I genitive I dative I accusative I vocative I ablative
	NUM_**Gender** = m I f I n;	# masculine I feminine I neutral
	NUM_**Number** = s I p;	# singular I plural
Conjunctions	C_**Type** = coord + subord;	# coordinating I subordinating

3   Grammars

3.1   Pronouns

In this paper, we continue to deal with challenges since Latin is a highly inflected language. Latin pronouns are inflected for number (2), case (6) and gender (3). The inflection of most pronouns differs from the inflection of nouns; the main difference is in the genitive and dative cases.

Unlike in classical Latin, in medieval Latin there is a lot of confusion and inconsistencies in the writing and usage of pronouns: the widespread *michi* in the dative singular instead of *mihi* 'to me'; the feminine singular nominative and the neuter plural nominative/accusative of relative pronouns often has the form *qua* instead of *quae* 'which'; confusing the reflexive pronoun with *is, ea, id* 'he, she, it; this, that' and reflexive possessive pronouns *suus, -a, -um* 'belonging to himself, herself' with *eius/eorum* 'his, her, their', etc. [6].

In creating a morphological inflectional grammar for non-compound pronouns (personal, possessive, reflexive, demonstrative, relative, interrogative), we propose 15 paradigms. We used some paradigms of common nouns (LUPUS, TERRA, VERBUM, etc.) as embedded rules for annotating declensions of possessive pronouns. The descriptions of paradigms were written according to the following model:

```
EGO = <E>/Nom+s + <B3>(mei/G+s + mihi/D+s + me/Acc+s
+ me/Ab+s + nos/Nom+p + nostri/G+p + nostrum/G+p
+ nobis/D+p + nos/Acc+p + nobis/Ab+p);
MEUS = (:LUPUS):MASC + <B3>i/Voc+s+m
+ <B2>a(:TERRA):FEM + <B1>m(:VERBUM):NEUTR;
```

Compound pronouns (two compound indefinite relative and nine indefinite pronouns) were excluded from the list. Namely, one of two compound indefinite relative pronouns (*quicumque, quecumque, quodcumque* – 'whoever, whatever') and eight of nine indefinite pronouns (*aliquis, aliquid / aliqui, aliqua, aliquod* – 'someone, something'; *quilibet, quidlibet / quilibet, quelibet, quodlibet* – 'anyone' etc.) are formed from *quis, quid* (for the substantive form) and/or *qui, que, quod* (for the adjective form) and the invariable prefix *ali-* or the invariable suffixes *-libet, -quam, -que, -vis, -dam, -piam, -cumque*). Furthermore, the indefinite pronoun *unusquisque* has two inflected elements consisting of *unus, unum* and *quis, quid* (for the substantive form) or *unus, -a, -um* and *quis, que, quod* (for the adjective form) followed by the enclitic particle *-que* (see Table 2; the forms are given only in the masculine gender).

Table 2. The declension of compound indefinite relative and indefinite pronouns.

Case			
N	*aliqui*	*quilibet*	*unusquisque*
G	*alicuius*	*cuiuslibet*	*uniuscuiusque*
D	*alicui*	*cuilibet*	*unicuique*
Acc	*aliquem*	*quemlibet*	*unumquemque*
e	etc	etc	etc

The indefinite relative pronoun *quisquis, quidquid* 'whoever, whatever' has a duplicated form of *quis, quid*, and both elements are declined. However, only their nominative and ablative forms are used (N **quisquis, quidquid**, Ab **quoquo**).

In compiling an inflectional grammar for these types of pronouns, we initially created 15 rule inflectional paradigms for 8 of them. We had to include two paradigms for most of them, taking into consideration their forms, which are used as substantives and as adjectives. We were sometimes able to use paradigms of relative and interrogative pronouns as embedded rules. For example,

```
QUISPIAM1 = <L4>(:QUIS);
QUISPIAM2 = <E>/Nom+s+m + <L4>(<B4>c(uius/G+s+m
+ ui/D+s+m + uius/G+s+f + ui/D+s+f
+ uius/G+s+n + ui/D+s+n) + <B2>(em/Acc+s+m
+ o/Ab+s+m + i/Nom+p+m + orum/G+p+m
+ ibus/D+p+m + os/Acc+p+m + ibus/Ab+p+m
+ e/N+s+f + a/N+s+f + am/Acc+s+f + a/Ab+s+f
+ e/Nom+p+f + arum/G+p+f + ibus/D+p+f
+ as/Acc+p+f + ibus/Ab+p+f + od/N+s+n
+ od/Acc+s+n + o/Ab+s+n + e/Nom+p+n
```

```
+ a/Nom+p+n + orum/G+p+n + ibus/D+p+n
+ e/Acc+p+n + a/Acc+p+n + ibus/Ab+p+n));
```

However, we came to the conclusion that it would be more elegant to create a morphological grammar for these compound pronouns in the graphical editor (see Fig. 1).[2]

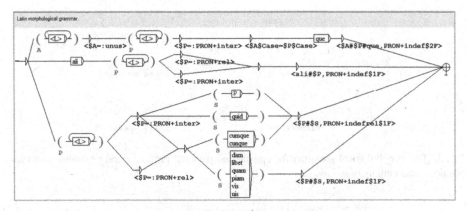

Fig. 1. The morphological grammar for compound pronouns.

When this grammar is applied, and annotations are added to the text, results show that NooJ recognizes all inflective forms of compound pronouns (see Fig. 2).

Before	Seq.	After
peruenerint ad etatem, volens, quod	quicquid	in hoc suo ordinauerit testamento
non possumus euitare discrimen, recte	unicuique	iminet precauendum ne in oculto
uel aliquorum et legiptimi comissarii	alicuius	defunti habent et habere possunt
procurator erit comunis Iadre, uel	quencumque	.... sufficienciorem et meliorem inuenire potue
et legitimus comissarius alicuius uel	aliquorum	habet uel habere potest in
dicta insula Pagy, et medietatem	quarumdam	salinarum in uale Pagy, et
uxore equali porcione per vnum	quenquam	tam masculum quam feminam. Et
a Francischina ipsorum suorum filiorum	unumquemque	.... mandatis eius a se expellere
urationis et quodlibet aliud instrumentum	cuiuslibet	generis necessarium faciendi et recipiendi

Concordance for text: OPORUKE tekst bez zagrada.not

Reset | Display: | 5 ⊂ characters before, and | 5 after. Display: ☑ Matches ☑ Outputs
⊙ word forms

Fig. 2. Concordance for compound pronouns.

Considering the fact that personal pronouns can be emphasized with the intensive suffix-*met*, e.g., *egomet* – 'I myself', *tibimet* – 'to you yourself', we created a morphological grammar for their recognition (see Fig. 3). However, there is another feature of

---

[2] We would like to express our gratitude to Kristina Kocijan (Department of Information and Communication Sciences of Faculty of Humanities and Social Sciences in Zagreb) for her help in creating this graph.

this grammar. Namely, the preposition *cum* with some pronouns in the ablative case appears postpositionally, and it merges with them into one word (*mecum* – 'with me', *tecum* – 'with you', *nobiscum* – 'with us', etc.), so this grammar can also annotate these compound words as a prepositional phrase.

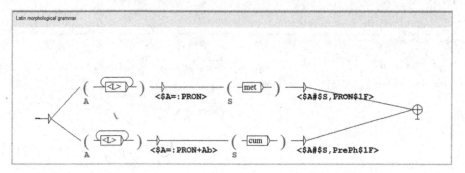

Fig. 3. The morphological grammar for emphasized personal pronouns and pronouns with the postpositional conjunctions *cum*.

A similar grammar (see Fig. 4) can be used for the processing of the enclitic conjunctions *-que* and *-ve*, which can be added to all groups of inflected words and adverbs. For example,

vitaque (noun)
firmumque (adjective)
eorumque (pronoun)
darique, dansque (verb)
deinque (adverb), etc.

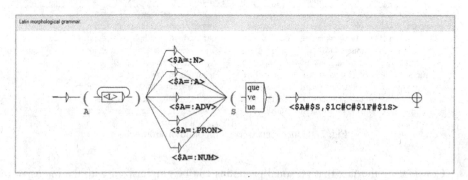

Fig. 4. The morphological grammar for enclitic conjunctions.

3.2 Numerals

Just like pronouns, ordinal numerals and most cardinal numerals are inflected for number (2), case (6) and gender (3). Regarding cardinal numerals, the first three numerals have a specific inflection, numerals from 4 to 100 are indeclinable, the hundreds over one hundred are declinable as adjectives of the first and second declensions, but only in plural form.

Before presenting the way we processed numerals in NooJ, we should point out some peculiarities in how they are written in medieval Latin documents. In the Middle Ages, cardinal and ordinal numerals were written either as Roman or Arabic numbers or as words, and sometimes partially both as numbers and words, as presented in examples 1 through 5 below. Furthermore, numerals were sometimes accompanied by a super-scripted minuscule letter. This is mostly the case with ordinal and cardinal numerals 4 and 100, for example:

Annis incarnationis eiusdem MCCC sexto, indictione IIII^a(...)'In the year of his incarnation 130 six, the fourth indiction(...)'(lat.*sexto* = engl.sixth)

$$(1)$$

Anno ab incarnatione eiusdem M$^\circ$CCC$^\circ$XLVIIII, indictione tercia(...)'In the year of his incarnation 1349, the third indiction(...)' $$(2)$$

(...)*exigere debeat et recipere XXXIIII^{or} libras*(...)'(someone)should get 34 livres(...)'

$$(3)$$

(...)*predicta comissaria mea dare debeat libras VIIII*$^1/_2$(...)'the above mentioned executrix of my will should give 9, 5 livres(...)'

$$(4)$$

(...)*XX libras deueniant Nicolao*(...)'Nicolaus should get 20 livres(...)' $$(5)$$

Furthermore, numerals in medieval Latin underwent numerous morphological changes: recomposition (e.g., *sedecim* > *sexdecim* or *sexdecem* 'sixteen'); classical subtractive double digit compounds ending in eight or nine were replaced by additive compounds (e.g., *duodeviginti* > *decem et octo* 'eighteen'); analogical formations (*octoginta* 'eight hundred' according to the *septuaginta* > *octuaginta*); misspellings (*quattor* for *quattuor* 'four'), etc. [6].

We designed an inflectional grammar with five paradigms in the rule editor for numerals, for example.

```
UNUS = <E>/Nom+s+m + <B2>(ius/G+s+m + i/D+s+m
+ um/Acc+s+m + o/Ab+s+m + a/N+s+f + ius/G+s+f
+ i/D+s+f + am/Acc+s+f + a/Ab+s+f + um/N+s+n
+ ius/G+s+n + i/D+s+n + um/Acc+s+n + o/Ab+s+n);
SINGULI = <E>/Nom+p+m + <B1>(orum/G+p+m + is/D+p+m
+ os/Acc+p+m + is/Ab+p+m + e/Nom+p+f + arum/G+p+f
+ is/D+p+f + as/Acc+p+f + is/Ab+p+f + a/Nom+p+n
+ orum/G+p+n + is/D+p+n + a/Acc+p+n + is/Ab+p+n);
```

Furthermore, we designed a grammar that recognizes multi-digit numbers with all the abovementioned peculiarities, as it is shown in the Contract (see Fig. 5).

We modified the grammar for the recognition and numeric value of Roman numerals presented in [7] by adding some characteristic peculiarities for medieval Latin (see Fig. 6).

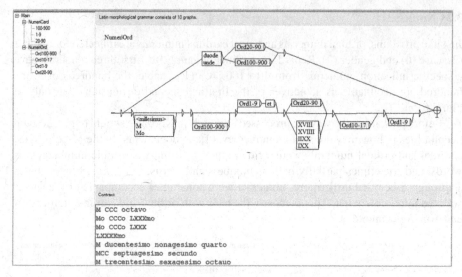

Fig. 5. The morphological grammar for multi-digit numbers.

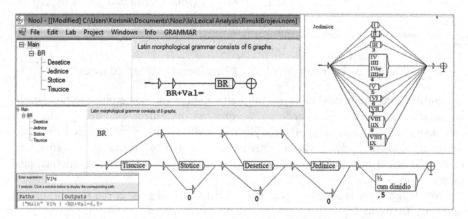

Fig. 6. The morphological grammar for the value of the Roman numerals.

3.3 Prepositions

Classical Latin prepositions are regularly used either with the accusative or the ablative case. Some of them can be used with both, depending on whether they indicate motion or state. The prepositions *causa* 'on account of' and *gratia* 'in favor of' are almost always postpositionally used with the genitive case.

There were many inconsistencies in the matter of prepositions in medieval Latin [6]. Due to the disintegration of the classical case system, numerous examples of case substitution with prepositions have been confirmed [8]. The most common was the case confusion in prepositional phrases, especially in the documents from the early medieval period.

In MedTest, a small number of inconsistencies are recorded, and they are marked with an exclamation mark in brackets, which in the published archival documents indicates some morphological or syntactical error, e.g., *ad sancta* (!) *Anastasia* (!) instead of *ad sanctam Anastasiam* 'to (sc. Church) Saint Anastasia'.

We also created a syntactic grammar for Latin prepositions (see Fig. 7).

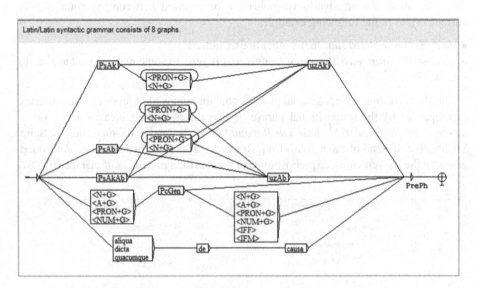

Fig. 7. The syntactic grammar for the prepositional case government.

Using the designed grammar (Fig. 7), it is possible to extract both simple and complex prepositional phrases, which can include several nouns followed or not followed by their attributes (adjectives, pronouns, numerals, nouns in the genitive case) and appositions. In such prepositional phrases, nouns can be separated by commas or linked/separated by various conjunctions (in bold), e.g.,

- *in Arbo, Pago, Nona, Iadera, Sclauonia* 'in Rab, Pag, Nin, Zadar, Slavonia' – several nouns separated by commas
- *in administratione et gubernatione* 'in administration and government' – two nouns coordinated with the conjunction 'and'
- *in dote siue repromissa* 'in the dowry or marriage portion' – two nouns coordinated with the conjunction 'or'
- *in ea parte et quantitate* 'in that part and quantity' – an attribute (pronoun) + two nouns coordinated with 'and'
- *in aliis operibus misericordie et pietatis* 'in other deeds of mercy and piety' – an attribute (pronoun) + a noun in the ablative case + two nouns in the genitive case coordinated with 'and'
- *in die obitus* 'on the day of (sc. His/her) death' – a noun in the ablative case and a noun in the genitive case

- *in augmento, utilitate **et** profectu ipsius filii mei* 'for the increase, utility and profit of my own son' – three nouns in the ablative case + an attribute (demonstrative pronoun) + a noun in the genitive case + an attribute (possessive pronoun)
- *in Andreasium fratrem* 'to brother Andrew' – a noun and an apposition in the accusative case

Also, an adverb or adverbs (in bold) can be inserted between the noun and its attribute(s), as in the following examples:

- *in domo **uero** altera sua* 'in his other house, indeed'
- *in aliquibus **tam** masculis **quam** feminis propinquis* 'to some male as well as female relatives'

In MedTest, many prepositional phrases contain names of churches or monasteries accompanied by the prepositional phrase *de* that refers to their location (e.g., *super terram monasterii sancti Michaelis de Rogoua* 'above the land of the monastery of Saint Michael (sc. Instead of Saint John) from Rogova'). Therefore, we added an embedded graph for the abovementioned prepositional phrases in the syntactic grammar (see Fig. 8).

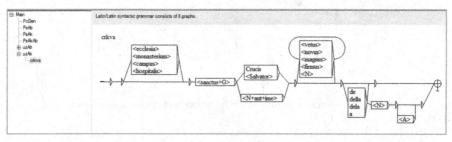

Fig. 8. The embedded graph for prepositional phrases containing an additional prepositional phrase.

The most complex prepositional phrases are those which include personal names because they were not as uniform as they are today. A medieval full name could contain various quantities of data in different word orders [see examples in 4]. For the recognition of medieval complex full names, we created two grammars [4]. Examples (6) through (8) show types of full names in prepositional phrases:

> *coram nobis Grisogono condam ser Damiani de Begna, Iohanne condam ser Francisci de Varicassis et Francischo condam ser Iohannis de Zadulinis, rectoribus Iadre* 'in the presence of us, Grisogonus of the late ser Damianus de Begna, Iohannes of the late ser Franciscus de Varicassis et Franciscus of the late ser Iohannes, rectors of Zadar'   (6)

> *super loco heredum Petri de Matafaris* 'above the place of the heirs of Petrus de Matafaris'   (7)

> *a Catiça, uxore Marci calegarii* 'from Catiça, wife of Marcus the shoemaker'   (8)

After successfully applying two grammars for the recognition of full male and female names with a higher priority level to the corpus, it was far too difficult for NooJ to apply the third grammar for prepositional phrases containing full names. The results in the debugger show that the grammar is functional, but the main problem is that the grammars are too complex due to numerous varieties of full names.

Except this problem with prepositional phrases containing medieval full names, the results obtained via the syntactic grammar for other prepositional phrases are good.

Still, there are some ambiguities. Since the dative and the ablative case have the same form, sometimes the object in the dative (in bold) is treated as part of the prepositional phrase (underlined), as can be seen in the example (9).

(...)[*ordino quod*]*soluatur solidos* ... grossorum, quos apud me hab**eo** <u>**in pecunia**</u>

<u>**presbytero Martino,**</u> **apatrino meo**(...)'I order to be paid shillings.. .which I have

with me in money(i.e., in cash)to the priest Martin, my confessor(...)'

(9)

As the word order in Latin is not strict, it is difficult for NooJ to differentiate between the accusative in a prepositional phrase and the following object in the accusative case (example 10 marked in bold).

(...)quarum vnam terciam partem <u>in Grisogonum filium suum</u> ***et aliam terciam partemin***

Franciscum filium condam Iohannis nepotem suum predictum voluit deuenire(...)'he

wanted one third of that to go to his son Grisogonus and another third to Franciscus,

the son of the late John, his aforesaid grandson(...)'.

(10)

There are ambiguities regarding the nouns *causa* and *gratia* in the ablative case because they can also be prepositions, for example:

- *Insuper <u>caritatis causa</u> Dobrice, filie condam Cressii de Calçina, legavit* (...) 'Moreover, for the sake of charity, he bequeathed Dobrica, the daughter of the late Cressius de Calçina (...)' – *causa* used as a preposition
- *ex quacumque causa et racione* 'from any cause and reason' – *causa* used as a noun

4 Conclusion and Future Work

By processing pronouns, numerals, prepositions and conjunctions, we have augmented the NooJ medieval Latin dictionary by approximately 400 lemmas, and at this stage, it contains about 6,000 entries.

The results of the lexical analysis show that there are no unknown pronouns, numerals and prepositions in the list of all the tokens that have no associated annotation. Still, since we only added lexical and morphological annotations, there are ambiguities, as mentioned before. In order to reduce them, we will have to create syntactic grammars after having completed the morphological processing of the whole corpus. Therefore, our future work will focus on the remaining word class of medieval Latin, i.e., verbs.

References

1. Silberztein, M.: Formalizing Natural Languages: The NooJ Approach. Wiley-ISTE, London (2016)
2. Reyes, S.S.: Formalizing the ancient greek participle inflection with NooJ. In: González, M., Reyes, S.S., Rodrigo, A., Silberztein, M. (eds.), Formalizing Natural Languages: Applications to Natural Language Processing and Digital Humanities. 16th International Conference, NooJ 2022, Rosario, Argentina, 14–16 June 2022, Revised Selected Papers, pp. 26–38. Springer, Cham (2022). https://doi.org/10.1007/978-3-031-23317-3_3
3. Mijić, L., Bartulović, A.: Formalizing latin. an example of medieval latin wills. In: Bekavac, B., Kocijan, K., Silberztein, M., Šojat, K. (eds.), Formalising Natural Languages: Applications to Natural Language Processing and Digital Humanities. 14th International Conference, NooJ 2020, Zagreb, Croatia, 5–7 June 2020, Revised Selected Papers, pp. 24–36. Springer, Cham (2021)
4. Bartulović, A., Mijić, L.: NooJ anotacije antroponima i toponima iz zadarskih srednjovjekovnih oporuka. In: Botica, I., Galović, T., Karbić, D., Miljan, S., Šimetin Šegvić, F., Šimetin Šegvić, N., Trogrlić, M. (eds.), Zbornik u čast Mirjane Matijević Sokol. Književni krug Split, Split (in press)
5. Mijić, L., Bartulović, A.: Pridjevi i prilozi srednjovjekovnih latinskih oporuka u NooJ formatu (to appear)
6. Stotz, P.: Handbuch zur lateinischen Sprache des Mittelalters. Formenlehre, Syntax und Stilistik, Bd. 2, pp. 116–139 (pronouns), 163–172 (numerals), 272–287 (prepositions). Verlag C. H. Beck, München (1996–2004)
7. Silberztein, M.: NooJ Manual (2003). www.nooj-association.org
8. Tekavčić, P.: Uvod u vulgarni latinitet. Sveučilište u Zagrebu, Zagreb (1970)

Towards a Linguistic Annotation of Arabic Legal Texts: A Multilingual Electronic Dictionary for Arabic

Khadija Ait ElFqih$^{(\boxtimes)}$ [ID], Maria Pia Di Buono [ID], and Johanna Monti [ID]

UNIOR NLP Research Group, University of Naples 'L'Orientale', Naples, Italy
{k.aitelfqih, mpdibuono, jmonti}@unior.it

Abstract. Terminology translation plays a significant role in domain-specific machine translation. However, some knowledge domains and languages still suffer from the lack of high-quality machine translation results due to the mistranslation of terminology. This is the case in the legal domain and the Arabic language. Most machine translation systems fail in their results to produce the exact equivalence of most legal terms for Arabic into other languages, mainly English and French. This failure highlights the lack of terminology resources related to the legal domain, the unfamiliarity of the legal systems to render the appropriate equivalences and the terminology linguistic characteristics of this type of discourse. This difficulty recalls the need for more legal terminology resources. In fact, even though there are many Arabic legal dictionaries, most of them are not machine-readable, and cannot be used in machine translation or other Natural Language Processing applications. As a pipeline, we first extract our terms using NooJ grammars, and then proceed with the creation of our dictionary using NooJ morpho-syntactic information (part of speech (POS), gender, number, etc.), syntactic information (transitive, intransitive, Naqis, etc.), and the creation of our semantic tags that describe our domain-knowledge terms including legal, Juri-religion, etc., and geoUsage to indicate where a given term is adapted to express a legal practice. Finally, we propose the translation. In this phase, the process relies on consulting many sources, including EUR-Lex, EuroVoc and IATE, to be then validated by our legal expert. Our electronic dictionary should enable the automatic annotation of the majority of legal documents in Arabic.

Keywords: Legal Terminology Resources · Multilingualism · Arabic Legal Dictionary · Machine Translation · NooJ

1 Introduction

In the field of natural language processing (NLP), linguistic and multilingual annotation of corpora plays a pivotal role in training and evaluating language models and applications [1]. The legal domain is no exception, with the need for accurately annotated legal texts in Arabic becoming increasingly important [2]. To ensure the quality and consistency of annotations in legal corpora for Arabic, the use of terminology resources

A. Bartulović et al. (Eds.): NooJ 2023, CCIS 1816, pp. 51–63, 2024.
https://doi.org/10.1007/978-3-031-56646-2_5

is paramount. These resources are particularly pivotal to improving the machine translation (MT) results for domain-specific terms [3]. Nevertheless, there is a significant upsurge of multilingual and standardized terminology resources in the legal domain for Arabic, especially in MT. This absence led to the incorporation of foreign terms or the adoption of imprecise and makeshift expressions, which may not accurately capture the intended legal concepts that are mostly affected by the culture, linguistic and legal system used therein. For instance, the example below shows the comparison between the results from the two MT systems, i.e., Google Translate (GT), Reverso Context (RC) and Human Translation (HT):

AR (source): يعتبر الفراش بشروطه حجة قاطعة على ثبوت النسب, لا يمكن الطعن فيه إلا من الزوج عن طريق اللعان, أو بواسطة خبرة تفيد القطع.

EN (GT): The **mattress**, with its conditions, is considered a definitive proof of paternity, and it can only be **challenged** by the husband through **li'an** or by means of experience that proves the **severance**.

EN (HT): The **marriage consummation** is considered strong proof of paternity; it can be **rebutted** only by the husband through **accusation** or **certain** evidence.

FR (RC): La **literie** selon ses termes est un argument concluant pour établir la filiation, qui ne peut être **contestée** par le mari que par la **baise**, ou par l'expérience de la coupe, par deux conditions : le mari en question apporte une preuve solide de sa demande; Un **mandat** a été émis pour cette expertise.

FR (HT): La **consommation du mariage** est considérée comme une preuve solide signifiant la paternité, il ne peut être **réfutée** que par le mari soit à travers **l'accusation** ou bien une **certaine** preuve.

The bold terms in the above example are domain-specific and context-dependent, so their correct translation requires the consideration of the context, as well as of the cultural, lexical, morphological and semantic properties of the terms in addition to their equivalences across languages and legal systems (i.e., English and French), as the HT does. This failure, caused by the upsurge of terminology resources for Arabic, affects the legal system's integrity, and creates confusion for those involved in legal proceedings and for legal scholars and researchers involved in accessing and annotating legal texts when conducting comparative studies or legal research [4].

Therefore, there is a great need for terminology resources in which each entry is explicitly associated with a set of fully defined linguistic properties. To contribute to filling this research gap, we use NooJ [5, 6], which gives the possibility of processing different natural languages and their related linguistic information, including morphosyntactic and semantic information. In this paper, we present the development of a multilingual AR-EN-FR legal dictionary using NooJ that will be capable of solving context-dependent issues, automatizing the process of annotating Arabic legal texts and obtaining the automatic translation of technical legal terms from Arabic into English and French. It consists of 1949 entries (70% are single terms and 30% are MWEs) extracted from various legal documents, mainly codes, decrees, contracts, provisions and constitutions of different Arab countries.

2 Workflow Methodology

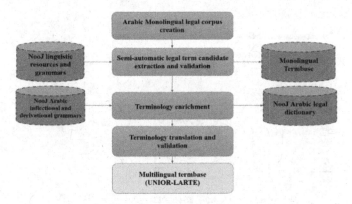

Fig. 1. Methodology Workflow.

The pipeline set up to develop the AR-EN-FR legal dictionary foresees our following steps (Fig. 1):

a. creation of Arabic monolingual legal corpus;
b. extraction and validation of semi-automatic legal term candidates using NooJ linguistic resources and grammars;
c. monolingual termbase as the semi-automatic extraction outcome, validated by a legal expert;
d. terminology enrichment, i.e., the creation of our dictionary, in which we:

- associate and/or enrich each entry with its grammatical and semantic properties;
- associate the translations after the validation;
- develop a dictionary incorporating Arabic inflectional and derivational rules.

e. translation of the terminology and submission of the termbase for validation to a legal expert;
f. the multilingual termbase UNIOR-LARTE (UNIOR Legal ARabic TErmbase) as the final result.

2.1 Arabic Monolingual Corpus Creation for the Legal Domain

As an initial step, we first created a legal corpus that we called ARLC (ARabic Legal Corpus) based on contracts, provisions, codes and regulations of different Arab countries (see Fig. 2). Data were collected from the official websites of Ministries of Justice, and others were provided by lawyers (contracts and provisions). This corpus is created using NooJ, consisting of 127 text files and 4,867,981 tokens. We then launch a pre-processing operation on our corpus where we eliminate common typographical errors such as confusion between Alif (ﺍ) and Hamza (ﺀ) or the substitution of (ﺓ and ﻩ) at the end of the word, the false writing of Hamza, the addition or omission of a character in a word, and any additional space that might be found in terms. Then, it is pre-annotated using NooJ linguistic resources for Arabic [6].

				Characters
Corpus Language is "Arabic(ar)";				Tokens
Original Text File format is "WORD".				Digrams
Corpus consists of 127 text files				Annotations
Text Delimiter is: "\n"				Ambiguities
Corpus contains 3780 text units delimited by "\n"				Unambiguous Words

File Name	Size	Last Modif.
DOC (33)	3588	28/05/2023
DOC (34)	3674	28/05/2023
DOC (35)	3936	28/05/2023
DOC (36)	4057	28/05/2023
DOC (8)	3938	28/05/2023
DOC (9)	3964	28/05/2023
إقرار بالنسب	1820	28/05/2023
انحلال العقد	97591	28/05/2023
حجة رجعة	1758	28/05/2023
طلاق إتفاقي قبل البناء	4405	28/05/2023
طلاق بائن مقابل الإبراء بعد الدخول	1904	28/05/2023
عقد الزواج	4924	28/05/2023

Fig. 2. ARabic Legal Corpus (ARLC) creation in NooJ.

2.2 Semi-automatic Legal Term Candidates' Extraction and Validation

Building upon the initial step, the focus now shifts toward the semi-automatic extraction of legal terms. In this phase, we semi-automatically extract single and multiword expressions (MWEs) using NooJ regular expressions and/or grammars. The results are then submitted for filtration and examination, where we delete irrelevant or inaccurate terms (i.e., terms that do not express a legal practice), and add new ones that were missed by the automatic process, and choose to process 1949 entries (70% are single terms and 30% are MWEs). In addition to this, all the entries are set in the base form to automatically extract other forms generated by the inflectional/derivational grammars we created accordingly (Sect. 6).

Then, all the listed entries were voweled manually so that NooJ could recognize unvoweled, semi-voweled and fully voweled entries. In some cases of Arabic legal terms, we can find entries that have different ways of vocalization and different meanings. For example, the term القِطَع with (.) means 'pieces', but القَطْع with (') means 'certainty'. Therefore, manual vocalization is a crucial step since it allows us to vowel entries depending on their semantic connotation. This helps reduce linguistic ambiguities in Arabic legal texts. After the consistency check of the Arabic legal term candidates' is done, the result is our ARabic Legal TErmbase (UNIOR-LARTE).

Terminology Translation and Validation. Terminology translation plays a significant role in domain-specific machine translation (MT). In this paper, we hypothesize that some knowledge domains and languages still suffer from the lack of high-quality MT results due to the mistranslation of terminology, and this is the case in the legal domain and the Arabic language [3]. Hence comes this project of creating an AR-EN/AR-FR legal dictionary using NooJ, where each entry is associated with its grammatical and semantic information and translations to enable not only the automatic annotation of any possible legal term in any possible legal corpus in Arabic but also use it in NLP tasks mainly MT.

However, equivalence in legal translation from Arabic into English and French is problematic; it requires careful consideration. Legal texts are highly specialized, and contain terminology and concepts that may not have exact equivalences in the target language. Therefore, we must carefully analyze the source text to identify the intended meaning, and choose appropriate terminology that accurately reflects the target legal concept in the target language.

Our approach to translating and/or checking the equivalences of legal terminology in AR-EN/AR-FR pairs involves three critical steps. Firstly, we developed a NooJ grammar containing all the terms in a node, and applied it to the corpus.

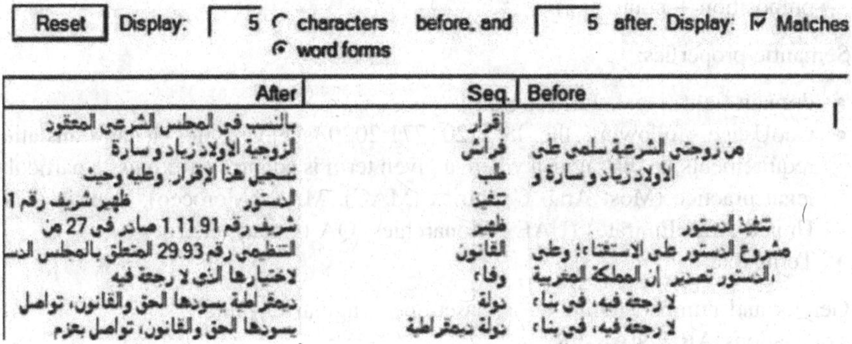

Fig. 3. Concordance sequences for capturing the context.

This operation assists in concordancing the entries' occurrences to capture the context where each term occurs, and which legal practice it conveys (Fig. 3) to then pre-decide the translations. Secondly, we use MT as a first attempt in compliance with consulting online gateways to EU laws, including EUR-Lex,[1] IATE[2] and Jeremy,[3] the intelligent online concordance search tool in EU law data in all 24 EU languages.

Following the completion of data preprocessing, the third and last crucial stage is the validation process. In this phase, the translations of the entries are subject to validation by our legal expert, whose language skills are perfect. This hybrid approach involves ensuring the accuracy, consistency and appropriateness of the extracted legal terms from Arabic into English and French, as it also allows for the incorporation of contextual information, domain expertise and linguistic knowledge. The outcome of this process is a comprehensive and validated list of multilingual legal terms poised for subsequent augmentations and enhancements in the coming sections.

---

[1] Available at: https://eur-lex.europa.eu/homepage.html?locale=fr.

[2] Available at: https://iate.europa.eu/.

[3] Available at: https://www.juremy.com/.

3   NooJ Arabic Legal Dictionary Creation (UNIOR-LARTE)

3.1   Terminology Enrichment

Following the validation process undertaken for the Arabic multilingual legal termbase, we proceed to initiate the creation of our dictionary, incorporating the validated and refined terminology as a foundational component. In this phase, we associate each entry with a set of properties as follows:

a. Part of speech (POS) tags:

- single terms;
- provision of the syntactic phrase structure composition for Arabic legal MWEs, giving each entry its component elements (noun + noun, noun + adj, noun + preposition + noun, etc.).

b. Semantic properties:

- domain field (legal, Juri-religion);
- GeoUsage, following the ISO 20 771:2020 standard, for legal translation requirements, to distinguish where a given term is adapted to express a particular legal practice (Most Arab Countries (MAC), MAR (Morocco), Tunisia (TN), United Arab Emirates (UAE), Monarchies, QA (Qatar), etc.;
- TermNote.

c. Gender and number: feminine or masculine, singular or plural.
d. Translations AR-EN/AR-FR.

The properties are encoded in a NooJ dictionary, and they are added to our entries. These codes are instantly available, and can be used in any NooJ query or grammar.

4   Inflectional and Derivational Rules

The development of an inflectional and derivational dictionary is a fundamental undertaking in the field of linguistics, aimed at capturing and organizing the intricate system of word forms and morphological processes within a language [7]. This academic endeavor involves meticulous analysis and documentation of inflectional patterns and derivational relationships, providing invaluable resources for researchers, language learners and computational linguists alike. By systematically cataloging the inflected forms and derived lexemes, such a dictionary enables a comprehensive exploration of the language's morphological structure, shedding light on its grammatical intricacies, lexical productivity and semantic nuances [8].

In this phase, we create a NooJ dictionary of inflectional and derivational rules[4] for Arabic. This step consists of the inflection and derivation process of the entries using grammars and the transformation of grammars into transducers [5]. For encoding the base form of our entries, this dictionary includes information about gender, number and

---

[4] https://github.com/Kaitelfqih/NooJ-Inflectional-derivational-dictionary-for-Arabic.git.

case needed to inflect our entries, as well as any irregular inflection pattern that may apply, such as vowels or the so-called الشكل in Arabic.

4.1 Inflection

Consider the following example in Table 1:

Table 1. Annotation of the entry خَبِيرٌ 'expert'.

		Annotation						
Entry	POS	Number	FLX	Sem	DOM	GeoUsage	EN	FR
خَبِيرٌ	N	S	FLX1	Hum	Legal	MAC	expert	expert

The term خَبِيرٌ 'expert' refers to a person recognized as a source of expertise in a branch of knowledge, particularly in the legal field, commerce, etc.[5] The rule of inflection -FLX1- applied to this entry inflects its masculine noun, feminine noun, masculine singular forms, feminine singular forms, masculine plural forms and feminine plural forms. This grammar also encodes the dual forms of both masculine and feminine genders. Consider these results:

- feminine dual form: خبير,خبيرَتَيْنِ+ f + d + a
- feminine plural form: خبير,خبيرَاتٌ+ f + p + u
- masculine dual form: خبير,خبيرَيْنِ+ m + d + a
- masculine plural form: خبير,خبيرُونَ+ m + p + u.

To inflect the later forms -FLX1-, is a rule based on diacritics or the so-called الشكل, which plays a vital role in conveying grammatical information about nouns. In NooJ grammar rules, they are referred as {a, u, i}: {a} for *fatha*, {u} for *damma* and {i} for *kasra*. They can be added to Arabic nouns to indicate their grammatical functions, and form different case endings and gender markers. For example, the addition of the vowel {a} or (*fatha*) and the {<T>} (ة: *Tah marbouta*) to the end of a noun can indicate the nominative case for feminine nouns, as in خبير,خبيرَةُ, while the addition of the vowel {u} or (*dama*) indicates the genitive case for masculine noun, as in خبير,خبيرُ.

Arabic diacritics form an essential component of Arabic language processing in computational linguistics, i.e., they must be taken into careful consideration as they play a crucial role in forming cases and gender markers for our terms. Furthermore, automatic diacritization techniques are needed to accurately process our corpus, as they provide important cues for disambiguating the morphological and syntactic structures and distinguishing between different concepts, which is what we will discuss more with the derivational descriptions of our entries.

---

[5] Available at: https://www.almaany.com/ar/dict/ar-ar/خبير/.

4.2   Derivation

Derivation in Arabic linguistics is the process of forming new words by adding affixes to a root. A root is a set of consonants that carries a core meaning, and can be modified by adding various vowels and affixes, suffixes or infixes to create different words. However, in addition to deriving words from roots, it is also possible to derive words from other words, even if they are not based on a root. Consider the following term مَسْؤُولٌ 'responsible' in Table 2:

Table 2. Annotation of the entry مَسْؤُولٌ 'responsible'.

	Annotation							
Entry	POS	No	FLX	Sem	DOM	GeoUsage	EN	FR
مَسْؤُولٌ	ADJ	s	FLXDRV	Hum	legal	MAC	responsible	résponsable

The term مسؤول 'responsible' is an adjective that describes a person or entity that is accountable for their actions or decisions, and who accepts the consequences of their behavior.[6] This term can be transformed into a noun by adding the suffix (ـيَّة) : مَسْؤُولِيَّة 'responsibility' using the NooJ grammar rule -FlxDRV- to indicate the state or quality of being accountable for one's actions, duties, decisions and obligations.[7]

Besides, this term can at the same time be inflected to indicate different cases and gender markers by the application of the same NooJ grammar rule -FlxDRV- that uses suffixes, prefixes, infixes and diacritization, and the results are the following:

- masculine form: مسؤولٌ,مسؤول +m+s+un
- feminine form: مسؤولةٌ,مسؤول +f+s+un
- feminine dual form: مسؤولتَيْنِ,مسؤول +f+d+a
- feminine plural form: مسؤولاتٌ,مسؤول +f+p+un
- masculine dual form: مسؤولَيْنِ,مسؤول +m+d+a
- masculine plural form: مسؤولونَ,مسؤول +m+p+u.

Transducers. So far, we have explained how to generate all possible noun cases and gender markers for our entries marked by the suffixes and الشكل: diacritics at the end of each entry in our dictionary. Now, we shall explain how to generate forms for entries that need suffixes, prefixes and infixes to be inflected and derived using NooJ transducers.

NooJ formalizes the inflectional and derivational paradigms by means of a finite state transducer [5]. They are based on morphological operators performing transformations within the input lemmas. These transformations are based on the use of certain predefined generic commands, and can be associated with two types of argument presented by Mesfar [7] in chapter 4 (see 4.4.1 "Generic morphological operators"). To illustrate the use of these transformational operators, consider entries in Table 3:

---

[6] Available at: https://iate.europa.eu/search/result/1689279604635/1.

[7] Available at: https://iate.europa.eu/search/result/1689279604635/1.

Table 3. Annotation of the terms عَقْد 'contract' and وَثِيقَة 'document'.

	Annotation						
Entry	POS	Number	FLX	DOM	GeoUsage	EN	FR
عَقْد	N	S	Oqoudon	legal	MAC	contract	Contract
وَثِيقَة	N	S	Wataaiq	legal	MAC	document	Document

To inflect the term عَقْد 'contract', the following transducer is created:

[Oqoudon=<LW><R><R>وَ<R><SW>/N+p;].

It contains the generic commands mainly<LW>(go to the beginning of the word) and <R> (right arrow); while doing so, we have to insert the diacritic of each letter as follows '<R><R>', and then add the infix وَ after the latter generic commands to form the plural noun of عُقُود 'contracts'.

To form the plural of the term وَثِيقَة 'document', the following transducer with the infix ائ and the genitive case {i} *kasra* is created which results in وَثَائِق 'documents':

[Wataaiq= <LW><R><R>ائ<S><R><S><SW>/N+p;]

Multiword Expressions. Our UNIOR-LARTE contains MWEs; hence, classifying and annotating them would have a major impact on the disambiguation of applications at the linguistic and multilingual levels working with Arabic texts [9]. The diverse parsers, based on morphological aspects, are not able to recognize MWEs [6]. In addition to that, morphological parsers usually separate MWEs into single terms. Therefore, recognizing MWEs as single lexical units is essential to preserve the semantics of texts. Consider the entry in Table 4:

Table 4. Annotation of the term مِسْطَرَة جِنَائِية 'criminal procedure law'.

	Annotation						
Entry	Unit POS	Pattern composition	FLX	DOM	GeoUsage	EN	FR
مِسْطَرَة جِنَائِية	N	N_ADJ	F1<P>F1	Legal	MAC	criminal procedure law	droit de la procédure pénale

This term consists of two terms مِسْطَرَة 'procedure' and جِنَائِية 'criminal'. To annotate it, we provide the POS as a single lexical unit <N> and its syntactic structure composition <N_ADJ> along with other properties, including domain, geoUsage, translations, etc. Note that the terms مِسْطَرَة 'procedure' and جِنَائِية 'criminal' already exist in the dictionary, so to obtain the inflected forms of the MWE, NooJ can reuse the inflectional paradigms *-FLX = F1<P>F1-* of the components without the need for separating or duplicating them. As a result, NooJ recognizes the following forms:

- مسطرتَيْن جنائيتَيْن,مسطَرةٌ جِنائية, d + i.
- مسطرتَانِ جنائيتَانِ,مسطَرةٌ جِنائية, d + u.
- مسطرتَيْن جنائيتَيْن,مسطَرةٌ جِنائية, d + a.

Fixed Terms. Fixed terminology refers to a set of standardized and defined terms that are used in a specific field or domain to ensure consistent and accurate communication [10]. Given that we are working with highly technical data from the legal domain in Arabic, most of our entries are fixed semantically and, in some cases, morphologically as well. Hence, no inflectional or derivational grammar rules are needed. Consider the following single fixed term and MWE القَطعُ, طَلَاق بَائن بيْنُونَة كُبْرَى in Table 5.

Table 5. Annotation of fixed terms and MWEs.

Entry	POS	Pattern composition	No	DOM	GeoUsage	EN	FR
				Annotation			
القَطعُ	N	-	s	Juri-religion	MAC	rebuttal	contre-preuve
طَلَاق بَائن بيْنُونَة كُبْرَى	N	N_ADJ1_ADJ2_ADJ3	s	Juri-religion	MAC	major irrevocable divorce	divorce irrévocable majeur

After the dictionary creation (Fig. 4), the following actions are taken:

a. Store the derivational/inflectional grammar and the properties definitions in the same folder as the dictionary.

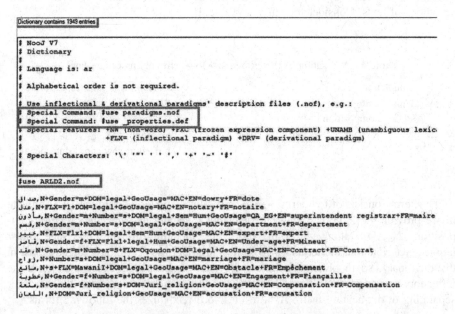

Fig. 4. Extract from the UNIOR-LARTE dictionary.

b. Add the commands to use the inflectional/derivational and the properties definitions paradigms in the dictionary.

c. Inflect the dictionary, and display the list of inflected and derived word forms, and then check if the dictionary is successfully compiled in lexical analysis.

We developed a large legal dictionary for Arabic, which, to the best of our knowledge, is the first electronic dictionary in the NooJ community that can:

a. recognize all the potential inflected forms;
b. annotate single terms and MWEs in Arabic legal texts;
c. improve the lexical coverage of the Electronic Arabic dictionary El_DicAr [6];
d. get a better semantic representation;
e. get automatic translations of Arabic legal terms in multilingual forms AR-EN/AR-FR;
f. reduce the lexical ambiguity.

5 Evaluation and Results

The complexity of analyzing Arabic legal terminology stems firstly from the intricate nature of the language itself; in other words, Arabic is a highly inflected language with a complex system of prefixes, suffixes and internal changes within words. This complexity poses challenges for translators and annotators who need to understand and convey the precise meaning of legal terms. The accurate identification and analysis of the root, pattern and grammatical features of legal terms are essential for their proper translation and annotation. Secondly, the cultural and historical context in which it operates, the lack of standardization, the need for precision and the interdisciplinary knowledge are required. These challenges highlight the importance of skilled professionals with expertise in both linguistics and law to ensure accurate translations and linguistic annotations of legal documents.

In this work, we develop a legal electronic dictionary for Arabic that contains 1949 entries. We believe this rate is high, especially considering all the variations that result in 2910 inflectional/derivational forms. Our electronic legal dictionary represents 70% of single terms and 30% of MWEs.

To test the lexical coverage of our UNIOR-LARTE, we first undertake the linguistic analysis of our corpora that contains 127 text files (Fig. 2). Afterward, we develop a NooJ grammar of recognition (Fig. 5), and calculate the precision (0.91) and recall (0.85). The results indicate that we have achieved high-quality recognition results. However, these are possible interpretations for the low rate of the recall:

a. false vocalization of terms: misplaced vowels;
b. common typographical errors: substitution of errosand (ه ,ة) at the end of the word and the substitution of (أ) هَمْزة القَطْع and (ا) هَمْزة الوَصْل at the beginning, middle or end of the word;
c. lack of entries in our dictionary;
d. typographical errors, etc.

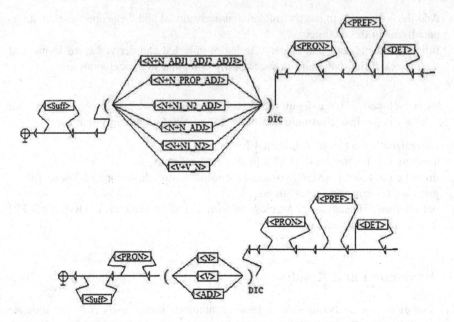

Fig. 5. Grammar of recognition for MWEs and single legal entries.

6 Conclusion and Future Work

This paper presents the development of a multilingual AR-EN-FR legal dictionary using NooJ. This dictionary is targeted toward solving context-dependent issues, automatizing the process of annotating Arabic legal texts and obtaining the automatic translation of technical legal terms from Arabic into English and French. It consists of 1949 entries (70% are single terms and 30% are MWEs). We believe that our method reduces linguistic, multilingual and terminological ambiguities, and improves the precision of the results.

The findings demonstrate that developing terminology resources for annotating legal corpora in Arabic improves understanding, standardizes legal terminology, enhances information retrieval, aids translation and comparative law research, supports legal education and training, enables legal technology applications, and promotes transparency and access to justice. These resources play a vital role in facilitating effective legal communication, research and the efficient functioning of the legal system. Nevertheless, developing legal terminology resources for Arabic is a challenging task due to the lack of existing resources and methodologies and the need for expertise in the legal domain. In future works, we intend to develop an automatic system that automatically translates the inflectional and derivational forms of our entries using NooJ grammars.

References

1. Garcia, M., Salido, M. G., Sotelo, S., Mosqueira, E., Ramos, M.A.: Pay Attention when you pay the bills. a multilingual corpus with dependency-based and semantic annotation of collocations. In: Korhonen, A., Traum, D., Màrquez, L. (eds.), Proceedings of the 57th Annual Meeting of the Association for Computational Linguistics, pp. 4012–4019. ACL, Florence (2019)
2. Moreno-Schneider, J., Rehm, G., Montiel-Ponsoda, E., Rodriguez-Doncel, V., Revenko, A., Karampatakis, S. et al.: Orchestrating NLP services for the legal domain. In: Calzolari, N. et al. (eds.) Proceedings of the Twelfth Language Resources and Evaluation Conference, pp. 2332–2340. European Language Resources Association, Marseille (2020)
3. Haque, R., Hasanuzzaman, M., Way, A.: Analysing terminology translation errors in statistical and neural machine translation. Mach. Transl. **34**(2–3), 149–195 (2020)
4. Halimi, S.: Arabic legal phraseology in positive law and jurisprudence: the historical influence of translation. Comparative Legilinguistics **46**(1), 37–64 (2021)
5. Silberztein, M.: La formalisation des langues : l'approche de NooJ. ISTE Editions, London (2015)
6. Mesfar, S.: Analyse morpho-syntaxique automatique et reconnaissance des entités nommées en arabe standard. Thèse de doctorat. Université de Franche-Comté, Besançon (2008)
7. Mesfar, S.: Towards a cascade of morpho-syntactic tools for arabic natural language processing. In: Gelbukh, A. (ed.) Computational Linguistics and Intelligent Text Processing, pp. 150–162. Springer, Berlin & Heidelberg (2010)
8. Najar, D., Mesfar, S., Ghezela, H. B.: A large terminological dictionary of arabic compound words. In: Okrut, T., Hetsevich, Y., Silberztein, M., Stanislavenka, H. (eds.), Automatic Processing of Natural Language Electronic Texts with NooJ. 9th International Conference, NooJ 2015, Minsk, Belarus, 11–13 June 2015, Revised Selected Papers, pp. 16–28. Springer, Cham (2016)
9. Constant, M., et al.: Multiword expression processing: a survey. Comput. Linguist. **43**(4), 837–892 (2017)
10. Cabré, M.T.: Terminology and translation. Handbook Transl. Stud. **1**, 356–365 (2010)

Recognition of Frozen Expressions in Belarusian NooJ Module

Yauheniya Zianouka[✉], David Latyshevich, Mikita Suprunchuk, and Yuras Hetsevich

United Institute of Informatics Problems of the National Academy of Sciences of Belarus, Minsk, Belarus
ssrlab221@gmail.com

Abstract. The article describes the resources for the automatic extraction of phraseological units in Belarusian within the research of syntagmatic delimitation of Belarusian prosody using NooJ. It comprises the dictionary of Belarusian phrasemes in NooJ format and 12 syntactic grammars for automatically searching different types of frozen expressions (phrasemes, nominal, adverbial, verbal, adjectival and mixed frozen expressions). Their implementation is essential for the computerized search of different types of syntagms for automatic speech delimitation to improve applications with voice accompaniment in the Belarusian language.

Keywords: Frozen Expression · Phraseological Unit · Syntactic Grammar · Intonation · Syntagma · Prosodic Delimitation · Segmentation

1 Introduction

In modern science, the question of the initial structural unit and perception of speech has no unambiguous solution because of various approaches and principles. However, speech is syntagmatic and comprises lexical units that form syntagms. The author's delimitation and proper intonation provide an adequate perception of speech. But synthesized speech, presented in various applications with voice accompaniment, is absorbed as unnatural, illegible and inexpressive. The way to solve this problem is to develop specific methods and algorithms for analyzing and processing intonation features of natural speech, its automatic syntagmatic separation and the implementation of all intonation constructions of a given language in NooJ [1]. It will lead to the automated reproduction of arbitrary text in the manner of human reading.

In the previous stages of the research, we composed syntactic grammars for extracting syntagms at the punctuational and lexical levels, highlighting the intonation boundaries [2–5]. The next task is to form a syntactic grammar for delimiting phraseological units or frozen expressions [6]. These phenomena are reproducible; at least two-component linguistic units that combine with words of free use and are integral in meaning. As a rule, they are stable in their composition and structure (that is, idioms). However, due to structural units, many frozen expressions in Belarusian are complicated to identify. For instance, the composition of phraseological expressions can be replaced by synonyms or other separate words. Or combinations, where one of the components is used in a phraseologically related sense and the other in a free one. Another problem is the order of units: in the phraseology, it can be fixed, or, more often, it is used in the reverse order.

So, the core of the research is to develop resources for searching and extracting phraseological units using NooJ [1]. Firstly, it is necessary to compile a phraseological dictionary of the Belarusian language in NooJ format based on the etymological dictionary of the Belarusian phraseological units and annotate it [7]. The next step is to build syntactic grammars for searching the most typical groups of frozen expressions. And finally, to test them on the literary corpus of the Belarusian NooJ module [1]. This will contribute to studying the automatic processing of phraseological units for further extraction into separate syntagms and forming their intonation portraits.

2 Syntactic Grammars for Extracting Punctuation and Lexical Syntagms

Our research on Belarusian prosodic segmentation focuses on three main problems: (1) the absence of research in the field of Belarusian prosody and intonology (practically unexplored); (2) the lack of automatic prosodic segmentation into syntagms; (3) the lack of deep syntactic parsing for the automatic selection of syntagms. They lead to the search for new approaches to developing machine algorithms, methods and techniques by defining sequences of linguistic elements associated with certain semantic relationships.

There are no general rules for syntagma extraction in Belarusian speech. However, the statistical analysis results based on experimental data provide a basis for developing a general algorithm for syntagma delimitation. The system planned for finding the intonational boundaries of syntagms is based on a superficial parsing with emphasis on the grammatical features of the part of speech (POS) categories. The primary task of this research is to develop formal syntactic grammar rules and algorithms that divide sentences into syntagms. To implement the algorithm, it is necessary to consider all punctuation marks' phraseological units and to create a list of formal rules for splitting sentences into lexical syntax.

When dividing a text into syntagms, one should consider the following aspects: sentence structure, word order, the presence of members of the same kind, the nature of word combinations and other linguistic parameters. In addition, each language has its own rules regarding syntactic relations and their application. Most sentences can be read purely syntactically, based on a superficial syntactic structure fully indicated by punctuation in Belarusian texts. However, syntactic structure alone may not be sufficient for correct delimitation, especially when the context is ambiguous due to the diversity of writing styles and genres.

As was noted in previous papers [2–5], we have distinguished three groups of syntagms for this project: punctuation, grammatical and lexical.

A *punctuation syntagma* (PS) refers to a sentence or part of a sentence that is limited to punctuation marks. A *grammatical syntagma* (GS) marks stable word combinations (phraseological units and collocations). A *lexical syntagma* (LS) is a short sentence of two or three words or a part of a sentence that is not limited to punctuation marks, and is expressed according to personal lexical signs (through certain words or phrases) or rules [8]. The task of this study is the correct extraction of all syntagms (PS, GS, LS) by developing, testing and improving syntactic grammars based on NooJ. For example,

- Дзе бацька той (PS): | недзе круціцца ў віры на калу (GS), | што ніхто не знае (PS), | дзе і што (PS). 'Where is the father (PS): | somewhere spinning in a whirlpool of the feces (GS), | that no one knows (PS), | where and what he is doing (PS)'.
- Ён нібы з неахвотаю (LS) | прыклаў да яе спіны далоні (PS). 'He seemed reluctant (LS) | to put his hands on her back (PS)'.
- Рыцар беларускасці (LS) | ніколі не ганяўся за славай (LS) | па прынцыпе пеўня (PS) | калі не даганю (PS), | дык хоць сагрэюся (PS). 'The knight of Belarus (LS) | never chased fame (LS) | on the principle of the rooster (PS) | (so) if I don't catch up (PS), | at least I'll warm up (PS)'.

Based on the theoretical analysis and applied computer processing of text material, we propose a step-by-step algorithm for determining syntagms and intonation boundaries in the text. It comprises three significant blocks according to the definition of syntagms (punctuation, grammatical, lexical) (Fig. 1).

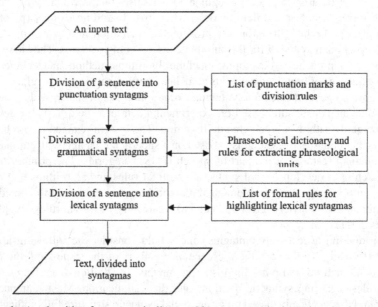

Fig. 1. An algorithm for automatically searching syntagms in the Belarusian language.

So, at previous stages, we developed syntactic grammars for exporting punctuation and lexical syntagms. Syntactic grammar for extracting punctuation syntagms is an automatic phrase segmentation technique at the punctuation level that marks phrase intonation types in Belarusian electronic texts using NooJ [2, 3]. This tool separates syntagms, drawing on the syntactic structure of a sentence and punctuation. It may be helpful to improve the Belarusian NooJ module for so-called prosodic transcription. The main drawback of grammar is the selection of phrases or sentence fragments only by punctuation marks. Without punctuation marks, the system highlights long phrases that are not syntagms. Syntactic grammar for automatically extracting lexical syntagms solves this problem [2, 4, 5]. The central core of grammar is a morphological and syntactic principle that lies in the ability of a particular POS category to agree with other words and word forms and occupy a specific position in a sentence. Its concept is based on a superficial syntactic analysis of different texts (based on corpora in the literary and medical domains), emphasizing the grammatical features of the parts of speech that combine the accusative units. To complete the algorithm presented in Fig. 1, it is necessary to develop a methodology for extracting phraseological units in the text, which is what the research aims at.

3   Phraseological Units of the Belarusian Language

According to NooJ terminology, *Atomic Linguistic Units* (ALUs) are the smallest elements that make up the sentence, i.e., the non-analyzable units of the language (simple words, affixes, multiword units, frozen expressions) [6]. *Frozen expressions* (FE) are ALUs spelled as potentially discontinuous sequences of word forms. Frozen expressions or phraseological units are reproducible, at least two-component linguistic units that combine with words of free use and are integral in meaning.

For the Belarusian language, there is only one source of phraseological units: the *Etymological Dictionary of Phraseological Units* by Lepeshau in 2 volumes (editions of 1981 and 1993) [7]. It received a historical and etymological reference of more than 1,300 phraseological units. Many dictionary entries, especially in the 1981 edition, have been corrected, supplemented or shortened. The books combine the old and new etymologies, and reveal the origin of about 1,750 phraseological units of the modern Belarusian language.

Within the research, the most frequent types of FE were singled out. They are:

a. phrasemes,
b. FE with lexical variation,
c. FE with obligatory right context,
d. FE with limited meaning,
e. FE with mandatory left and right context,
f. FE similar to free-word combinations.

A phraseme is a semantically indivisible unit, the meaning of which is wholly inferred from the sum of the values of its components. Their semantic independence is entirely lost. They are idioms, collocations, clichés, pragmatemes, e.g.,

- З вышыні птушынага палёту 'a bird's eye view'
- Да мозгу касцей 'to the core'
- З агню ды ў полымя 'from fire to flame'
- Абое рабое 'the kettle calling the pot black'

The group of phrasemes can be characterized by lexical variation. It means that one word can be replaced by its synonym. For example,

- Выбываць (*выбыць; выходзіць, выйсці*) са строю 'drop out (exit) from the line'
- Выводзіць (*вывесці; спісваць, спісаць*) у расход каго 'take out (write off) at the someone's expense'
- Порах(-у) не выдумляць (*не выдумаць*). 'Do not invent gunpowder.'

- Праз (*скрозь*) зубы 'through (thru) the teeth'
- Заставацца пры сваіх інтарэсах (*пры сваім інтарэсе*) 'remain in one's interests'

Many phraseological units cannot be used without an obligatory object environment ("right context"). Their meaning is realized only in a strictly defined context. For example,

- Адальюцца слёзы *каму чые*. 'Someone's tears will go away.'
- Зуб за зуб зайшоў *у каго, з кім*. 'Tooth for tooth went to someone.'
- Клюнуць на вудачку *чыю, каго, чаго, якую* 'to peck with someone else's fishing rod'

Some phraseological units have valently limited meanings. It is expressed only in a combination of phraseology with strictly defined words. For example, the expression куры не клююць 'a lot of' comes into contact only with the word грошы 'money'.

There are phraseological units with double obligatory right and left context, e.g.,

- *Станавіцца/стаць* і *пад/на* роўную нагу з кім 'to be on an equal footing with someone'
- Як *што/чаго* хоча (захоча) левая нага *каго, чыя*. 'What does/will someone's left leg want.'
- <*Адны*>скура ды косці засталіся *на кім, у каго, ад каго*. '<Only>skin and bones remained on someone, from someone.'

The last group can be confused with general word combinations. Their meaning may be interpreted only due to their semantics. Let us analyze the phrase божая кароўка' 'ladybug' in the next sentences. Its general meaning is 'red, yellow or white speckled bug'. Its FE meaning is 'a quiet, harmless person who does not know how to stand up for themself'.

- Прыгрэтая на падаконніку божая кароўка раптам заварушылася і пацёпала сваімі чырвонымі падкрылкамі. 'The **ladybug** warmed on the windowsill, suddenly stirred and fluttered its red wings'.
- Ня можа быць, каб ён быў шпіён, ён жа божая кароўка. 'He can't be a spy, he's **a ladybug**.'

The first sentence is used in general meaning, and the second is FE. Only the context and the meaning of the phrase can indicate whether it is a FE of a free word combination. Other examples of this type are represented below:

- Агульнае месца 'common place'
- Ад рукі пісаць 'write by hand'
- Без гальштукаў 'no ties'

As a part of the complex analysis of phraseological units, some specific features of phrasemes in Belarusian were identified. Firstly, the word order of some combinations can vary (гонар трымаць = трымаць гонар 'to keep honor'). Secondly, some phrasemes admit lexical insertions (у той жа момант –>у той жа [самы] момант 'at the same moment'). Finally, one or two lexical elements can often change their form. In the case of nominal phrasemes (multiword units) of the type [ADJECTIVE + NOUN], both elements are declined: вадзяная курачка, вадзяных курачак 'water hen'.

Also, we emphasized the types of FE according to the syntactic function: nominal, verbal, adjectival, adverbial and phrasal frozen expressions. This classification depends on the main component of FE (Fig. 2).

Nominal

ADJECTIVE+NOUN]: вадзяная курачка *('a water hen')*;
[NOUN+ADJECTIVE]: свет ясны *('a clear light')*;
[NOUN+NOUN]: зямля маці *('the mother Earth')*;
[NOUN+PREPOSITION+NOUN]: бочка з порахам *('a hornet's nest')*.

Verbal

[VERB+NOUN]: выскаляў зубы *('bare one's teeth')*;
[NOUN+VERB]: гонар трымаюць *('to keep honor')*;
[VERB+ADVERB]: кінуліся прэч *("they rushed away")*;
[NOUN+NOUN+VERB]: круг нагамі вытаптала *('I trampled the circle with my feet')*;
[VERB+PREPOSITION+NOUN]: бурчаў пад нос *('grumbled under his breath')*;
[VERB+CONJUNCTION+NOUN]: бягуць, як шалёныя *("they run like mad')*;
[VERB+ADJECTIVE+NOUN]: меў вялікія надзеі *('had high hopes')*.

Adjectival

[PREPOSITION+NOUN]: з капрызамі *('with whims')*;
[ADVERB+ADJECTIVE]: смяротна перапалоханы *('terrified to death')*;
[NUMERAL+ADJECTIVE]: першае лепшае *('the first best')*;
[ADJECTIVE+CONJUNCTION+NOUN]: белыя як снег *('white as snow')*;
[CONJUNCTION+ADJECTIVE+NOUN]: як парахавая бочка *('like a powder keg')*.

Adverbial

[PREPOSITION+NOUN]: з замілаваннем *('with emotion')*;
[ADJECTIVE+NOUN]: апошні раз *('last time')*;
[PREPOSITION+ADJECTIVE+NOUN]: з вераб'іныя нагавіцы *('with sparrow pants')*;
[CONJUNCTION+PREPOSITION+NOUN]: як па струны *('as if on cue')*;
[PREPOSITION+NOUN+PREPOSITION+NOUN]: ад краю да краю *('from edge to edge')*.

Phrasal (phrasemes)

[NOUN+ADJECTIVE]: дзень добры *('Good afternoon')*;
[CONJUNCTION/PARTICLE+NOUN] як ястраб *('like a hawk')*, як свіння *('like a pig')*;
[NOUN+WORD COMBINATION] лярва, хоць і у барве *('larva, though in barva')*;
[ADJECTIVE+PRONOUN+NOUN] мяккая яму зямля *('the earth is soft to him')*.

Fig. 2. Types of FE according to the syntactic function.

Thus, the next step of the research after classifying the types of frozen expressions is an application of NooJ as a suitable software product for the automatic extraction of phraseological units.

4 Syntactic Grammars for Extracting FE in NooJ

To fulfill the automatic extraction of frozen expressions, NooJ offers two ways to format frozen expressions. NooJ's syntactic grammars can represent and recognize all possible contexts for a given expression. Also, NooJ allows linguists to link a dictionary describing the possible components of a frozen expression with a grammar describing its syntactic behavior. We combined two approaches according to the variety of FE types. There is a dictionary of phrasemes as well as a limited number of syntactic grammars for searching frozen expressions represented in the article. Two main strategies were realized within the research:

a. NooJ Dictionary of phrasemes (idioms, collocations, clichés, pragmatemes) was collected and compiled. The reason is that there are a lot of phrasemes that do not vary grammatically, and do not admit any insertion. For such phrasemes, one must construct a dictionary, and there is no need to elaborate a local grammar. For example,

Кожнаму свая шкура даражэй,PHRASEME + PHRType = PHRASE 'Everyone's skin is more expensive.'

b. We developed syntactic grammars for searching nominal, adverbial, verbal, adjectival and mixed frozen expressions. Some phrasemes have a similar structure (as ад краю да краю 'from stern to stern', ад цямна да цямна 'from dawn to dusk'), and can admit lexical insertions. They should be organized in groups, and each of these groups requires a separate local grammar.

4.1 NooJ Dictionary of Phrasemes

For collecting and compiling the NooJ Dictionary of phrasemes, all possible fixed phraseological units, namely idioms, collocations, clichés and pragmatemes were chosen from [7]. The total number of phrasemes in the dictionary is 760 entries. The fragment of the dictionary is shown below:

Абы дзень давечара,PHRASEME + PHRType = PHRASE
Абы з рук, PHRASEME + PHRType = PHRASE
Авохці мне!, PHRASEME + PHRType = PHRASE
Агнём і мячом, PHRASEME + PHRType = PHRASE
Ад Адама,PHRASEME + PHRType = PHRASE
Ад а да я,PHRASEME + PHRType = PHRASE
Ад альфы да амегі,PHRASEME + PHRType = PHRASE
Ад варот паварот,PHRASEME + PHRType = PHRASE
Адвод вачэй,PHRASEME + PHRType = PHRASE
Адваротны (другі) бок медаля,PHRASEME + PHRType = PHRASE
Ад гаршка паўвяршка,PHRASEME + PHRType = PHRASE
Адданне чэсці,PHRASEME + PHRType = PHRASE
Ад дошкі да дошкі,PHRASEME + PHRType = PHRASE

We tested the dictionary of phrasemes by applying it to NooJ Belarusian Corpus "Kalasy 01_12". Locating the pattern "PHRASE" produces the list of frozen phrasemes as output. The function "Show Text Annotation Structure" confirms the use of the dictionary (Fig. 3).

NooJ cannot identify frozen expressions that contain one interchangeable component that depends on the author's usage, e.g., Ва ўсякім (у кожным) выпадку 'In any (every) case'. The same is true for the use of different cases for nouns and tenses for the verb, e.g., Шмат (многа, нямала, колькі, столькі) вады сплыло (сплыве) 'a lot of (how much, so much) water has floated away (will float away)'. A significant problem in using a dictionary is the insertion of an additional word inside a phraseme, e.g., Вось табе<бабка>і Юр'еў дзень! 'Here's to you<grandma>and St. George's Day!' The last one is the elimination of an object of action in phraseologism in the postposition of a transitive/intransitive verb with a controlling preposition, e.g., Волас з галавы не ўпадзе ў каго, з чыёй. 'A hair will not fall off/from anyone's head.' We solved this problem by constructing a separate syntactic grammar for similar phraseological units.

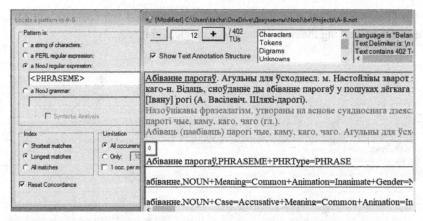

Fig. 3. An application of the dictionary of phrasemes in the Belarusian NooJ Corpus.

4.2 Syntactic Grammars for Searching FE

To process the remaining 1,000 examples of changeable phraseological units, we have created two syntactic grammars for each type (nominal, verbal, adjectival, adverbial and phrasal frozen expressions). The total number of syntactic grammars is 12. For each grammar, an average number of subgraphs are 5–8-word combinations.

A syntactic grammar for searching for some adjectival frozen expressions is shown in Fig. 4. It includes such phraseological units as:

•Заднім розумам моцны. 'The hindsight is strong.'
•I жук i жаба 'and the beetle and the frog'
•Лёд разбіты/паламаны 'to break the ice'
•Мамчын/мамін сынок 'mother's/mum's son'

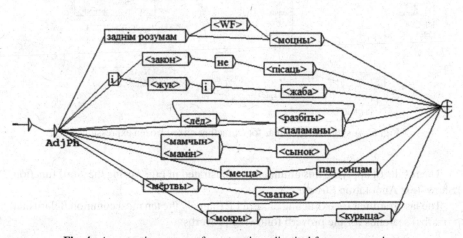

Fig. 4. A syntactic grammar for extracting adjectival frozen expressions.

The grammar depicts subgraphs in which the right and left contexts and FE are represented, preserving the core of the phraseological unit (Fig. 5).

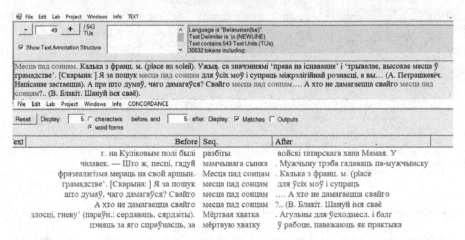

Fig. 5. An output of syntactic grammar for extracting adjectival frozen expressions.

The following syntactic grammar searches mixed verbal and adjectival frozen expressions with the main component вочы 'eyes' (Fig. 6). For example,

- Вочы вялікія адкрыць/раскрыць/адчыняць/рабіць (**verbal FE**) 'eyes wide open'
- Зрабіць вялікія вочы (**verbal FE**) 'make big eyes'
- Вочы на мокрым месцы (**adjectival FE**) 'eyes on a wet place'

Fig. 6. A syntactic grammar for extracting mixed frozen expressions.

The results of applying this grammar are illustrated in Fig. 7 using the NooJ function "Show Text Annotation Structure".

The last grammar for extracting phrasal FE (namely the ten most common Belarusian proverbs) searches for the proverb following proverbs:

- Да Абрама на піва трапіць. 'Go to Abram for a beer.'
- Дзяліць скуру незабітага мядзведзя. 'Split the skin of an unkilled bear.'

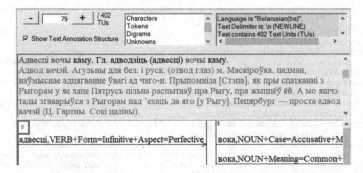

Fig. 7. An output of syntactic grammar for extracting mixed frozen expressions.

- Забіць двух зайцаў. 'Kill two birds with one stone.'
- Узяцца за гуж 'to take the buzz'
- Ухваціцца за саломінку 'grasping at straws'
- З'есці пуд солі 'to eat a pinch of salt'
- З мухі зрабіць слана 'to make an elephant out of a fly'
- Есці з сямі печаў хлеб 'to eat bread from seven ovens'
- Калоць вочы 'to sting eyes'
- Лезці са сваім статутам у чужы манастыр 'to go with your charter to someone else's monastery'

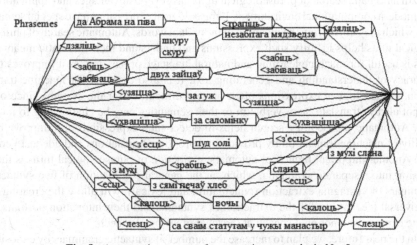

Fig. 8. A syntactic grammar for extracting proverbs in NooJ.

The syntactic grammar, shown in Fig. 8, indicates the proverb 'калоць вочы' 'to sting eyes'. It illustrates not only the word combination 'калоць вочы', but also the phrase with an opposite word order of this proverb with different time intervals ('калоў вочы', 'вочы калоць будуць', 'не будзе калоць вочы') (Fig. 9). As you can see, the grammar works, illustrating the results of searching for the proverb 'калоць вочы' 'to sting eyes'.

lay: [5] ○ characters   before, and   [5] after. Display: ☑ Matches ☑ Outputs
       ● word forms

Before	Seq.	After
...ыняй — разбурэннем, гібеллю ад персаў.	Калоць вочы/Phrasemes	каму. Агульны для ўсходнесл. м
што наш дастатак коле людзям	вочы/Phrasemes	, усе зайздросцяць, таму і плятуць
Ніхто яму, Вадзіму, не будзе	калоць вочы/Phrasemes	былымі памылкамі (І. Шамякін. Атланты
Выраз паходзіць з прыказкі Праўда	вочы коле/Phrasemes	, у складзе якой абазначае 'вельмі
развіўся варыянт кідаць (кінуць) у	вочы/Phrasemes	каму, каго што: Моладзь выбягала
Моладзь выбягала наперад і ў	вочы/Phrasemes	паліцыянтаў кідала гэтыя воклічы (Ц
пальчатку каму, чаму. Кінуць у	вочы/Phrasemes	каму, каго што. Гл. кідаць
пакрыць, пабіць карту праціўніка'. Куды	вочы/Phrasemes	нясуць (панясуць). Уласна бел. Адпаведн
а тады сабе пойдзеш куды	вочы/Phrasemes	панясуць (Л. Родзевіч. Пакрыўджаныя). `
з тым жа значэннем: куды	вочы/Phrasemes	глядзяць + куды ногі нясуць (панясуць
сцяну. Гл. на сцяну лезці.	Лезці са сваім статутам у чуж...	. Агульны для ўсходнесл. м. Умешвацца
двары з суседам. — Прабач, што	лезу са сваім статутам у чужы...	, — сказаў той. — Але шкада цябе
абшчыны манахаў. Лезці сляпіцай у	вочы/Phrasemes	<каму>. Уласна бел. Ужыв. са
так і лезеш сляпіцаю ў	вочы/Phrasemes	(М. Лынькоў. Векапомныя дні). Праз
снег усё ішоў лез у	вочы/Phrasemes	сляпіцай (Я. Брыль. У Забалоцці
на аснове фразеалагізма лезці ў	вочы/Phrasemes	(каму) шляхам пашырэння яго кампанент

Fig. 9. An output of syntactic grammar for searching the proverb 'калоць вочы'.

5   Conclusion

Within the current research, we performed several essential tasks: we created the NooJ dictionary of Belarusian phrasemes (nearly 760 entries), and developed 12 complex syntactic grammars for searching nominal, adverbial, verbal, adjectival and mixed frozen expressions. We verified them using NooJ corpus "Kalasy 01-12.noc".

An automatic search of phraseological units has several advantages and applications in a modern computational environment. Phraseological expressions have special semantics, which may differ from the meaning of individual words. Automatic search of phraseological units helps identify such expressions and understand their idiomatic meaning. This is useful for machine learning and natural language processing, as it improves the accuracy of understanding and generating text. It is also essential for machine translation. Phraseological expressions often present difficulties for the systems since one cannot always translate them verbatim or their semantics may be challenging to interpret. Automatic phraseology search helps to detect such expressions and improve the quality of machine translation by providing appropriate translations and adequate context. Another important branch of automatic extraction of phraseological turns is their division into a separate syntagma, which, in the general combination of two syntactic grammars of syntagma extraction (punctuation and lexical), will allow the creating of a universal mechanism for the extraction of syntagms and their intonation portraits to create expressive emotional speech at the level of artificial speech.

In the near future, we plan to increase the number of syntactic grammars by choosing the most popular and typical FE for Belarusians. Another one is to unify syntactic grammars for extracting punctuation, grammatical and lexical syntagms in one syntactic grammar as a single algorithm for automatic syntagma extraction. The results obtained will be used for further research in the automatic processing of Belarusian prosodic structure, in particular for computer systems with voice accompaniment.

References

1. NooJ: A Linguistic Development Environment, http://www.nooj4nlp.org/. Last accessed 21 July 2022
2. Okrut, T., Hetsevich, Y., Lobanov, B., Yakubovich, Y.: Resources for identification of cues with author's text insertions in belarusian and russian electronic texts. In: Monti, J., Silberztein, M., Monteleone, M., di Buono, M.P. (eds.) Formalising Natural Languages with NooJ 2014, pp. 129–139. Cambridge Scholars Publishing, Newcastle upon Tyne (2015)
3. Hetsevich, Y., Okrut, T., Lobanov, B.: Grammars for the sentence into phrase segmentation: punctuation level. In: Okrut, T., Hetsevich, Y., Silberztein, M., Stanislavenka, H. (eds.), Automatic Processing of Natural-Language Electronic Texts with NooJ. 9th International Conference, NooJ 2015, Minsk, Belarus, June 11–13, 2015, Revised Selected Papers, pp. 74–82. Springer, Cham (2016)
4. Zianouka, Y., Hetsevich, Y., Latyshevich, D., Dzenisiuk, Z.: Automatic generation of intonation marks and prosodic segmentation for belarusian nooj module. In: Bigey, M., Richeton, A., Silberztein, M., Thomas, I. (eds.) NooJ 2021. CCIS, vol. 1520, pp. 231–242. Springer, Cham (2021). https://doi.org/10.1007/978-3-030-92861-2_20
5. Zianouka, Y., Hetsevich, Y., Suprunchuk, M., Latyshevich D.: Prosodic segmentation of belarusian texts in NooJ. In: González, M., Reyes, S.S., Rodrigo, A., Silberztein, M. (eds.), Formalizing Natural Languages: Applications to Natural Language Processing and Digital Humanities. 16th International Conference, NooJ 2022, Rosario, Argentina, June 14–16, 2022, Revised Selected Papers, pp. 50–62. Springer, Cham (2022)
6. Silberztein, M.: Formalizing Natural Languages: The NooJ Approach. Wiley-ISTE, London (2016)
7. Lepeshau, I.Y.: Etymological Dictionary of Phraseological Units. Bielaruskaja encyklapiedyja, Minsk (1993)
8. Lobanov, B.: Computer Synthesis and Cloning of Speech. Bielaruskaja navuka, Minsk (2008)

Syntactic and Semantic Resources

A Proposal for the Processing of the Nucleus Verb Phrase of Pronominal (SVNPr) Verbs in Spanish

Andrea Fernanda Rodrigo[1]([✉]), Rodolfo Bonino[2], and Silvia Susana Reyes[1]

[1] Facultad de Humanidades y Artes, CETEHIPL, Universidad Nacional de Rosario, Rosario, Argentina
andreafrodrigo@yahoo.com.ar, sisureyes@gmail.com
[2] CETEHIPL, IES "Olga Cossettini", Rosario, Argentina
rodolfobonino@yahoo.com.ar

Abstract. The *Centro de Estudios de Tecnología Educativa y Herramientas Informáticas de Procesamiento del Lenguaje* (CETEHIPL) focuses on the pedagogical application of the NooJ tool created by Silberztein [1]. In this line of work and based on our Spanish Module Argentina, available on the NooJ platform [2], we have been addressing the formalization of lexical categories such as the adjective and the adverb. We will now go further into the processing of the verb, a complex lexical category that is a central element of the sentence. When dealing with the verb in Spanish, it is essential to include clitics since they always and only occur in construction with it. Following Bès [3], we will describe pronominal (SVNPr) verbs in Spanish. According to our usual methodology, a corpus of authentic texts written in Rioplatense Spanish was created. Specifically, in this case, a corpus of popular songs allowed us to account for the current use of pronominal verbs, as well as their distinctive particularities. For the sake of formalization, we introduced changes in the morphological grammar and the dictionary of the Spanish Module Argentina, and developed a syntactic grammar to recognize nucleus pronominal verb phrases (SVNPr). This syntactic grammar will be defined in contrast with nucleus transitive verb phrases (SVNTr) since the comparison between transitive and pronominal verbs is one of the most emblematic.

Keywords: Spanish · Verb · NooJ · Pronominal Verbs · SVNPr

1 Introduction

The *Centro de Estudios de Tecnología Educativa y Herramientas Informáticas de Procesamiento del Lenguaje* (CETEHIPL) focuses on the pedagogical application of the NooJ tool created by Silberztein [1]. The central ideas of this proposal are developed in our book *Aprendo con NooJ* [4]. In this line of work and based on our Spanish Module Argentina, available on the NooJ platform [2], we have been addressing the formalization of lexical categories such as the adjective and the adverb. We will now go further into the processing of the verb, a complex lexical category that is a central element of

A. Bartulović et al. (Eds.): NooJ 2023, CCIS 1816, pp. 79–89, 2024.
https://doi.org/10.1007/978-3-031-56646-2_7

the sentence. When dealing with the verb in Spanish, it is essential to include clitics since they always and only occur in construction with it. In this presentation, the focus is on the pronominal verbs of a specific corpus. However, since the complex nature of the verb in Spanish makes some verbs behave differently depending on their syntactic context, we designed dictionaries and grammars to account for this syntactic behavior. Our proposal is based on the contrast between pronominal and transitive verbs, which are one of the most emblematic.

1.1 The Nucleus Verb Phrase (SVN) in Spanish

Following Bès [3], we will formalize the nucleus verb phrase of pronominal (SVNPr) verbs in Spanish. From this perspective, the phrase ends in its nucleus, and phrase components place constraints on or arrow to the nucleus.[1] On the other hand, the nucleus phrase is integrated into a larger phrase that contains it. In the case of pronominal verbs, the clitic specifies constraints on the pronominal verb. Addressing pronominal verbs and clitics involves a challenge in automatic processing. The compulsory presence of the clitic with this type of verb tallies with Bogard's statements [6], who precisely points out that the "formal nature of clitics complicates the structure of the verbal word, whereas a verbal word plus one or more clitics produces the same verbal word."[2]

Defining the nucleus pronominal verb phrase without contrasting verbs in different syntactic contexts is challenging. It will be indispensable to compare pronominal and transitive senses. Nevertheless, nucleus verb phrases are integrated into a larger verb phrase (SINVERB).

Many verbs are transitive in some contexts and pronominal in other contexts, as in the case of *dar/darse* 'to give'/'to take to' or 'to arise', as seen in the following example of our corpus. For instance, in a sentence like *Va a perderse de vista* 'She/he/it is going to get out of sight', we will interpret the verb *perderse* 'to get out' as forming part of a nucleus pronominal verb phrase (SVNPr) included within a larger verb phrase (SINVERB): SINVERB [SVNPr <Va a perderse> de vista]. Instead, the same verb but with a transitive sense can form part of a nucleus transitive verb phrase (SVNTr), as in *He perdido un corazón* 'I have lost a heart'. The nucleus *he perdido* 'I have lost' stands at the end of the nucleus transitive verb phrase (SVNTr), and the larger verb phrase SV (SINVERB) also comprises the direct object *un corazón*.

How can we account for this?

2 Working with NooJ

For the sake of formalization, it was necessary to introduce changes in the morphological grammar and the dictionary of the Spanish Module Argentina. We also had to develop a syntactic grammar to recognize and generate possible expressions in Spanish containing nucleus pronominal verb phrases (SVNPr) to contrast them with others containing nucleus transitive verb phrases (SVNTr). We are particularly interested in the use of pronominal verbs in Rioplatense Spanish, although, in principle, there are no significant differences for Peninsular Spanish.

---

[1] We follow Bès's and Hagège's [5] statements about *fléchage* "arrowing" properties.

[2] The translation is ours.

2.1 The Corpus

According to our usual methodology, a corpus of authentic texts written in Rioplatense Spanish was created. Specifically, in this case, we chose popular songs to account for the current use of pronominal verbs and their idiosyncratic peculiarities. The corpus contains 32 songs written by Gilda, who was a famous Argentinian singer. She enjoyed great popularity in the 90s [7].

2.2 Methodology

Several procedures were followed to process the nucleus verb phrase of pronominal verbs in Spanish (SVNPr). We reformulated dictionaries and inflectional grammars by incorporating the required tags for new ALUs. We designed syntactic grammars so that they can recognize two entries for verbs that can be transitive or pronominal. Furthermore, we developed a general grammar for pronominal verbs considering the canonical order of clitics, and included negation, always within the nucleus verb phrase (SVN). We also developed a syntactic grammar to generate expressions that agree with the natural uses of pronominal verbs. To account for the behavior of pronominal verbs in authentic texts, we selected some sentences from the corpus,[3] and compared them with other transitive or pronominal structures. These verses are analyzed in the following subsections:

- *Me niego a comer* 'I refuse to eat' / *No me lo niegues* 'Don't deny it to me'
- *¡Cómo te voy a olvidar!* 'How am I going to forget you!' / *¡Cómo olssvidarme de ella!* 'How to forget her!'
- *La chica se pierde* 'The girl gets lost' / *Se me ha perdido un corazón* 'A heart has been lost by me'
- *Se enamora de todas* 'He falls in love with every woman' / *Enamora a las mujeres* '(He) makes women fall in love with him' / *Nadie más que tú para enamorarme* '(There is) no one but you to win my heart'
- *Dame tu amor* 'Give me your love' / *Me doy por vencido* 'I give myself up.'

Negar/Negarse: **Transitive/Pronominal Verbs.** Two lemmas had to be included in our dictionary, *negar* 'to deny' and *negarse* 'to refuse to':

negar,V+tr+FLX=JUGAR

negar,V+pron+FLX=JUGAR[4]

Figure 1 shows the "Main" grammar of *No me lo niegues*. There is a tacit or null PRO-DROP (pronoun dropping) subject [8] <SNN_SUJETO_PRO_DROP> and then a combination of proclitics, *me lo*, preceded by negation <ADV + 2c2> [9, p. 137] before the verb *negar* in the SVNTr.

---

[3] We compared expressions taken from our corpus of songs with other possible expressions in Spanish in order to account for the contrast between pronominal and transitive verbs.

[4] We entered lexical entries into our dictionary marking them with the same tags used in the RAE (Royal Spanish Academy) Dictionary [10], + [tr] and + [pron].

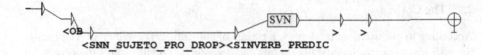

Me niego a comer
No me lo niegues

Fig. 1. Main grammar of the embedded nucleus verb phrase (SVN).

The transitive (SVNTr) and pronominal (SVNPr) nucleus verb phrases are shown below:

SVN

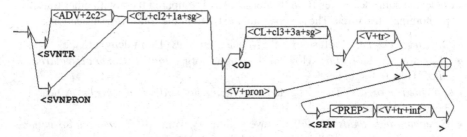

Fig. 2. Embedded graph of the nucleus verb phrase (SVN) that includes the transitive and pronominal senses of the verb *negar(se)*.

We validated these verses with "Locate > Grammar":

- *Me niego a comer*: pronominal verb *me niego* + prepositional phrase *a comer*.
- *No me lo niegues*: negation + indirect object + direct object + transitive verb.

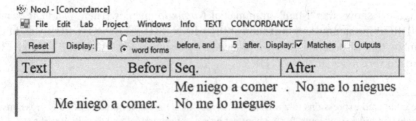

Fig. 3. Applying "Locate" to the grammar presented in Fig. 1.

Olvidar/olvidarse: **Transitive/Pronominal Verbs.** We compared and checked both occurrences, and modified our dictionary to include both the transitive and the pronominal sense, as we did with the verb *negar*:

olvidar,V+tr+FLX=AMAR

olvidar,V+pron+FLX=AMAR

To analyze the exclamatory sentences ¡*Cómo te voy a olvidar!* 'How am I going to forget you!' and ¡*Cómo olvidarme de ella!* 'How to forget her!', we added the future verbal periphrasis *ir + a + infinitive*, and specified that only the intransitive auxiliary *ir* 'to go' should be inflected:

ir a hacer,V+FLX=<P2>IR

ir a correr,V + FLX =<P2>IR.

ir a olvidar,V+FLX=<P2>IR

This grammar considers the possibility of processing these sentences with or without exclamation/interrogation marks in the transitive and pronominal sense of the verb. The validation of this grammar by applying "Linguistic Analysis" to both sentences is shown in Figs. 5 and 6:

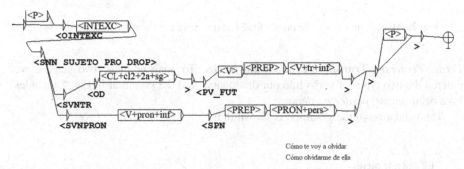

Cómo te voy a olvidar
Cómo olvidarme de ella

Fig. 4. Main grammar for the transitive and pronominal senses of the verb *olvidar(se)*.

0	5		15	18
OINTEXC				
cómo,INTEXC	SVNPRON			
		olvídame,V+V+pron+inf	SPN	
			de,N+fem+sg	ella,PRON+pers+3a+fem+sg+nom
			de,PREP	ella,PRON+pers+3a+fem+sg+obl

Fig. 5. Grammar validation of ¡*Cómo te voy a olvidar!* (SVNTr) and verb phrase (VP).

	5	8	12	14
ƆINTEXC				
:ómo,INTEXC	SVNTR			
	te,CL+cl2+2a+sg	ir a olvidar,V+pres+ind+1a+sg		
	OD	PV		
		ir,V+pres+ind+1a+sg	a,PREP	olvidar,V+tr+inf
				olvidar,V+pron+inf

Fig. 6. Grammar validation of *¡Cómo olvidarme de ella!* (SVNPr) and verb phrase (VP).

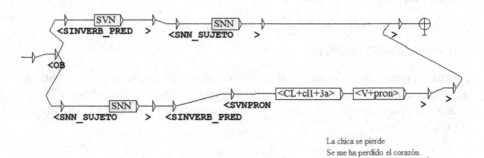

La chica se pierde
Se me ha perdido el corazón.

Fig. 7. Main grammar for the pronominal and transitive senses of the verb *perder(se)*.

Perder/Perderse: **Transitive/Pronominal Verbs.** To analyze these two senses, we entered the two types of verbs into our dictionary. And the grammar in Fig. 7 includes both occurrences: *perder/perderse*.

The validation of the grammar is shown in Fig. 8:

La chica se pierde

0		9	12	
OB				
SNN		SINVERB		
la,DET+artdet+fem+sg	chico,ADJ+fem+sg	SVNPRON		
la,CL+cl3+3a+sg+fem+ac	chico,N+fem+sg	se,CL+cl1+3a+sg	perder,V+pron+pres+ind+3a+sg	

Fig. 8. Linguistic analysis of *La chica se pierde* (SVNPr).

For reasons of space, the validation of the grammar of the pronominal sense of the verb is not included here.

To analyze the sentence *Se me ha perdido un corazón* (SVNPr), a grammar of compound tenses of the indicative mood was added to "Info > Preferences". We combined two grammars: the compound tense grammar of the present perfect indicative and the "Main" grammar involving the whole sentence. We ordered them by priority: the smaller grammar (compound tenses) has low-level priority, and the larger (involving the entire sentence) has high-level priority. For reasons of space, the compound tense grammar of the present perfect is not included here.

***Enamorar/Enamorarse:*Transitive/pronominal Verbs.** The following grammar in Fig. 9 recognizes two senses of the verb *enamorar*, both the pronominal sense of *enamorarse* in *Se enamora de todas* (SVNPr), as well as the transitive sense of *enamorar* in *Enamora a las mujeres* (SVNTr). In the first case, there is an implicit PRO-DROP subject plus and then a VP that contains a nucleus verb phrase (SVN) made up of the pronominal verb *se enamora* followed by the prepositional phrase *de todas.* In the second case, there is again a tacit PRO-DROP subject and then a VP with the transitive verb *enamora* but followed by a prepositional direct object, *a las mujeres.* It should be noted that *se enamora* can only be followed by the preposition *de* (SPN), whereas *enamora* can only be followed by *a* (SPN1):

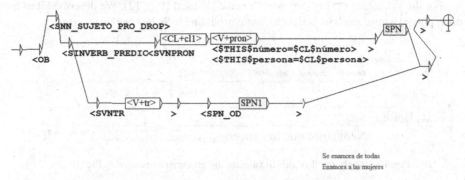

Fig. 9. Grammar for the pronominal and transitive senses of the verb *enamorar(se).*

In the following example, the transitive verb *enamorar* is no longer a finite verb (*enamora*) but an infinitive followed by the first person singular accusative clitic *me*, *enamorarme.* Here, we can pinpoint another grammatical requirement of the Spanish language. A non-finite verb does not admit clitics to be orthographically separated since clitics must attach to them as inflections, forming a unit with them.

To process *enamorarme*, we designed and constructed an inflectional grammar according to a model that could recognize this entry.

The grammar in Fig. 10 analyzes the transitive verb *enamorar* in *Nadie más que tú para enamorarme* '(There is) no one but you to win my heart'. There is an NP whose head is the indefinite pronoun *nadie*, followed by the comparative structure *más que tú*, and by an indirect modifier, the prepositional phrase *para enamorarme*, where the infinitive *enamorarme* made up of the transitive infinitive *enamorar* + the enclitic direct object me, follows the preposition *para.* The "Main" grammar is displayed in Fig. 10:

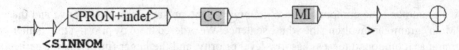

Fig. 10. Main grammar of *Nadie más que tú para enamorarme*.

Figure 11 shows the embedded graph of the indirect modifier, that is, of the prepositional phrase that includes the transitive infinitive + the enclitic direct object *me*:

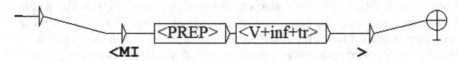

Fig. 11. Embedded graph that includes a transitive infinitive plus an enclitic.

For the validation of this sentence, "Locate" is used (Fig. 12). We described it as a noun phrase whose nucleus is the indefinite pronoun *nadie* 'no one'.

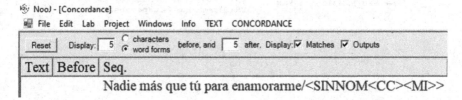

Fig. 12. Applying "Locate" to validate the grammar presented in Fig. 10.

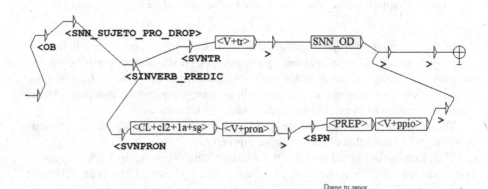

Fig. 13. Grammar for the pronominal and transitive senses of the verb *dar/darse*.

***Dar/Darse*: Transitive/Pronominal Verbs.** Figure 13 shows the grammar that can process the two senses of the verb *dar(se)* in D*ame tu amor* 'Give me your love' and in *Me* *doy por vencido* 'I give myself up'. For reasons of space, validation of the grammar is not included here.

2.3 Towards the Formalization of a Grammar for the Nucleus Pronominal Verb Phrase (SVNPr): Model *Jactarse*

Here, we propose a possible formalization of the pronominal verb *jactarse*, which will be our model for pronominal verbs. The grammar is shown below in Fig. 14.

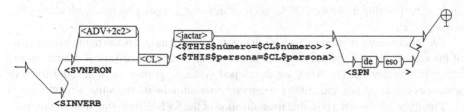

Fig. 14. A possible formalization of pronominal verbs taking as a model *jactarse*.

Applying this grammar generates many phrases, such as phrases made up of a pronominal verb followed by a prepositional phrase, phrases where the pronominal verb follows a negation, and phrases where the pronominal verb follows a negation plus a clitic or only one clitic (Fig. 15).

```
# Dictionary generated automatically
#
<ADV+2c2> <CL> <jactar>,+<+<>
<ADV+2c2> <CL> <jactar> de eso,+<+<+>+<+>
<CL> <jactar>,+<+<>
<CL> <jactar> de eso,+<+<+>+<+>
```

Fig. 15. Generation outputs after applying this grammar for SVNPr with the model *jactarse*.

Finally, in Fig. 16, the function "Locate > Matches > Outputs" is displayed to obtain expressions with the verb *jactarse* to validate the grammar presented in Fig. 14.

Text	Before	Seq.	After
		me jacto/<SINVERB<SVNPRON>>	no te jactes me jactaré
	me jacto	no te jactes/<SINVERB<SVNPRON>>	me jactaré de eso no
	me jacto no te jactes	me jactaré de eso/<SINVERB<SVNPRON><SPN>>	no me jactaré de eso
	jactes me jactaré de eso	no me jactaré de eso/<SINVERB<SVNPRON><SPN>>	

NooJ - [Concordance]
File Edit Lab Project Windows Info TEXT CONCORDANCE
Reset   Display: 5 ☐ characters / ☑ word forms before, and 5 after. Display: ☑ Matches ☑ Outputs

Fig. 16. Applying "Locate" with the grammar presented in Fig. 14.

3   Conclusion

This paper presented an analysis of nucleus pronominal verb phrases (SVNPr) following Bès's [3] statements. The analysis was conducted on a corpus comprising many songs from a famous Argentinian singer, Gilda [7].

After analyzing the verbs in this corpus, we noticed that according to the syntactic context, a verb can either be transitive or pronominal, i.e., a verb can form a nucleus pronominal verb phrase (SVNPr) or a nucleus transitive verb phrase (SVNTr). We showed that when a pronominal verb forms an SVNPr, it is usually followed by a nucleus prepositional phrase (SPN), such as *negarse a*, *enamorarse de*, *olvidarse de*, *darse por*, etc.

We modified our dictionary by adding tags that helped us characterize the two entries of the same verb as transitive or pronominal. Then, we designed lexical grammars to recognize the new ALUs. Also, we developed syntactic grammars to account for six sentences of our corpus and always compared pronominal with transitive structures.

Finally, we achieved a possible formalization of the SVNPr by taking the pronominal verb *jactarse* as a model and generated pronominal structures that include negation and a prepositional phrase.

4   Perspectives

We have not discussed the ethical datives here, such as *me*, which occur between the clitic and the verb (for example, in the sentence *no te me arrepientas*) since they are exceptional and typical of orality. We will study these latter strings as well as verbs that appear with different combinations of clitics in future work.

In our dictionary, there is not yet a complete list of verb entries that can be contrasted in their pronominal and transitive meaning. We have only presented a limited number of entries directly related to the pronominal verbs that appear in our corpus of songs. Therefore, our priority is to complete the entries of pronominal verbs and other classes of verbs. In each case, we must create labels for these classes.

We will continue to classify verbs according to their syntactic behavior, and add the corresponding tags.

References

1. Silberztein, M.: Formalizing Natural Languages: The NooJ Approach. Wiley-ISTE, London (2016)
2. Spanish Module Argentina, https://atishs.univ-fcomte.fr/nooj/resources.html, last accessed 2023/09/09
3. Bès, G.G.: La phrase verbal noyau en français écrit. Recherches sur le français parlé **15**, 273–358 (1999)
4. Rodrigo, A., Bonino, R.: Aprendo con NooJ: de la lingüística computacional a la enseñanza de la lengua. Editorial Ciudad Gótica, Rosario (2019)
5. Bès, G. G., Hagège, C.: Properties in 5P. [Research Report] GRIL, Université Blaise-Pascal, Clermont-Ferrand (2001). hal-01147889

6. Bogard, S.: Los clíticos pronominales del Español. Estrutura y fonción. Nueva Revista de Filología Hispánica LXIII(1), p. 1–38 (2015)
7. Lyrics of Gilda's songs. Available at: https://www.letras.com/gilda/, last accessed 2023/09/10
8. Rodrigo, A., Reyes, S., Mota, C., Barreiro, A.: Causal Discourse Connectors in the Teaching of Spanish as a Foreign Language (SFL) for Portuguese Learners Using NooJ. In: Fehri, H., Mesfar, S., Silberztein, M. (eds.) Formalizing Natural Languages with NooJ 2019 and Its Natural Language Processing Applications. 13th International Conference, NooJ 2019, Hammamet, Tunisia, June 7–9, 2019, Revised Selected Papers, pp. 161–172. Springer, Cham (2020)
9. Rodrigo, A., Reyes, S., Bonino, R.: Some Aspects Concerning the Automatic Treatment of Adjectives and Adverbs in Spanish: A Pedagogical Application of the NooJ Platform. In: Mbarki, S., Mourchid, M., Silberztein, M. (eds.) Formalizing Natural Languages with NooJ and Its Natural Language Processing Applications. 11th International Conference, NooJ 2017, Kenitra and Rabat, Morocco, May 18–20, 2017, Revised Selected Papers, pp. 130–140. Springer, Cham (2018)
10. Real Academia Española (Asociación de Academias de la Lengua Española): Nueva gramática de la lengua española. Espasa-Calpe, Madrid (2009)

German *selbst*-Compounds: Towards a NooJ Grammar

Marco Angster[✉]

University of Zadar, Zadar, Croatia
mangster@unizd.hr

Abstract. In this paper, we will describe the first steps taken to build a NooJ grammar able to annotate German *selbst*-compounds, a rather productive compound pattern that has attracted the attention of scholars in the domains of grammatical description, word formation and typology. After defining *selbst*-compounds, we will review the existing NooJ German module. We will then detail the procedure to get to an in-depth description of the phenomenon through the analysis of a sample of a thousand occurrences of *selbst*-compounds in a huge Web-based corpus of German. We will show the first version of our grammar based on the insights obtained from analyzing the corpus data, describe its output, and evaluate its performance. Finally, we will outline the future steps needed for improving the performance of the grammar.

Keywords: Compounds · Contrastive Coreference · German · NooJ

1 Introduction

In this section, we will introduce *selbst*-compounds in word formation and in the wider domain of intensifiers and define the general motivation of this study. In Sect. 2, we will review the NooJ German module in light of our aim at annotating German *selbst*-compounds. Section 3 sketches the procedure to identify the morphological (more specifically, derivational) complexity of *selbst*-compounds. Section 4 describes the preliminary results of building a NooJ grammar for *selbst*-compounds. Section 5 contains the conclusion and outlook of the paper.

1.1 German *Selbst*-Compounds

It is disputed whether compounding is a language universal [1], but Štekauer et al. [2, p. 308 ff.] attest the use of compounding in 50 out of the 55 languages included in their typological sample (90.91%) between suffixation (53/55, 96.36%) and prefixation (44/55, 80%). In Štekauer et al. [2], it is also observed that Indo-European languages display a tendency to use compounds at a higher than random frequency.

Compounding in German is particularly productive even when compared to English and Dutch, two closely related Germanic languages. The most productive pattern of compounding in German is, both in synchrony and diachrony, that of nominal N–N

© The Author(s), under exclusive license to Springer Nature Switzerland AG 2024
A. Bartulović et al. (Eds.): NooJ 2023, CCIS 1816, pp. 90–101, 2024.
https://doi.org/10.1007/978-3-031-56646-2_8

Table 1. Patterns of German nominal and adjectival compounds [4]

Left constituent	Right constituent	
	Noun	Adjective
Noun	*Finger·nagel* 'fingernail'	*fuß·kalt* 'having a cold floor'
Adjective	*Schwarz·brot* 'black bread'	*dünn·flüssig* 'thin runny'
Verb	*Tret·mühle* 'treadmill'	*denk·faul* 'mentally lazy'
Preposition	*Hinter·hof* 'courtyard'	*über·glücklich* 'overjoyed'
Numeral	*Drei·eck* 'triangle'	–
Adverb	*Jetzt·zeit* 'present times'	*rechts·extrem*
		'right-wing extreme'
Proper name	*Bunsen·brenner* 'Bunsen burner'	*merkel·spezifisch*
		'Merkel-specific'
Combining form	*Mikro·darlehen* 'micro loan'	*multi·national* 'multinational'
Cranberry morph	*Him·beere* 'raspberry'	–
Phrase	*Dritte-Welt-Phänomen*	*Lilien-und-Astern-blau*
	'Third World phenomenon'	'lily-and-aster blue'

compounds [3]. However, a variety of patterns involving different left constituents is nonetheless available, mainly having as outputs nouns and adjectives [4].

Beyond the combinations seen in Table 1, also minor, closed word classes can occur in compounds, e.g., pronouns:

- *Ich·form* 'narration in first person'
- *Wir·bewusstsein* 'group consciousness'

The examples above have as left constituent the German pronouns *ich* 'I' and *wir* 'we', respectively [5].

The case of *selbst*-compounds and of the lexical class of the left constituent *selbst* has often been considered in the German morphological literature, and with almost no exception, *selbst* is considered a pronoun, e.g., [5, 6]. This follows a tendency until recently widespread in the German grammatical tradition (see [7] for a short survey) to include *selbst* in the class of pronouns. This is probably due to historical reasons – Middle High German *sëlp*, from which German *selbst* derives, used as a kind of demonstrative pronoun [8] – but also due to the role of *selbst* in the reflexive construction in association with the reflexive pronoun *sich*.

1.2 Compounds and Intensifiers

A more current treatment of *selbst* links this element to the class of focus particles [9]. In their typological survey, König and Gast [10] connect *selbst* with the cross-linguistically heterogeneous functional class of intensifiers.

Despite the heterogeneity of the class, intensifiers share several functions, among others their frequent occurrence in the reflexive construction, especially the so-called heavy reflexive, as exemplified below.

- light reflexive: *er lobt sich* 'he praises himself'
- heavy reflexive: *er lobt sich selbst* 'he praises himSELF'

More often than not, the intensifiers occurring in the (heavy) reflexive construction have, similarly to German *selbst*, a role in word formation so that it is possible to recognize parallel series in different languages.

Table 2. Intensifiers and contrastive coreference markers: examples from German, English, Croatian

German	English	Croatian
Selbst·zerstörung	*self*-destruction,	*samo·uništenje,*
Zerstörung	*destruction,*	*uništenje,*
*er zerstört <u>sich</u> **selbst***	*he destroys <u>him</u>·**self**,*	*on uništi **samog** <u>sebe</u>,*
das Selbst	*the self*	*sam, sama, samo*
'the self' N	'ego, I' N	'alone' ADJ

In Table 2, we report an example of *selbst*-compound in German and in other European languages. The compounds in the first row are based on a deverbal action noun, reported in the second row. The third row contains a possible paraphrasis of the meaning of the compound, showing the use of an element (the intensifier, highlighted in bold) that corresponds to the marker in the compound above, and has the function to add to the (light) reflexive construction the idea that the coreferentiality of subject/agent and object/patient of the verb 'destroy' is remarkable, unexpected, i.e., in contrast with an expectation. Finally, in the last two rows, we report the possible syntactically free correspondent of the left constituent of the compound.

König [11] defines *selbst*-compounds and similar formations in other languages (cf. examples in Table 2) as "reflexive compounds". In this perspective, the bases with which *selbst*- and similar markers in other languages combine should display argument structures that allow for the coreferentiality of arguments. This is, however, not always the case (see) [7, 12-13]. On the one hand, it is possible to find formations with verbs displaying an anti-causative alternation – e.g., German *Selbst·entzündung* 'self-ignition' from the verb *entzünden* 'light, kindle' alternating with *sich entzünden* 'catch fire, ignite' – in which the interpretation keeps the idea of an unexpected state-of-affairs, but not of coreference, since in the anti-causative alternation the object of the transitive configuration is promoted to the subject in the intransitive configuration.

- transitive: *Er entzündet das Heu* 'He lights the hay'
- intransitive: *Das Heu entzündet sich* 'The hay catches fire'

On the other hand, if the interpretation of *selbst-* were always reflexive, there should not occur the case of complex words with this marker modified by prepositional phrases constituting the object of the embedded predicate, but only as subject.

- *the self-destruction of one's own writings* ≠ 'the destruction of oneself'
- *die Selbst·ernte von Obst und Gemüse* 'self-harvesting of fruit and vegetables' ≠ 'picking of oneself'

Contrast the examples above with the following ones:

John's self-destruction = 'John destroys/destroyed himself'
die Selbst·ernte von Luka = 'Luka performed the harvest by himself'

1.3   Motivation of the Study

Despite the interest in *selbst*-compounds and more generally in reflexivity – or contrastive coreference, as proposed in Angster [12, 13] – in word formation, few studies address the actual profitability (i.e., scalar productivity as opposed to availability [14]) of *selbst*-compounds with different types of bases (action nouns, agent nouns, different kinds of deverbal adjectives, etc.) or verbal roots. The presence of huge corpora of German allows for this kind of research question to be answered by providing a wide empirical basis. If obtaining long lists of *selbst*-compounds is trivial, cleaning the list, decomposing the compounds and analyzing them requires a lot of effort. If we add the variable of the possible different syntactic contexts in which the *selbst*-compounds occur, the steps mentioned above must be repeated for each relevant syntactic construction.

This constitutes the motivation of this study: devising a way to automatize the annotation process of *selbst*-compounds. The desired result of this automatization is to make the analysis of *selbst*-compounds (and possibly of other compounds or formations involving contrastive coreference markers) faster and more effective. This motivation translates into several more specific objectives:

a. identifying the bases of these compounds (their lexical class and word formation structure);
b. identifying the (types of) verbs embedded in (the majority) of these compounds.

In the paper, we will sketch our first steps in this enterprise that we will tackle using the NooJ platform [15]. In the next section, we will first consider the possibility of exploiting the existing resources developed for German by the NooJ community.

2   Compounds in NooJ German Module

A German module for NooJ [16] is available, and it includes a rich dictionary of 26,000 entries and an additional dictionary of 60,000 compounds. The module is also provided with a series of grammars for processing compounds generating more or less fine-grained outputs. However, the module was originally envisioned for the analysis of poetry and, in general, for the syntactic analysis of (literary) texts.

We tried to analyze a small sample corpus including a higher than random amount of *selbst*-compounds (see Sect. 3 below) using the resources of Müller's [16] German module. A first test showed that the module works, correctly identifies the words in the text, and provides an acceptable syntactic annotation. We have not performed a thorough evaluation of the resource, though.

Carrying out some additional tests, we could observe some of the limits of the use of the German module for the purposes laid out above in Sect. 2. First, only a few *selbst*-compounds are listed in the dictionary, while the ones not listed are not analyzed.

Even if we change the priority between the dictionary and the grammar devised for analyzing German compounds so that compounds are forcedly analyzed before the dictionary-based tagging, we get an output that does not meet our objectives. Although the grammars successfully process *selbst*-compounds splitting *selbst*- from the relevant bases, the objective of Müller's compounding grammar is the identification of the lexemes that make up compounds, without any further insight into the word formation structure of the bases, let alone a more fine-grained identification of the verbal bases.

By testing Müller's German module, it becomes evident that the objectives laid out above ask for a special treatment of compounds allowing to:

a. identify the derivational processes involved in *selbst*-compounds;
b. identify the verbs (verbal bases) involved in *selbst*-compounds.

To fulfill these objectives, we have to put aside for now the available NooJ German module, and we must start developing (almost) from scratch the resources needed for the analysis of *selbst*-compounds.

3 Identifying the Patterns of *selbst*-Compounds

Developing an effective algorithm to decompose and annotate complex words implies an in-depth knowledge of the phenomenon. This can be achieved by thoroughly describing a sample of formations rich enough to get a precise picture of the most frequent patterns and of the types of lexemes and lexeme-forming processes involved in the phenomenon of interest.

To get these preliminary insights into *selbst*-compounds, we employed the deTenTen13 corpus of the TenTen family [17]. We extracted a sample of 1,000 occurrences of the strings starting with the case-insensitive sequence of characters "selbst". The 1,000 tokens yielded 312 different strings, 306 after some cleaning of a few uninteresting typos. In case typos correspond to rarer bases, they have been corrected to enhance the representativity of the sample.

We report here below some examples of the complex lexemes obtained from the query, i.e., sequences of the marker *selbst*- and of a base of increasing morphological complexity.

- $[selbst\ [bild]_N]_N$
- $[selbst\ [sicher]_A]_A$
- $[selbst\ [[bau]_V]_N]_N$
- $[selbst\ [[führ]_V\ ung]_N]_N$
- $[selbst\ [[er\ [fahr]_V]_V\ ung]_N]_N$
- $[selbst\ [[wahr\ [nehm]_V]_V\ ung]_N]_N$

We will refer to the examples above and similar structures as {SELBSTK}. This constitutes the core of interest of this study and of the NooJ formalization that we will sketch in Sect. 4 below. However, the patterns above do not exhaust nor the level of complexity nor the type of patterns found in the sample. Here below, we further exemplify the sample showing compounds that add rounds of derivation or of compounding (highlighted in bold) outside {SELBSTK}; namely affixes or compound heads added on the right of {SELBSTK}.

- $[[selbst [bild]_N]_N \textit{nis}]_N$
  $\leftrightarrow [\{SELBSTK\} \textit{nis}]_N$

- $[[selbst [[er [fahr]_V]_V ung]_N]_N s \textit{[fähig]}_A]_A$
  $\leftrightarrow [\{SELBSTK\}s \textit{[fähig]}_A]_A$

- $[[selbst [[er [fahr]_V]_V ung]_N]_N s \textit{[wille]}_N]_N$
  $\leftrightarrow [\{SELBSTK\}s \textit{[wille]}_N]_N$

- $[[[selbst [[wirk]_V sam]_A]_A \textit{keit}]_N s \textit{training}]_N$
  $\leftrightarrow [[\{SELBSTK\} \textit{keit}]_N s \textit{[training]}_N]_N$

It is worth noting that our objective is to obtain a picture as detailed as possible of the patterns included under {SELBSTK}, while we will not give an in-depth account of the external rounds on the right of {SELBSTK}. From the variety of patterns attested in the sample, we can at least identify the following slots in a linear structure.

Table 3. Linear structure of *selbst*-compounds: attested slots

{SELBSTK}					External					
PP-	PREV-	ZU-	PREF-	ROOT	-CONV	-SUFF	-FUGE	-SUFF_EXT	-FUGE_EXT	-COMP
				bild						
				bau	V → N					
				führen		-ung				
			er-	fahren		-ung				
	wahr-			nehmen		-ung				
				bild				-nis		
			er-	fahren		-ung	-s			-fähig
				wirken		-sam		-keit	-s	-training
ge-				dremel	N → V I -t					
		zu-		nähen						

It goes without saying that the leftmost element is always the marker *selbst*-. The other constant ingredient in the compounds we analyze is a root (ROOT), which can also be the head of the compound (e.g., *Bild* 'image') or just the base of a derivational process. The derivational processes that we have observed include instances of conversion (CONV; *bauen* 'to build' → *Bau* 'the action of building') and suffixation (SUFF; *führen* 'to lead' → *Führung* 'the action of leading') on the right of the root and prefixation (PREF;

fahren 'to drive' → *erfahren* 'to find out; to experience') on the left. Additional lexeme-changing morphological modifications of a verbal root can be the effect of preverbs of different kinds (PREV; *nehmen* 'to take' → *wahrnehmen* 'to perceive'; → *annehmen* 'to accept'). There is no room here for an in-depth discussion of the properties of preverbs. What is relevant for the present study is the fact that, in contrast with prefixes, preverbs are less cohering, and allow some markers to be inserted between them and the root, for example *zu(-)* (ZU), used in the infinitive construction (e.g., *Er braucht mehr zu den Projekten zu erfahren* 'he needs to learn more about the projects'; *Er braucht dies Gestank wahrzunehmen* 'he needs to feel this smell'). The inflectional prefix *ge-* (PP), which marks the past participle, is the leftmost possible modification. Along with this position for which we have devised a slot in Table 3, *ge-* can also be inserted between a preverb and the root, similarly to *zu*. However, given that it is in complementary distribution with derivational prefixes, we have not devoted a special slot for this more internal position.

Table 3 also includes slots dedicated to word formation processes that are added outside (i.e., further on the right of) {SELBSTK}. As mentioned above, we have not aimed to provide a fine-grained analysis of this domain, so we have only defined three slots here. The most internal one is the slot dedicated to the linking elements (German *Fugenelemente* or *Fugen*; FUGE) that attach to {SELBSTK}, and precede more external compound elements (COMP). Between FUGE and COMP, we have defined slots for an additional round of suffixation (SUFF_EXT) and possibly for a linking element that attaches to this more external suffix (FUGE_EXT). We come up in this way with eleven different slots (including ROOT) that can be filled with morphological operations, which are usually – apart from the instances of conversion – also phonologically filled. We have not mentioned until now the fact that some processes, especially conversion and some types of suffixation, can affect the phonological form of the root via stem allomorphy (e.g., *vorwerfen* 'to reproach' → *Vorwurf* 'accusation'; *helfen* 'to help' → *Hilfe* 'help'). These cases are not very frequent in terms of type, but they might have a rather high token frequency.

In our sample, we have attested a limited number of combinations of filled slots. To get a quantitative idea of the complexity of *selbst*-compounds, we have built Table 4, in which we report the number of different patterns of filled slots and the number of types that represent the relevant patterns. The level of complexity corresponds to the number of different slots that are filled. The lowest level of complexity corresponds to the presence of at least a ROOT. From level 2, we have combinations involving a ROOT and one of the ten slots described above. It is worth noting that the levels of complexity higher than 4 in Table 4 all involve the presence of layers of derivation or compounding outside {SELBSTK}.

Interestingly, the most varied level of complexity as far as the variety of patterns is concerned is level 3, which is also the level characterized by the highest productivity. Moreover, the first three levels of complexity account for 52% (14/27) of the attested patterns but for 81% of the types (249/306).

In Table 5, the 27 attested patterns ordered by decreasing type frequency is listed.

The first five patterns, which account for 174 types (57% of the sample), are all characterized by a complexity equal or lower than 3.

Table 4. Complexity of *selbst*-compounds: number of patterns and types

Complexity	# of patterns	# of types
1	1	30
2	4	79
3	9	140
4	6	28
5	4	22
6	3	7
TOTAL	27	306

Table 5. Morphological patterns in *selbst*-compounds

	Pattern	Type frequency	Complexity
1	ROOT-SUFF	58	2
2	PREF-ROOT-SUFF	42	3
3	ROOT	30	1
4	PP-ROOT-CONV	23	3
5	PREF-ROOT-CONV	21	3
6	PREV-ROOT-SUFF	18	3
7	PREF-ROOT-SUFF-FUGE-COMP	18	5
8	PREF-ROOT-CONV-SUFF	14	4
9	ROOT-CONV	13	2
10	ROOT-CONV-COMP	11	3
11	ROOT-SUFF-COMP	10	3
12	PREV-ROOT-CONV	7	3
13	PREF-ROOT-SUFF-SUFF_ext	6	4
14	ROOT-SUFF-SUFF_ext	6	3
15	ROOT-SUFF_ext	5	2
16	PREF-ROOT-CONV-SUFF-FUGE-COMP	4	6
17	ROOT-SUFF-FUGE-COMP	4	4
18	ROOT-COMP	3	2
19	PREV-ROOT-SUFF-COMP	2	4
20	PREV-ROOT-CONV-SUFF-FUGE-COMP	2	6
21	ROOT-CONV-SUFF	2	3

(*continued*)

Table 5. (*continued*)

	Pattern	Type frequency	Complexity
22	ROOT-SUFF-SUFF_ext-FUGE_ext-COMP	2	5
23	PREV-ROOT-SUFF-FUGE-COMP	1	5
24	PREF-ROOT-SUFF-SUFF_ext-FUGE_ext-COMP	1	6
25	PREV-ROOT-CONV-SUFF	1	4
26	PREF-ROOT-CONV-SUFF-SUFF_ext	1	5
27	PREV-PREF-ROOT-CONV	1	4

The exploration of the sample of *selbst*-compounds has shown that these formations can achieve a rather high level of complexity involving different morphological devices, but this complexity is balanced by the fact that a small number of patterns account for the majority of the types. We can thus expect that the prospective NooJ grammar will quickly allow us to effectively treat a fair number of formations.

4   Towards a NooJ Grammar for *selbst*-Compounds

In this paragraph, we will sketch our first results in building a grammar to analyze German *selbst*-compounds. The scope of this study is rather limited, and our aim did not include developing a full-fledged grammar of German, but rather a tool to gain quick access to the structure and the lexemes that characterize a narrow family of German complex words. If limiting the scope of the grammar reduces its complexity and so the difficulty of the task, on the other hand, completing the task starting from scratch implies developing – at least to a limited extent – the linguistic resources needed for the analysis. We therefore chose to further reduce our aims.

First of all, we decided not to develop any inflectional component in our grammar, with the consequence that the grammar will not be able to process inflection, apart from citation forms – i.e., singular forms of the nouns and the predicative form of the adjectives. Secondly, we decided to leave aside the analysis of any round of derivation or compounding outside {SELBSTK}: this corresponds to 248 of the 306 types, namely 81% of the types and 701 out of the sample of 1,000 tokens. A third limitation is linked to the lack of a dictionary. As mentioned earlier, we decided not to exploit the dictionary available in the German component developed by Müller [16], so we decided to draw up a limited dictionary capable of accounting for at least the lexemes identified, analyzing the 1,000-token sample. The resulting dictionary includes verbs, nouns and adjectives for a total of 254 entries. The entries are, for the most part, simple roots, with the exception of prefixed verbs (e.g., *be·dienen* 'to serve') and verbs displaying a preverb (e.g., *wahr·nehmen* 'perceive'), whose verbal bases are also included as simple roots (e.g., *dienen* 'to be in service' and *nehmen* 'to take'). Finally, the present version of the grammar is still unable to analyze and annotate the output of derivational process characterized by conversion and stem allomorphy, i.e. non-concatenative processes implying the absence of an overt phonological exponent (e.g., *bauen* 'to build' → *Bau* 'the action of building'), or that imply phonological changes in the base (with or without the co-occurrence of an affix; e.g., *helfen* 'to help' → *hilfe* 'the action/an act of helping'; *stehen* 'to stand' → *stand* '(standing) position, state' → *ständ·ig* 'constant, permanent').

The present version of the grammar is reported in Fig. 1 below.

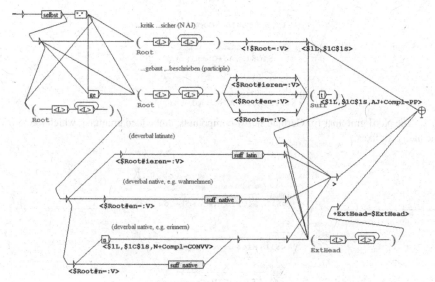

Fig. 1. The NooJ grammar for German *selbst*-compounds: main grammar

The grammar has two embedded grammars, which process the most productive concatenative exponents of native and non-native stratum. The grammar that deals with native suffixes (suff_native, see Fig. 2) is able to annotate the suffixes *-ung* (which forms action nouns), *-er* (which outputs agent nouns) and the adjectival suffixes *-sam*, *-end* and *-bar*.

The grammar which deals with non-native suffixes, most of which are in German of Latin or Romance origin (suff_latin, see Fig. 3), is devised to treat the suffixes *-ation* and *-age*, which form action nouns and *-anz*, a nominal suffix which can be interpreted as forming deadjectival abstract nouns – in turn derived from Latin deverbal adjectives in *-ans*, *-antis* Lat. *fragrans* 'fragrant', see e.g., Ger. *Fragranz* 'fragrance'.

The output of the grammar is an annotation in two parts. The first part (<\$ 1L, \$ 1C\$ 1S,...) reports the lexical, morphological and syntactic-semantic information of the verbal roots identified in the dictionary via one of the constraints in the main grammar (e.g., < \$Root#en = :V >). The second part of the annotation (e.g., ...,N + Compl = ung) identifies the lexical class and the relevant (concatenative) derivational process that a verbal root undergoes – if any: see the upper part of the main grammar, which filters all bases of *selbst*-compounds which cannot be recognized as deverbal (e.g., the noun *(Selbst)kritik* '(self-)critic' or the adjective *(selbst)sicher* '(self-)confident').

In the lower right part of the graph, we added a third level of annotation, which allows to process more complex compounds, the ones which add some derivational or

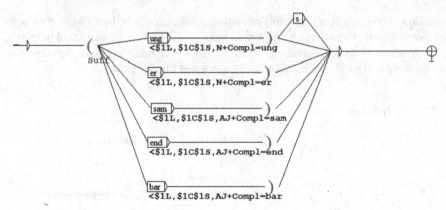

Fig. 2. The NooJ grammar for German *selbst*-compounds: embedded grammar, which identifies some native suffixes

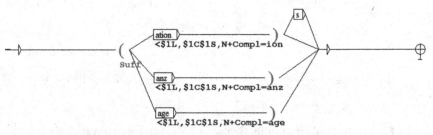

Fig. 3. The NooJ grammar for German *selbst*-compounds: embedded grammar which identifies some non-native suffixes, especially those of Latin origin

compound element on the right of {SELBSTK}. At this stage, the annotation is very rough, simply repeating the string stored in "ExtHead", but it is useful because it allows the grammar to annotate also the *selbst*-compounds embedded in larger structures.

To give a quantitative assessment of the results, the grammar can correctly annotate 148 compounds (48.4%), a number which rises to 193 (63%) with the addition of the "ExtHead" variable. If we consider only 148 out of 248 "simpler" compounds, the grammar successfully annotates 60% of the compounds that constituted our initial objective.

5 Conclusion

In this paper, we sketched our work in progress to create a tool to annotate German *selbst*-compounds using the NooJ platform. We started from scratch, creating a small dictionary and a grammar that would ideally be able to annotate at least "simpler" compounds (see {SELBSTK} in Sect. 3) displaying concatenative derivational processes identifying the underlying verbal root. The version of the grammar we presented in Sect. 4 can successfully annotate 60% of our sample. The rate of success is not high, and this is probably due to the fact that (fully or partially) non-concatenative derivational processes are quite widespread in German word formation. In NooJ, these processes are probably best treated in a dictionary, so our future aim is to further enrich the dictionary we built for this first project but also to consider to what extent we can exploit the existing German module and its dictionary to process *selbst*-compounds and their constituents.

References

1. Libben, G.: Why Study Compound Processing? An Overview of the Issues. In: Libben, G., Jarema, G. (eds.) The Representation and Processing of Compound Words, pp. 1–22. Oxford University Press, Oxford (2006)
2. Štekauer, P., Valera, S., Körtvélyessy, L.: Word-Formation in the World's Languages. A Typological Survey. Cambridge University Press, Cambridge (2012)
3. Schlücker B.: Die deutsche Kompositionsfreudigkeit. Übersicht und Einführung. In: Gaeta L., Schlücker B. (eds.) Das Deutsche als kompositionsfreudige Sprache: Strukturelle Eigenschaften und systembezogene Aspekte, pp. 1–26. De Gruyter, Berlin & Boston (2012).
4. Schlücker, B.: Wortbildung. In: Angelika Wollstein (ed.) Duden. Die Grammatik. 10. Auflage, pp. 608–637. Dudenverlag, Berlin (2022).
5. Fleischer, W., Barz, I.: Wortbildung der deutschen Gegenwartsprache, 2nd edn. Niemeyer Verlag, Tübingen (1995)
6. Fleischer, W., Barz, I.: Wortbildung der deutschen Gegenwartsprache, 4th edn. De Gruyter, Berlin & Boston (2012)
7. Angster, M., Gaeta, L.: Being itself: on German *selbst* in synthetic compounds. Zeitschrift für Wortbildung/J. Word Form. **7**(2), 89–120 (2023)
8. Paul, H.: Mittelhochdeutsche Grammatik, 25th edn. Niemeyer Verlag, Tübingen (2007)
9. Siemund, P.: Reflexivum. In: Hoffmann, Ludger (ed.) Handbuch der deutschen Wortarten, pp. 707–725. De Gruyter, Berlin & New York (2007)
10. König, E., Gast, V.: Focused Assertion of Identity: A Typology of Intensifiers. Linguistic Typology **10**, 223–276 (2006)
11. König, E.: Reflexive nominal compounds. Studies in Language **35**(1), 112–127 (2011)
12. Angster, M.: Le marche di coreferenza contrastive nella formazione delle parole. Una panoramica delle lingue d'Europa. PhD Thesis. University of Pavia, Pavia (2012).
13. Angster, M.: At the Boundaries of Word-Formation. Contrastive Coreference in 30 European Languages. University of Zadar/morepress, Zadar (2023)
14. Bauer, L.: Morphological Productivity. Cambridge University Press, Cambridge (2001)
15. Silberztein, M.: Formalizing Natural Languages: The NooJ Approach. Wiley-ISTE, London (2016)
16. Müller, R.: NooJ as a Concordancer in Computer-Assisted Textual Analysis: The Case of the German Module. In: Koeva, S., Mesfar, S., Silberztein, M. (eds.) Formalising Natural Languages with NooJ 2013: Selected Papers from the NooJ 2013, pp. 197–208. Cambridge Scholars Publishing, Newcastle upon Tyne (2014)
17. Jakubíček, M., Kilgarriff, A., Kovář, V., Rychlý, P., Suchomel, V.: The TenTen Corpus Family. In: 7th International Corpus Linguistics Conference CL, pp. 125–127. Lancaster University, Lancaster (2013).

Disambiguation Grammars for the Ukrainian Module

Olena Saint-Joanis[1,2]([⊠])

[1] C.R.I.T., University Bourgogne Franche-Comté, Besançon, France
olena.saint-joanis@inalco.fr
[2] CREE, INALCO, Paris, France

Abstract. Grammatical ambiguity is one of the problems to be solved when preparing a morphosyntactic analyzer because when they are not solved, users have to spend a lot of time removing them manually. In Ukrainian, ambiguities result from grammatical homonymy, which affects all grammatical classes. The grammatical homonyms that make up a homonymous pair or set may belong to different classes but also to a single class or paradigm. In this article, we will outline the typology of grammatical homonyms in Ukrainian and present some contextual grammars for disambiguation.

Keywords: Grammatical Ambiguity · Contextual Grammar · Ukrainian · NooJ

1 Introduction

Linguists and sociologists often use morphosyntactic text analyzers to study discourse or verify linguistic hypotheses. As a result, they need software that enables them to produce reliable statistics. Such software must be able to access large corpora, be error-free in its tagging and eliminate ambiguities.

There are currently very few open-source software tools available for the Ukrainian language. These include Sketch Engine [1], TreeTagger [2] and GRAC [3]. The first two are based on an empirical approach, and contain many errors [4]. GRAC is a large corpus tagged according to the formal approach, but ambiguities are not removed. We aim to prepare the Ukrainian module for NooJ and remove as many ambiguities as possible using contextual grammars.

The current version of NooJ consists of a dictionary containing 167,128 lexical entries and 21 morphological grammars. To these, we add the 11 syntactic grammars that resolve ambiguities related to grammatical homonymy.

2 Typology of Grammatical Homonyms

Grammatical homonymy is a well-known phenomenon in Ukrainian linguistics. This topic has been studied by Hriaznukhina et al. [5], Demska [6, 7], Kuzmenko [8], Shypanivska [9, 10], Sokolova [11], Bunio [12], Hlibtchuk [13], Holubenko [14]. Moreover, there is no well-defined classification of grammatical homonyms. So, we propose one adapted to NLP software. According to our classification, homonyms are divided into the following groups:

© The Author(s), under exclusive license to Springer Nature Switzerland AG 2024
A. Bartulović et al. (Eds.): NooJ 2023, CCIS 1816, pp. 102–113, 2024.
https://doi.org/10.1007/978-3-031-56646-2_9

a. inflectional homonyms,
b. homoforms,
c. lexico-grammatical verbal homonyms,
d. transposed homonyms,
e. mixed homonymous sets.

Inflectional homonyms belong to the same paradigm, and have the same graphic composition but have one or more different grammatical properties. For example, there are two inflected forms of the word сестра [sestra] 'sister' with flexion -и [y] → сестри [sestry]. The first refers to the genitive singular, while the second to the nominative plural. The flexions of these two inflected forms are also called homonymous flexions. In Ukrainian, inflectional homonyms account for 98% of all grammatical homonyms [9].

Homoforms can belong to the same or different grammatical classes, and their graphic composition is identical in one or more inflected forms. For example, ніс [nis] 'nose' (the masculine singular noun in the nominative) and ніс [nis] '(he) carried' (the imperfective verb in the masculine past tense). Or else, спала [spala] '(she) slept' (the imperfective verb in the feminine past tense) and спала [spala] '(she) fell off' (the perfective verb in the feminine past tense). We also note that there are several types of homoform pairs. The most common are noun-verb, adjective-verb, verb-adverb, noun-adverb, adjective-adverb [9].

Verbal lexico-grammatical homonyms have the same graphic composition in all arrow forms but do not have the same verbal aspect. For example, заносити [zanosyty] 'bring (something) inside' – the imperfective verb of the aspectual pair заносити [zanosyty] IPF/занести [zanesty] PF, and заносити [zanosyty] 'wear out (clothes)'– the secondary perfective verbs.

Transposed homonyms have been created through conversion, i.e., the transposition of the lexical unit from one class to another without any change in form. So, homonyms of this type have an etymological link, and belong to two or more different classes. For example, коло [kolo] belongs to two classes: the singular neuter noun in the nominative 'circle' and the preposition 'next to'; так [tak] belongs to three classes: the adverb 'so', the particle 'yes' and the conjunction 'but'. In this case, it is not a couple but a homonymous set. This group of homonyms also includes adjective–nominalized adjective pairs, such as зоряний [zorianyi] 'stellar'– the adjective masculine and Зоряний [zorianyi] masculine proper noun.

Mixed homonymous sets are made up of several homonyms that can belong to several homonym types, as mentioned above. In this case, we find за [za] as the preposition 'behind', the adverb 'for', the particle 'what kind', or we find коли [koly] as the conjunction 'when', the adverb 'when', the imperative of the verb колоти [koloty] 'to prick' in the second-person singular, feminine noun кола [kola] 'Coca-Cola' in the genitive singular and masculine noun кіл [kil] 'picket' in the nominative plural.

In this article, we will first present contextual grammars that allow us to remove ambiguities linked to inflectional homonyms. Then, we introduce a grammar for disambiguating homoform pairs in which one member is a verb. We will also propose a grammar for distinguishing conjunctions in transposed or mixed homonymous sets. Finally, we will suggest a few ways to complete our work.

3 Inflectional Homonyms

Ukrainian is an inflectional language. This means that the ending of a lexical unit can change under the influence of grammatical factors, creating inflected forms. Inflected forms constitute a paradigm. All lexical units are divided into grammatical classes with the same morphological and syntactic properties. A grammatical class composed of units that have inflected forms is called a grammatical variable class. Ukrainian traditionally distinguishes ten grammatical classes, five of which are variable: noun, verb, adjective, numeral and pronoun.

Paradigms of different classes do not include the same properties. For example, the nominal paradigm involves cases (nominative, genitive, accusative, dative, instrumental, locative, vocative) motivated by the word's role in the sentence and then numbers (singular and plural) inspired by quantity. Thus, each nominal paradigm comprises a minimum of 14 inflected forms. Note that some properties, such as animate/inanimate[1] and gender (masculine, feminine, neuter), do not have any variation inside the nominal paradigm.[2] But they are included in the adjectival paradigm, as an adjective must accord with the noun it describes. In addition, Ukrainian adjectives can have long, contracted or short endings. As a result, the adjectival paradigm is composed of at least 38 inflected forms.

All paradigms, except verbal paradigms, include two or more forms with homonymous inflections. For example, in the nominal paradigm "СИН" [syn] 'son', illustrated in Fig. 1, there are five homonymous inflections.

```
СИН=

<E>/Nominative+Singular|      <E>a/Genitive+Singular|       <E>a/Accusative+Singular|
<E>y/Dative+Singular|         <E>oві/Dative+Singular|       <E>oм/Instrumental+Singular|
<E>y/Locative+Singular|       <E>oві/Locative+Singular|     <E>i/Locative+Singular|
<E>y/Vocative+Singular|       <E>и/Nominative+Plural|       <E>ів/Genitive+Plural|
<E>ам/Dative+Plural|          <E>ами/Instrumental+Plural|   <E>ів/Accusative+Plural|
<E>ах/Locative+Plural|        <E>и/Vocative+Plural;
```

Fig. 1. Nominal paradigm "СИН".

Adjectival paradigms have even more homonymous inflections, as masculine and neuter adjectives have the same inflections for all cases except the nominative. For example, the most frequently used adjectival paradigm, "ВЕЛИКИЙ" [velykyi] 'big' contains ten homonymous inflections.

The same applies to all grammatical classes that accord with the noun or personal pronoun, i.e., pronouns other than personal pronouns, numerals and participles.

As a result, if we do not disambiguate in context, we get multiple tags for almost all variable classes. To solve this problem, we need to build syntactic grammars capable of distinguishing inflectional homonyms.

---

[1] Animate = living being, inanimate = object or concept.

[2] The transition from masculine to feminine nouns can only be made through derivation, which involves deeper morphological changes.

3.1   Disambiguation in Nominal Group (NG) Agreements

The first step is to prepare a syntactic grammar capable of agreeing on the members of an NG. The nucleus of this group is the noun or personal pronoun, and the other members are a pronoun other than personal, a numeral, a participle and an adjective. The last two may be repeated, in which case a conjunction or virgule will link them. The particle не [ne] 'not' or adverbs like дуже [duzhe] 'very' and надто [nadto] 'too' can be inserted before the secondary members. As mentioned above, all these members agree in gender and case with the noun.

We, therefore, prepare a schema with the possible axes as can be seen in Fig. 2. Although there is a narrative order for the NG members, this order can be overturned in various situations. To avoid multiplying lines, we replace secondary members with the <ALU> operator.[3]

---

1. [PARTICLE "не"] *and*[4]/*or* [PRONOUN possessive invariable] *and/or* [ADVERB] → [ALU] → [NOUN] *or* [PRONOUN Personal].
2. [ALU] → [","] *and/or* [CONJUNCTION] → [ALU] → [NOUN] *or* [PRONOUN Pers.].
3. [[PARTICLE "не"] *and/or* [PRONOUN possessive invariable] *and/or* [ADVERB] → [ALU] → [","] *and/or* [CONJUNCTION] → [PARTICLE "не"] *and/or* [PRONOUN possessive invariable] *and/or* [ADVERB] → [ALU]→ [NOUN] *or* [PRONOUN Personal].
4. [NOUN] *or* [PRONOUN Personal] → [ALU].
5. [NOUN] *or* [PRONOUN Personal] → [PARTICLE "не"] *and/or* [PRONOUN possessive invariable] *and/or* [ADVERB] → [ALU].
6. [NOUN] *or* [PRONOUN Personal] → [ALU] → [","] *and/or* [CONJUNCTION] → [ALU].
7. [NOUN] *or* [PRONOUN Personal] → [PARTICLE "не"] *and/or* [PRONOUN possessive invariable] *and/or* [ADVERB] → [ALU] → [","] *and/or* [CONJUNCTION] → [PARTICLE "не"] *and/or* [PRONOUN possessive invariable] *and/or* [ADVERB] → [ALU].

Fig. 2.   Schema for agreeing the members of an NG.

The "Nominal group" grammar, shown in Fig. 3, is based on this scheme, and consists of 23 graphs. On the main graph (see Fig. 3), we see seven blocks, one for each case. Each block has subgraphs for masculine, feminine and neuter. Each subgraph represents the eight axes of our schema (see Fig. 2), except for the subgraph describing the vocative NG, which is made up of axes 1 and 5 only. We can see how the subgraphs are constructed in Figs. 4 and 5.

To evaluate our grammars, we use a corpus of several texts (excerpts from novels of the 19th to 21st centuries, excerpts from articles) corresponding to 199,996 (word forms) graphic forms. Before applying our grammar, the text contains 370,522 annotations (67,180 different) and 14,643 different types of ambiguity. After applying our grammars to the corpus, the number of annotations fell to 299,247 and the number of ambiguities to 9,509.

---

[3] At NooJ, the ALU operator means 'all language units'.

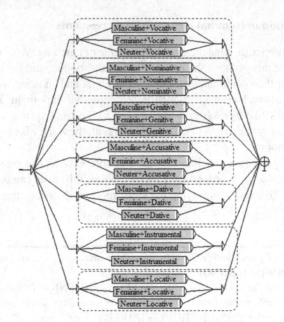

Fig. 3. Syntactic grammar "Nominal group".

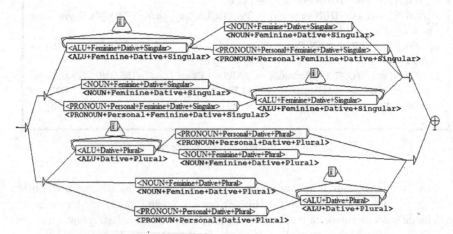

Fig. 4. Subgraph "Feminine+Dative" in "Nominal group" grammar.

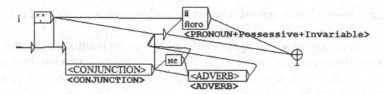

Fig. 5. Subgraph "i" in "Nominal group" grammar.

3.2 Disambiguation of Cases

The next step to eliminate ambiguities caused by inflectional homonyms involves creating separate syntactic grammars for each case. To accomplish this, we establish a specific schema for every case, identifying the place of the NG in question and how it relates to the other components of the sentence. Within this structure, we label all members of the NG as <ALU>.[4] In Fig. 6, the schema for the locative case can be seen.

---

1. [PREPOSITION] → [**ALU** (in locative)].
2. [PREPOSITION] → [**ALU** (in locative)] → [","] *and/or* [CONJUNCTION] → [**ALU** (in locative)].
3. [PREPOSITION] → [PRONOUN possessive invariable] *and/or* [PARTICLE не] *and/or* [ADVERB] → [**ALU** (in locative)].
4. [PREPOSITION] → [PRONOUN possessive invariable] *and/or* [PARTICLE не] *and/or* [ADVERB] → [**ALU** (in locative)] → [","] *and/or* [CONJUNCTION] → [PRONOUN possessive invariable] *and/or* [PARTICLE не] *and/or* [ADVERB] → [**ALU** (in locative)].

Fig. 6. Schema for the locative case.

This schema helped us prepare the grammar shown in Fig. 7. The "Locative" syntactic grammar consists of 3 graphs. The main graph describes the variants of the nominal group. The "Preposition" subgraph lists prepositions followed by the locative. The

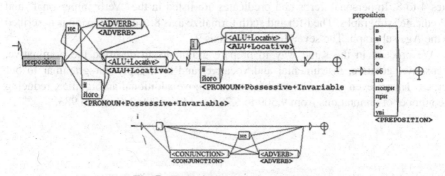

Fig. 7. "Locative" syntactic grammar.

---

[4] The nucleus is not distinguished from the peripheral members, as this grammar completes the previous one.

"I" subgraph describes connections between two homogeneous members of a nominal group.

This grammar is relatively straightforward, as the locative is utilized only after a few prepositions. However, the grammars describing the other cases are more intricate, as they must account for several turns without prepositions. For the dative, we need to add several axes (see Fig. 8).

---

1. [Intransitive VERB] → [ALU (in dative)] = "I call (VERB) my mother (ALU+Dative)".
2. [VERB] → [ALU (in Accusative = direct object)] → [ALU (in dative = indirect object)] = "I offer (VERB) a gift (ALU+Accusative) to my mother (ALU+Dative)".
3. [VERB] → [ALU (in accusative)] → [ALU (in genitive) = Noun complement] → [ALU (in dative)] = "I give (VERB) my phone (ALU+Genitive) number (ALU+Accusative) to my friend (ALU+Dative)."
4. [ALU (in dative)] → [VERB Impersonal] = "It seems (VERB Impersonal) to me (ALU+Dative)".
5. [VERB Impersonal] → [ALU (in dative)] = Axis 5 upside down.
6. ALU (in dative)] → [Predicate] = "It's necessary (Predicate) for me (ALU+Dative)"
7. [PREDICATE]→ ALU (in dative)] = Axis 7 upside down.
8. [ALU (in dative)] → [Age expression] = "I'm (ALU+Dative) 20 years old (Age)". And question about age: [PRONOUN] → [ALU (in dative)] → [Age] → ["?"]
9. [ALU (in dative)] → [VERB <бути> <стати>[6]] → [ADVERB expressing the state] (ALU+Dative) am (VERB) cold (ADVERB) = "He (ALU+Dative) felt (VERB <стати>) bad (ADVERB)".

Fig. 8. Schema for dative case.

Based on this schema, we have prepared the "Dative" syntactic grammar. The main graph is shown in Fig. 9 and the subgraphs in Figs. 10 and 11. The "Dative" syntactic grammar consists of seven parts. The first describes the use of dative after prepositions (axis 1 in our schema Fig. 8). The list of prepositions is given in the "Preposition" subgraph. The second graph describes axes 2, 3 and 4. The third and fourth graphs describe axes 4 to 8. Impersonal verbs and predicates are listed in the "Verb_impersonal" and "Predicate" subgraphs. The fifth and sixth formalize axis 8. Age expression is described in the Age subgraph. The seventh describes axis 9.

We proceed in the same way to prepare grammars to describe the nominative, accusative, genitive, instrumental and vocative, and then apply our grammar to our corpus. These seven grammars enabled us to remove additional ambiguities, reducing the number of annotations from 9,509 to 6,384 and from 299,247 to 226,983.

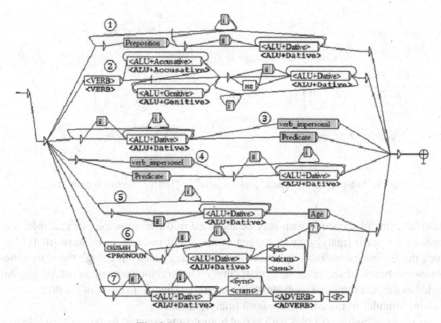

Fig. 9. "Dative" syntactic grammar.

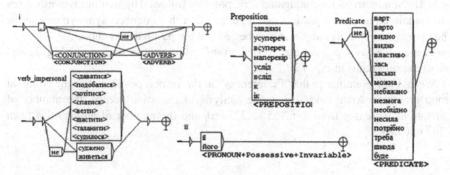

Fig. 10. Subgraphs "i", "repositio", "Verb_impersonal", "Predicate", "ii" in "Dative" syntactic grammar.

It is important to note that these grammars only take into account the links between NG members within a simple sentence. In Ukrainian, however, the nucleus of the group can be found in the main sentence, while the peripheral members are in the subordinate sentence or a secondary sentence, which is linked to the main one.

4   Disambiguation of Verbal Homoforms

As we pointed out above, pairs in which one member is a verb are very frequent, so it is important to find a solution to resolve ambiguities at this level. Moreover, these pairs are not always symmetrical, as they may be extended by several homoforms, or several

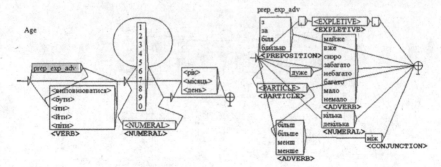

Fig. 11. Subgraphs "Age" and "prep-ex_adv" in "Dative" syntactic grammar.

inflected forms of the same verb may be included in different pairs. For example, the graphic form мати [maty] may be tagged as the infinitive of the verb мати [maty] 'to have', the feminine nominative plural of the noun мата [mata] 'matting', the masculine nominative plural of the noun мат [mat] 'mat'. The graphic form мала [mala] can be labeled as the past feminine singular of the verb мати [maty] 'to have' or the nominative feminine singular of the adjective малий [malyi] 'small'.

So, to disambiguate couples with verbal homoforms, we start by preparing a schema with four main axes: past, present, future and imperative. Each axis comprises a subject (<ALU+Nominative>), a conjugated verb, possibly followed by an infinitive verb. Axes also contain an adverb, a particle and a conjunction that connects synonymous verbs. The verb agrees with its subject in number, and in the past tense in gender.

This enables us to prepare the "Verbal group" grammar (see main graph Fig. 12 and one of the subgraphs in Fig. 13).

We add our grammar to the "Preferences" in the second position after the Nominal group grammar. After morphosyntactic analysis of the same corpus, the number of annotations increases from 226,755 to 223,061 and the number of ambiguities from 6,367 to 6,089.

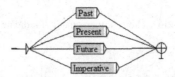

Fig. 12. "Verbal group" grammar: the main graph.

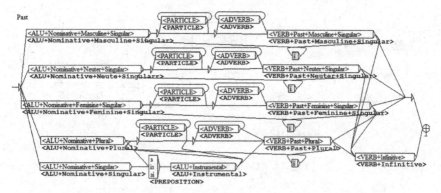

Fig. 13. "Verbal group" grammar: the subgraphs "Past".

5 Transposed or Mixed Homonymous Sets

5.1 Conjunction

According to the traditional view, the conjunction is an invariable linguistic unit that serves to link members of the NG that belong to the same grammatical class and have the same syntactic function (coordinating conjunction) and also the subordinate phrase to the main sentence and independent sentences in the discourse (subordinating conjunction). In Ukrainian, conjunctions are classified according to their structure (simple, compound, repetitive) and also according to their functionality (temporal, conditional, causal and others).

Many transposed or mixed homonymous sets include conjunctions, e.g., що [shtcho] pronoun – particle – conjunction, i [i] conjunction – particle, так [tak] conjunction – particle – adverb, a [a] conjunction – particle – interjection. The grammars we presented above already perform disambiguation of part of a conjunction, specifically the coordinating conjunctions that link identical elements. However, these grammars do not consider subordinating conjunctions, which establish a hierarchy between the parts of a compound sentence.

To eliminate such ambiguities, we formulated the initial grammar encompassing temporal and conditional subordinating conjunctions. This grammar is shown in Fig. 14. These subgraphs describe the place of the conjunction in the subordinate sentence. We would like to note that this grammar is not complete, and needs to be extended.

After applying this grammar to our corpus, the number of annotations falls from 223,061 to 215,157 and the number of ambiguities from 6,089 to 5,671.

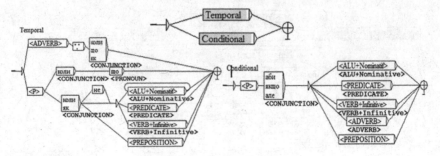

Fig. 14. "Conjunctions" grammar.

5.2 Adverb

In Ukrainian, adverbs are a class of invariable linguistic units used to specify the meaning of verbs, adjectives, other adverbs or the location of nouns. Transposed or mixed homonymous sets can include adverbs. We have already mentioned так [tak] adverb – conjunction – particle, геть [het] adverb – interjection – particle, добре [dobre] adverb – particle – adjective neuter nominative singular. Like conjunctions, adverbs have already been partially disambiguated by previous. To complete these grammars, we have prepared a straightforward grammar that explains the connections between adverbs and verbs as well as the connections between some adverbs and adjectives (see Fig. 15). This has enabled us to reduce the number of notations from 223,061 to 212,321 and the number of ambiguities from 5,671 to 5,614.

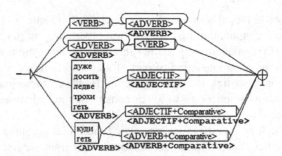

Fig. 15. "Adverbs" grammar.

6   Evaluation and Perspectives

We have built 11 syntactic grammars to remove ambiguities that result from grammatical homonymy. We have applied the new Ukrainian resources to a corpus of 100 texts (novel extracts from the 19th to 21st centuries and article extracts), corresponding to 199,996 graphical forms. An excellent result has been obtained as we were able to reduce the number of annotations by 158,201 (from 370,522 to 212,321) and the number of different types of ambiguity by 9029 (from 14,643 to 5,614).

We are planning to extend our "Conjunctions" and "Adverbs" grammars, and then prepare grammars for particles, interjections, expletives and nominalized adjectives. We have already started work on the disambiguation of proper nouns.

We can think about how to grant the peripheral members of a nominal group in the secondary sentence to the nucleus in the main sentence.

These resources are freely available and can be downloaded from the Resources page (The Ukrainian module) of NooJ's Web site: http://www.nooj4nlp.org.

References

1. Sketch Engine: https://www.sketchengine.eu/. Last accessed 21 Jul 2023
2. TreeTagger: https://www.cis.uni-muenchen.de/~schmid/tools/TreeTagger/. Last accessed 21 Jul 2023
3. GRAC: https://parasol.vmguest.uni-jena.de/grac_crystal/#dashboard?corpname=grac16. Last accessed 21 Jul 2023
4. Saint-Joanis, O.: A new set of linguistic resources for Ukrainian. In: Silberztein, M. (ed.) Linguistic Resources for Natural Language Processing: On the Necessity of Using Linguistic Methods to Develop NLP Software, pp. 85–102. Springer, Cham (2023)
5. Hriaznukhina, T.O., Bratyshchenko, L.H., Darchuk, N.P., Krytska, V.I., Puzdyrieva, T.K., Orlova, L.V.: Shliakhy unyknennia omonimii v systemi avtomatychnoho morfolohichnoho analizu. Movoznavstvo 5, 3–12 (1989)
6. Demska, O.M.: Leksychna ta leksyko-hramatychna omonimiia suchasnoi ukrainskoi movy. Dysertatsia. Institute of the Ukrainian Language (NAS of Ukraine), Kyiv (1996)
7. Demska, O.M.: 10 istorii pro omonimiiu. Ranok, Kharkiv (2019)
8. Kuzmenko, G.I.: Omonimiia: aspektolohiia, problematyka. Kyiv University Press, Kyiv (2000)
9. Shypanivska, O.O.: Strukturno-semantychni ta funktsionalni kharakterystyky mizhchastynomovnoi morfolohichnoi omonimii suchasnoi ukrainskoi movy. Dysertatsiia. Kyiv (2007)
10. Shypnivska, O.: Problema vydilennia mizhchastynomovnykh morfolohichnykh omonimiv. Leksykohrafichnyi biuleten 17, 83–89 (2008)
11. Sokolova, S.V.: Transpozytsiini peredumovy rozvytku funktsionalnoi omonimii v ukrainskii movi (na materiali leksyko-hramatychnoho klasu pryslivnykiv). "Alfa- M", Kyiv (2010)
12. Bunio, H. B.: Suchasni metody vyrishennia problemy hramatychnoi omonimii v teksti. Naukovi zapysky natsionalnoho universytetu "Ostrozka akademiia" (49), 12–16 (2014)
13. Hlibtchuk, N.: Prepozytsionalizatsiia u ploshchyni mizhchastynomovnoi omonimii [Prepositionalization in the Plane of Prepositionalization in the Plane of Cross-POS Homonymy]. Visnyk Lvivskoho universytetu. Seriia filolohichna 68, 58–67 (2018)
14. Holubenko, N.I.: Hramatychna omonimiia chastok u suchasnii ukrainskii movi: perspektyvy doslidzhen. Akademichni vizii 11, 61–70 (2021)

Automatic Disambiguation
of the Belarusian-Russian Legal Parallel Corpus
in NooJ

Valery Varanovich[1]([⊠]), Mikita Suprunchuk[2], Yauheniya Zianouka[3],
and Yuras Hetsevich[3]

[1] Belarusian State University, Minsk, Belarus
ssrlab221@gmail.com
[2] Minsk State Linguistic University, Minsk, Belarus
[3] United Institute of Informatics Problems of the National Academy of Sciences of Belarus,
Minsk, Belarus

Abstract. The article deals with the problem of lexical ambiguity in the legislative texts of the Belarusian legal codes. Specialists of the Speech Synthesis and Recognition Laboratory in Minsk translate law codes from Russian into Belarusian to ensure equal access to them for speakers of both official languages of our country. First, the texts are translated automatically and checked and edited by translators, linguists, and lawyers. Over 20 of the 26 codes have already been prepared. The article examines types of homonyms, their semi-automatic extraction and classification using the NooJ development environment. There are two dominant classes of ambiguity resolution mechanisms: automatic, implying a completely computerized solution to this problem and interactive (semi-automatic), supposing a joint solution by a person and a computer. It means the user has a set of alternatives from which he should choose one option. About 17% of words in the experimental corpus have homonyms. The article examines their types, and presents several syntactic NooJ grammars, which allow for removing different types of homonymy.

Keywords: Ambiguity · Automatic Translation · Disambiguation · Homonymy · Natural Language Processing · NooJ · Text Corpus · Text Tagging

1 Introduction

Homonymy (and ambiguity) is still the central problem of automatic text processing at the lexical level. The problem of the automatic (rarely semi-automatic) solving of lexical ambiguity was first formulated for creating Machine Translation systems. To date, this is a critical problem for improving the quality of systems for various branches of computational linguistics.

There are two dominant classes of ambiguity resolution mechanisms: (1) an automatic one, implying a fully computerized solution to this problem; (2) an interactive (dialogic, semi-automatic) one, supposing a joint solution by a person and a computer [1]. It means the user has a set of alternatives from which they should choose one option.

A. Bartulović et al. (Eds.): NooJ 2023, CCIS 1816, pp. 114–126, 2024.
https://doi.org/10.1007/978-3-031-56646-2_10

We are creating a legal text corpus in Belarusian and Russian for various software products, such as speech synthesis, machine translation, spell checkers, etc. As part of the project, we developed a trilingual dictionary of legal terms in Belarusian, Russian and English. Also, in forming the corpus, we compiled contextual dictionaries, which became the basis for dictionaries in the NooJ system. The dictionaries reflect contexts that show the preferred translation of a given term from Russian into Belarusian [2].

Our plan includes the creation of high-priority dictionaries for each of the 26 law codes in Belarus. We assume that many diagnostic contexts will be consistent across different codes (настоящий 'this' = гэты 'this' (code), not настоящий 'this' = сапраўдны 'real' (code)). Still, we hypothesize that in some cases, the contexts for the same values will be different. It is also possible that one polysemous word (or a homonym) will have different meanings in several codes.

The following examples of words with multiple meanings were identified during our work: данный – 1) гэты, 'this'; 2) дадзены, 'given'; отпуск – 1) выдача (тавараў), 'issuance', 'supply'; 2) адпачынак (даць), 'holiday,' 'vacation'. These meanings (translations) can be selected based on their neighboring words. Given that NooJ is an effective tool for resolving word ambiguity, we intend to utilize it for constructing syntactic grammars [3]. They will search for homonyms by analyzing the context (the sequence of words) and form a list of lexical units for different domains. This will aid in identifying terms within various thematic domains, a crucial step in compiling specialized vocabularies for the mentioned fields.

2 Linguistic Analysis of the Text Corpus

To handle the question of translating legislative documents into Belarusian, the Speech Synthesis and Recognition Laboratory of UIIP NASB (https://ssrlab.by/en/), in cooperation with specialists from Belarusian State University, has translated all 26 codes of the Republic of Belarus (*The Civil Code, The Labor Code, The Education Code, The Banks and Banking Code*, etc.) into the Belarusian using the automatic services of the website *corpus.by*. We constructed a corpus of texts on medical and social domains, and integrated it into NooJ to extend the research results to other fields of knowledge. Belarusian code links, the translation of each legal code into Belarusian and the dictionary of Regular substitutions are posted here: https://ssrlab.by/7804.

To determine the types of homonymy, we performed an experimental corpus of legal texts (Fig. 1). It consists of 5 first pages from 23 codes. The collection contains 4,572 text units (TUs), 52,463 tokens, including 40,647 word forms, 1,796 digits and 10,020 delimiters. The text comprises 95,184 annotations (11,891 different).

Thus, standard tools (the basic Belarusian module for NooJ) analyze legislative texts quite well, but not all forms receive an unambiguous grammatical characteristic. We suggest several ways to improve the results of automatic disambiguation.

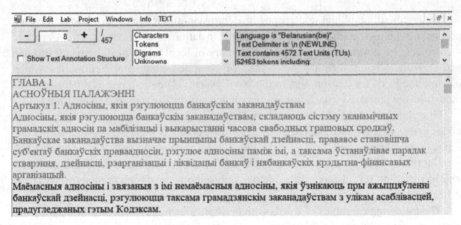

Fig. 1. A fragment of the corpus of the legal domain.

3 Linguistic Analysis of the Text Corpus: Homonymy Type Determination

In the following research stage, we exported the list of ambiguities computed by the NooJ linguistic analyzer. It comprises 3,172 examples of homonyms (Fig. 2).

We classified the selected homonyms with a frequency of ten or more. Sometimes, one-word form belongs to different types of homonymy. Such a case was marked as, for example, 6+1 гэты 'this' (Fig. 3).

For example, ambiguous forms of the word асобы, which can be a plural noun in the genitive case, a single noun in the genitive (a person) or a single adjective in the nominative or accusative case (special) according to the Belarusian NooJ dictionary:

```
<асобы,ADJECTIVE+FLX=AAЗICHЫ+Case=Accusative+Animation=Inanim
ate+Gender=Masculine+Meaning=Qualitative_Relative>
<асобы,ADJECTIVE+FLX=AAЗICHЫ+Gender=Masculine+Case=Nominative
+Meaning=Qualitative_Relative>
<асоба,NOUN+FLX=AБАЛОHA+Meaning=Common+Gender=Feminine+Case=G
enitive+Animation=Inanimate>
<асоба,NOUN+FLX=AБАЛОHA+Case=Accusative+Meaning=Common+Gender
=Feminine+Animation=Inanimate+Number=Plural>
<асоба,NOUN+FLX=AБАЛОHA+Meaning=Common+Gender=Feminine+Animat
ion=Inanimate+Case=Nominative+Number=Plural>
<асоба,NOUN+FLX=AБАТЫСA+Animation=Animate+Meaning=Common+Gend
er=Feminine+Case=Genitive>
<асоба,NOUN+FLX=AБАТЫСA+Animation=Animate+Meaning=Common+Gend
er=Feminine+Case=Nominative+Number=Plural>
```

Homonymy is widespread in Belarusian texts: almost every token has several variants of grammatical annotation (Fig. 3). Other examples of homonyms are presented in Fig. 4.

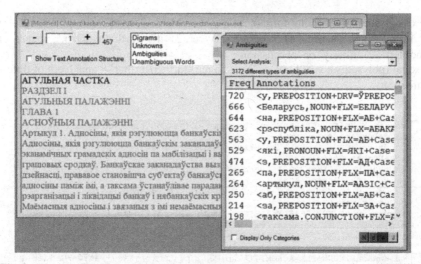

Fig. 2. The list of ambiguous words exported from the corpus of the legal domain in NooJ.

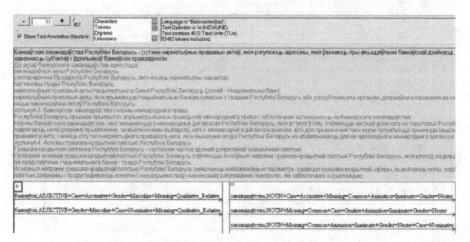

Fig. 3. Examples of ambiguous word annotations in NooJ.

Within the research, we identified the following types of homonyms:

a. grammatical (coincidence in case only or case and number): Беларусь 'Belarus' (nom. case = acc. case);

b. grammatical (coincidence in animacy: animate or inanimate): асоба 'a person' (animate) or 'a legal person' (inanimate);

c. preposition (different case management): у, на 'in, on', etc.;

d. partial homonyms (coincidence in parts of speech): рабочы – 1) 'employee, worker', 2) 'working'; таксама – 'also', 'too';

e. lexico-grammatical (homoforms): які – 1) 'which', 2) 'yak (animal)'; дзікі – 1) 'wild', 2) 'boar'; варта – 1) 'security, service', 2) 'it's worth doing sth.'; правы – 1) 'not left', 2) 'liberty' or 'permission';

f. lexical (polysemy): яго 'him' or 'his'; далей 'farther/further' – an adverb of time or direction.

7 9	`<права,NOUN+FLX=ПРАВА+Meaning=Common+Case=Genitive+Animation=Inani mate+Gender=Neuter+Number=Plural>`
	`<правіць,VERB+FLX=БАВІЦь+Person=2+Mood=Imperative+Aspect=Imperfect ive+Number=Singular>`
	`<прасці,VERB+FLX=КЛАСЦІ+Aspect=Imperfective+Mood=Indicative+Gender =Masculine+Tense=Past>`
		5

7 5	`<зямельны,ADJECTIVE+FLX=ААЗІСНЫ+Case=Genitive+Number=Plural+Meanin g=Qualitative_Relative>`
	`<зямельны,ADJECTIVE+FLX=ААЗІСНЫ+Number=Plural+Case=Prepositional+M eaning=Qualitative_Relative>`
	`<зямельны,ADJECTIVE+FLX=ААЗІСНЫ+Case=Accusative+Animation=Animate+ Number=Plural+Meaning=Qualitative_Relative>`
		1

7 4	`<дзейнасць,NOUN+FLX=АСКОМІСТАСЦь+Meaning=Common+Case=Dative+Gender =Feminine+Animation=Inanimate>`
	`<дзейнасць,NOUN+FLX=АСКОМІСТАСЦь+Meaning=Common+Case=Genitive+Gend er=Feminine+Animation=Inanimate>`
	`<дзейнасць,NOUN+FLX=АСКОМІСТАСЦь+Meaning=Common+Case=Nominative+Ge nder=Feminine+Animation=Inanimate+Number=Plural>`
	`<дзейнасць,NOUN+FLX=АСКОМІСТАСЦь+Meaning=Common+Case=Prepositional +Gender=Feminine+Animation=Inanimate>`
		1

7 4	`<зямельны,ADJECTIVE+FLX=ААЗІСНЫ+Case=Accusative+Animation=Inanimat e+Number=Plural+Meaning=Qualitative_Relative>` `<зямельны,ADJECTIVE+FLX=ААЗІСНЫ+Case=Nominative+Number=Plural+Mean ing=Qualitative_Relative>`	1

7 1	`<гэты,PRONOUN+FLX=ГЭТЫ+Group=Demonstrative+Case=Genitive+Gender=Ma sculine>`
	`<гэты,PRONOUN+FLX=ГЭТЫ+Case=Accusative+Animation=Animate+Group=Dem onstrative+Gender=Masculine>`
	`<гэты,PRONOUN+FLX=ГЭТЫ+Group=Demonstrative+Case=Genitive+Gender=Ne uter>`
	`<гэты,PRONOUN+FLX=ГЭТЫ2+Case=Genitive+Group=InterrogativeRelative+ Gender=Masculine>`
	`<гэты,PRONOUN+FLX=ГЭТЫ2+Case=Accusative+Animation=Animate+Group=In terrogativeRelative+Gender=Masculine>`
	`<гэты,PRONOUN+FLX=ГЭТЫ2+Case=Genitive+Group=InterrogativeRelative+ Gender=Neuter>`
		6 + 1

Fig. 4. The fragment of ambiguous homonyms of different types.

Table 1 shows which type of homonym is the most frequent among the word forms of the text (2 and 3 columns), as well as statistics on unique forms (4 and 5 columns) (cf. [4], as well). Grammatical homonymy is highly frequent and covers the maximum number of different lexemes.

4 Syntactic Grammars for Removing Grammatical Ambiguity

4.1 A Subsection Sample

It is known that the Slavic languages have well-developed inflection. The endings of verbs indicate gender, number, person, time, etc. For example, Belarusian and Russian nouns and adjectives have declension, i.e., six cases and two numbers. Due to this

Table 1. Statistical data on different types of ambiguity.

Type	Tokens		Other words (= "types")	
	Units	%	Units	%
1	2303	25	423	78
2	803	9	41	8
3	3548	37	20	4
4	702	8	19	3
5	1429	15	32	6
6	536	6	9	1
All	9321	100	544	100

paradigmatic abundance, some words coincide in all forms, while others only coincide in specific forms. In other words, it is observed that they are not complete homonyms but rather homoforms. The following examples with the word мае 1) 'has'; 2) 'my; mine' show this:

- <мой,PRONOUN+FLX=МОЙ+Case=Accusative+Animation=Inanimate+Number=Plural+Group=Possessive>
- <мой,PRONOUN+FLX=МОЙ+Case=Nominative+Number=Plural+Group=Possessive>
- <мець,VERB+FLX=МЕЦЬ+Person=3+Aspect=Imperfective+Mood=Indicative+Tense=Present+Number=Singular>

Банк **мае** права ажыццяўляць іншыя банкаўскія аперацыі. 'The bank **has** the right to carry out other banking operations.'   (1)

(...) кожны выбаршчык, удзельнік рэферэндуму **мае** адзін голас. '(...) each voter participant in the referendum **has** one vote.'

    (2)

We have implemented a syntactic grammar to remove this kind of ambiguity and assigned the correct verb tags (Fig. 5). All 48 ambiguous cases of the word мае were cleared out with this grammar.

The case when several forms of a word coincide within the same paradigm is more common. Consider the example of a noun's genitive and dative cases that coincide. Since the forms of the dative and the genitive cases of the words бюджэт 'budget' and фонд 'fund' are the same (G. sg. = D. sg. = бюджэту, G. sg. = D. sg. = фонду), then the automatic annotation, of course, attributed to them two tags of these cases.

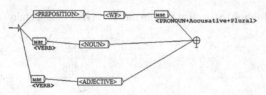

Fig. 5. Syntactic grammar for removing ambiguous forms of word мае 1) 'has'; 2) 'my; mine'.

Бюджэтны крэдыт – бюджэтныя сродкі, якія даюцца з вышэйстаячага **бюджэту** ніжэйстаячаму **бюджэту**, а таксама з рэспубліканскага **бюджэту**, **бюджэту** дзяржаўнага пазабюджэтнага **фонду** або з **бюджэту** дзяржаўнага пазабюджэтнага **фонду** рэспубліканскаму **бюджэту** на зваротнай аснове.   (3)

'Budget credit (budget loan) – budget **funds** provided from the higher **budget** to the lower **budget**, as well as from the republican **budget** to the **budge**t of the state extrabudgetary **fund** or from the **budget** of the state extrabudgetary **fund** to the republican **budget** on a reciprocal basis'.

Fig. 6.Syntactic grammar for extracting masculine nouns of dative and genitive cases.

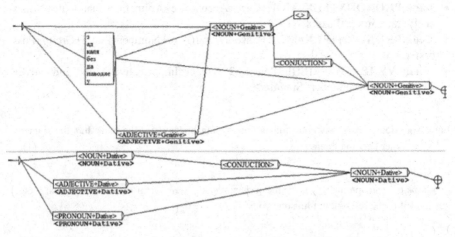

Fig. 6. Syntactic grammar for extracting masculine nouns of dative and genitive cases.

To remove this type of homonymy, we developed two grammars (Fig. 6). They analyze the left and the right contexts and allow users to define the genitive and dative cases, respectively.

4.2 Identification of Partial Homonyms

One more group of homonyms is partial homonyms, i.e., the same word is associated with multiple parts of speech categories. Parts of speech homonymous to each other have the same spelling; that is, they represent one homocomplex (term). This type of homonym may be extracted by analyzing left and right contexts.

We identified ten groups of partial homonymy, which are:

a. conjunction – particle (таксама, калі 'also', 'when'),
b. conjunction – adverb – verb (imperative) (калі, калоць 'when to split'),
c. conjunction – particle (ці, толькі 'if', 'only'),
d. adverb – preposition (пасля 'after'),
e. short adjective – adverb (юрыдычна, спецыяльна, пастаянна 'legal, special, permanent' vs. 'legally, specifically, permanently'),
f. noun – verb (справа, спрасці, справіць 'law case', 'to span, to fulfill'),
g. parenthesis – verb (можа, магчы 'maybe' vs 'can'),
h. adjective – participle (населены 'populated', 'with population'),
i. verb (gerund) – preposition (уключаючы 'switching' vs. 'including'),
j. noun – adjective (правы 'the right', 'right').

The group of short adjectives and adverbs exhibited the most frequent type of partial homonymy. Let us consider the coincidence between the short feminine adjective 'legal' and the adverb 'legally' that have the same graphics in Belarusian (юрыдычна). For example,

- <юрыдычны,ADJECTIVE+FLX=ААЗІСНЫ+Gender=Feminine+Case=Nominati ve+Meaning=Qualitative_Relative+Form=Short>

Банк – **юрыдычная** асоба, якая мае выключнае права ажыццяўляць у сукупнасці наступныя банкаўскія аперацы (...). 'A bank is a legal entity that has the exclusive right to carry out the following banking operations (...).'   (4)

- <юрыдычна,ADVERB+FLX=АБАВЯЗАЦЕЛЬНА+Type=Quality_Manner>

Судовыя дакументы ва ўстаноўленым парадку ўручаюцца **юрыдычна** зацікаўленым у зыходзе справы асобам на мове судаводства. 'Court documents are duly handed over to persons legally interested in the outcome of the case in the language of the proceedings'. (5)

The wordform спраў coincides with the plural noun in the genitive case (спраў 'law cases') and singular verbs of the past tense ('to span, to fulfill'). For the legal texts, the most typical usage is a plural noun in the genitive case, but still, the following syntactic grammar helps to find out all cases of the word спраў in all texts of different styles (Fig. 7).

Determining the coincidence of auxiliary parts of speech is more challenging in this case, as it requires consideration of the underlying meaning in the sentence. We tried to distinguish conjunction and particle таксама 'also', 'too'. To identify whether таксама is a conjunction or a particle, we used the following syntactic grammar (Fig. 8).

Another example of partial homonymy is the coincidence of the word калі (conjunction/adverb 'when'; imperative 'split, stab'). For legal texts, an adverb and a conjunction

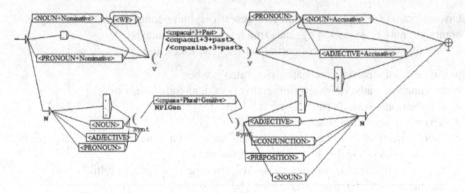

Fig. 7. Syntactic grammar for extracting the wordform спраў in NooJ.

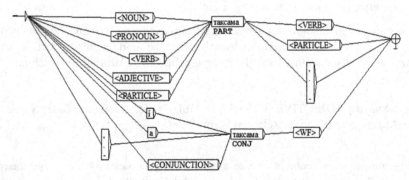

Fig. 8. Syntactic grammar for extracting conjunction or particle таксама 'also', 'too'.

are more typical. At the same time, the imperative form of the verb is used relatively rarely and primarily in literary texts (Fig. 9).

4.3 Identification of Lexical Homonyms

Lexico-grammatical homonyms belong to different parts of speech. They have different lexical meanings, and may also have differences in grammatical categories: які 'which; yak', дзікі 'wild; boar', варта 'security service; it's worth doing sth.', правы 'not left; liberty, permission').

The word form *правы* has the meanings of a noun and an adjective in different contexts. Linguistic analysis has shown that the noun is most often found in legal texts, which is natural since the word is a part of the legal vocabulary. Note that this pair of homonyms also have different accents, so this grammar can be used in text-to-speech synthesizers for correct voicing, depending on the context. For example,

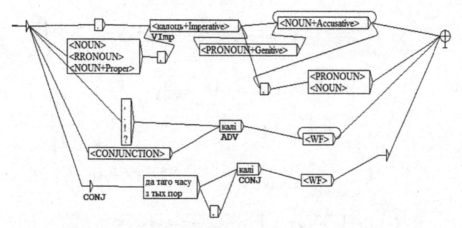

Fig. 9. Syntactic grammar for extracting калі (conjunction, adverb or imperative).

- <права,**NOUN**+FLX=ПРАВА+Case=Accusative+Meaning=Common+Animation =Inanimate+Gender=Neuter+Number=Plural>

Шлюбны дагавор, які прадугледжвае **правы** і абавязкі былых сужонкаў пасля спынення шлюбу, дзейнічае да іх выканання. 'The marriage contract, which provides for **the rights** and obligations of the former spouses after the termination of the marriage, is valid until their fulfillment.'

- <правы,**ADJECTIVE**+FLX=ААЗІСНЫ+Gender=Masculine+Case=Nominative+ Meaning=Qualitative_Relative>

Кіраўскі мост праз Дзвіну знаходзіцца ў цэнтры Віцебска, злучае вуліцы Кірава (**правы** бераг) і Замкавую (левы бераг). 'The Kirov Bridge over the Dvina River is located in the center of Vitebsk, connecting the streets of Kirov (**right** bank) and Zamkavaya (left bank).'

The developed grammar helps to determine the part-of-speech homonyms of the word *правы*, as well as its grammatical characteristics (Fig. 10).

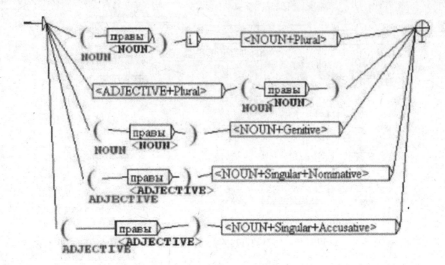

Fig. 10. Syntactic grammar for extracting part-of-speech homonym правы 'not left'; 'liberty', permission'.

In the Belarusian language, there is a case when a word form has a different lexical meaning but entirely coincides with a particular grammatical form. Thus, the words акт 'act' (masculine gender) and акт 'octave' (feminine gender) coincide in the plural form of the genitive case, and also have different accents. Therefore, the grammar developed for this case also helps the correct voicing of the word form by the text-to-speech synthesizer (Fig. 11). For example,

- <акт,NOUN+FLX=ААМІЦЭТ+Meaning=Common+Case=Genitive+Animation=
  =Inanimate+ Gender=**Masculine**+Number=Plural>

  Пацярджэнне адпаведнасці транспартных работ патрабаваннян тэхнічных нарматыўных правовых **áктаў** у галіне тэхнічнага нарміравання. 'Confirmation of compliance of transport works with the requirements of technical regulatory **legal acts** in the field of technical regulation.'

- Noun+Feminine:
  <актава,NOUN+FLX=АБЛАВА+Meaning=Common+Gender=**Feminine**+Case=
  Genitive+ Animation=Inanimate+Number=Plural>

  Белыя клавішы (...) заўсёды імкнуліся правільна перадаць гучанне асноўных тонаў музычных **актáў**. 'White keys (...) always tried to correctly convey the sound of the main tones of musical **octaves.'**

One can only use semantic features of words that form the context to recognize homonyms of this type. The developed grammar illustrates specific words that can indicate the semantic and generic affiliation of the noun актаў in the genitive plural.

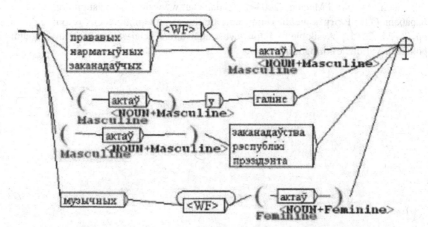

Fig. 11. Syntactic grammar for extracting plural noun актаў in the genitive case.

5 Conclusion

Specialists of the Speech Synthesis and Recognition Laboratory of UIIP of NASB translate legal codes from Russian into Belarusian to ensure equal access for speakers of both official languagess. First, the texts are translated automatically and checked and edited by translators, linguists and lawyers. More than 20 of the 26 codes have already been prepared (more details are available at https://ssrlab.by/en/7804). We used the NooJ system for optimization of work and research purposes. It incorporates tools that help in solving various types of ambiguity (homonymy and polysemy) in Belarusian legal texts: lexical, grammatical, part-of-speech homonymy and mixed homonymy. We prepared an experimental legislative corpus of some fragments for the study of homonymy in the language of legal texts. Ambiguities of various types are prevalent in Belarusian legal texts: 9,000 tokens of 52,500 tokens. The most common types are grammatical rather than lexical: homonymy of prepositions (government of different cases) and homoforms (coincidence of cases of the same word). Several NooJ grammars for reducing ambiguity are presented above. They make it possible to remove homonymy, to reduce the number of incorrect definitions of grammatical or lexical meaning, to distinguish a noun from a verb, an adjective from an adverb, etc. Our findings will be employed in the automatic linguistic analysis of Belarusian texts, machine translation and speech synthesis.

References

1. Bouarroudj, W., Boufaida, Z., Bellatreche, L.: Named Entity Disambiguation in Short Texts over Knowledge Graphs. Knowl. Inf. Syst. **64**(2), 325–351 (2022)

2. Воронович, В. В.: Словарь лексических валентно-стей в системе русско-белорусского машинного перевода. In: А. И. Головня (ed.) Третьи чтения, посвя-щенные памяти В. А. Карпова: сб. науч. ст., pp. 88–92. РИВШ, Минск (2009). Available at: http://elib.bsu.by/han dle/123456789/10645

3. Silberztein, M.: NooJ Manual. (2003–). Available at: www.nooj-association.org

4. Барабаш, О.В.: Разграничение омонимии и полисемии юридических терминов. Рема 2, pp. 39–51 (2015)]. Available at: https://cyberleninka.ru/article/n/razgranichenie-omonimii-i-polisemii-yuridicheskih-terminov

Syntactic-Semantic Analysis of Perception Verbs in the Croatian Language

Daša Farkaš[1](✉) [iD] and Kristina Kocijan[2] [iD]

[1] Department of Linguistics, Faculty of Humanities and Social Sciences, University of Zagreb, Zagreb, Croatia
dberovic@ffzg.unizg.hr

[2] Department of Information and Communication Sciences, Faculty of Humanities and Social Sciences, University of Zagreb, Zagreb, Croatia
krkocijan@ffzg.unizg.hr

Abstract. This study presents a corpus approach to verbs of perception for the Croatian language, considering the fact that there has not been a single corpus-based study of the Croatian language, which considers a large number of verb lemmas that express perception verbs. A total of 86 verbs were selected from the Croatian Morphological Lexicon and divided into five semantic subgroups: sight, hearing, taste, smell and touch. These verbs are processed using NooJ by adding the semantic tag +*prcp* to mark the semantic category of a perception verb and its semantic subgroup +*viz* [sight], +*sluh* [hearing], +*okus* [taste], +*miris* [smell] and +*dodir* [touch]. The verbs were next explored within three different domains (a corpus of medical texts, a corpus of parliamentary texts and a corpus of children's literature) to learn more about their syntactic and semantic features. The research corpus consisted of 214,387 forms of perception verbs in context. Corpus entries were manually validated, and linguistic information (syntactic complements and meanings of perception verbs) was assigned manually. In semantic annotation, information was added to each form of a perception verb concerning whether it expresses a prototypical, physical meaning or metaphorical meaning. In the syntactic processing, the types of predicate complements of perception verbs were annotated. The analysis showed eight different categories of predicate complements. This study includes many more perception verb lemmas than previous research, which is why it brings some new results, especially in semantic analysis.

Keywords: Perception Verbs · Croatian Language · Predicate Complements · Prototypical Physical Meanings · Metaphorical Meanings · NooJ

1 Introduction

1.1 Definition and Previous Research of Perception Verbs

Perception verbs express the internal ways and processes with which we perceive the world around us but also gather information from our surroundings. Their main feature is that they are ambiguous – i.e., they have their **prototypical**, physical meanings as

© The Author(s), under exclusive license to Springer Nature Switzerland AG 2024
A. Bartulović et al. (Eds.): NooJ 2023, CCIS 1816, pp. 127–138, 2024.
https://doi.org/10.1007/978-3-031-56646-2_11

well as **non-prototypical**, extended physical and metaphorical meanings. Perception verbs have been described by numerous linguists from different theoretical aspects: typological studies, lexical semantics, morphosemantics, cognitive linguistics, etc. [1–4]. The majority of researchers [2, 5–8] have dealt with perception verbs related to the sense of sight and hearing, reporting that perception verbs have senses which move beyond the expression of simple embodied experience as if it were a common feature of all verbs of that class. This premise, among others, is questioned in this paper.

Research on perception verbs for the English language has followed the development of linguistic theories: Vieberg [1] conducted a typological study of perception verbs for many languages; Atkins [2] presented a Frame Semantics approach to analyzing the verbs of seeing; Usoniene [3] carried out a statistical analysis of verbs of seeing and seeming in English and their direct/indirect perception; Whitt [5] explored evidentiality in perception verbs in English and German. Gisborne's [6] publication on the event structure of perception verbs is considered the most significant theoretical contribution to the literature on this topic. His analysis derives from word grammar as a part of cognitive grammar, and links argument structure, polysemy, and evidentiality to the theory of event structure.

Most analyses of perception verbs in English have explored evidentiality as their main feature. For the Croatian language, Gnjatović and Matasović [9] showed that evidentiality does not exist as a grammatical category but as a syntactic strategy with the perception verbs in Croatian in which it is possible to express the opposition between indirect and direct experience. Mihaljević [7] performed an extensive analysis of 12 Croatian perception verbs (from 3 of the 5 sensory modalities – 8 verbs expressing visual perception, 2 hearing verbs and 2 touching verbs). He explains the structure of complements of verbs of perception in Croatian from a generative grammar perspective. Raffaelli [4] defines and describes the processes involved in the lexicalization of perception verbs, essentially describing their morphosemantic features. Burić [8], on the other hand, analyzes prototypical and non-prototypical meanings of perception verbs in Croatian in terms of cognitive grammar. Her research is based on 16 perception verbs considered to be the basic verbs of perception.

1.2 Initial Hypothesis

In his famous typological study, Vieberg [1] showed that some perception verbs are more frequent in usage, and that they have a greater ability to express multiple meanings. Because this ability depends on sensory modalities, he devised a scale of sensory modalities that expresses how perception verbs express non-prototypical meanings (Sight > Hearing > Touch > Smell > Taste). Examining the Croatian language, Burić [8] examined only verbs from the top of the Vieberg scale, and found that approximately 70–75% of their meanings are metaphorical. We believe that the problem of these two large studies is that Vieberg explores many languages, but the small number of perception verb lemmas and the research is not corpus-based. Furthermore, Burić [8] uses HrWac, the internet corpus of the Croatian language, whose texts have features of spoken language.

We believe that, in order to make general conclusions about perception verbs, all lemmas of perception verbs should be included in the research, and that the research must be corpus-based. That was our basic motivation for this paper. Our initial hypothesis is that there are more verbs of perception that are not polysemous, and that the realization of metaphorical meanings depends on the choice of corpus type.

2 Data and Research

2.1 Data and Corpus Processing

With our research, we wanted to cover the most lemmas possible (if not all) of perception verbs in the Croatian language from all sensory modalities. We manually extracted all verb lemmas related to perception from the total list of verb lemmas from the Croatian Morphological Lexicon [10]. Lemmas of 86 verbs were selected and divided into five semantic subgroups: sight, hearing, taste, smell and touch (Table 1). All these verbs were processed by NooJ and explored within three different domains.

Table 1. List of perception verb lemmas.

Sensory modality	Verb lemmas
Sight	*blejati* (to bleat), *blenuti* (to gawk), *buljiti* (to stare), *gledati* (to look), *izvidjeti* (to scout), *motriti* (to observe), *nadgledati* (to supervise), *ogledati* (to reflect), *ogledavati* (to look around), *opaziti* (to notice), *opažati* (to notice), *opservirati* (to observe), *osmatrati* (to watch), *piljiti* (to stare), *pogledati* (to look), *pogledavati* (to glance), *pregledati* (to examine), *previdjeti* (to overlook), *prigledati* (to look after), *prigledavati* (to look after), *progledati* (to regain), *promotriti* (to observe), *providjeti* (to see through), *proviriti* (to peep), *provirivati* (to peep), *razgledati* (to look around), *razgledavati* (to sightsee), *razvidjeti* (to find out), *sagledati* (to realize), *sagledavati* (to realize), *škiljiti* (to squint), *ugledati* (to sight), *uvidjeti* (to realize), *uviđati* (to realize), *vidjeti* (to see), *viđati* (to see), *viriti* (to peep), *zagledati* (to gaze), *zagledavati* (to gaze), *zapaziti* (to note), *zapiljiti* (to stare)
Hearing	*čuti* (to hear), *dočuti* (to hear about), *načuti* (to overhear), *naslušati* (to listen), *osluhnuti* (to listen), *osluškivati* (to eavesdrop), *oslušnuti* (to eavesdrop), *počuti* (to hear), *posluhnuti* (to hear), *poslušati* (to listen), *prečuti* (to misheard), *preslušati* (to listen to), *prisluhnuti* (to listen), *prisluškivati* (to eavesdrop), *pročuti* (to get around [with subject *word* e.g., **word** got out / **word** got around]), *saslušati* (to hear), *saslušavati* (to question), *slušati* (to listen), *začuti* (to hear)
Smell	*namirisati* (to smell), *nanjušiti* (to scent), *omirisati* (to smell), *onjušiti* (to sniff), *pomirisati* (to take a smell at), *ponjušiti* (to nose), *primirisati* (to get close), *pronjuškati* (to sniff around), *vonjati* (to stink), *zasmraditi* (to leave a stink on), *zasmrditi* (to stink)
Touch	*dirkati* (to touch), *dodirivati* (to touch), *ispipati* (to feel out), *ispipavati* (to probe), *opipavati* (to examine with fingers), *pipati* (to grope), *pipkati* (to grope), *pipnuti* (to touch), *popipati* (to grope)
Taste	*iskusiti* (to experience), *okusiti* (to taste), *osladiti* (to sweeten), *ožednjeti* (to get thirsty)

NooJ dictionary of Croatian verbs has 4,901 main verb entries, all of which carry markers for category (**V**) and Aspect (**dual**, **fin**ite and **inf**inite) and an additional marker (**pov**) if they are reflexive verbs. Semantic markers were added for the purposes of this project, mainly the tag +**prcp** to mark all the verbs of **perce**ption and the additional tag to denote a specific sensory modality of sight (**+viz**), hearing (**+sluh**), smell (**+miris**), touch (**+dodir**) and taste (**+okus**).

Annotation of the verbs at the dictionary level facilitated the design of a rule-based algorithm for the detection of verbs within the corpus. Their distribution per corpus domain differs considerably, as portrayed in Table 2, where we also observe that statistically significant use of sensory modality verbs is strongly emphasized in the children's corpus and the least in the medical corpus. This is to be expected considering the diversity of the **domains** of each corpus (medical texts, speakers of the Croatian Parliament, children's literature), as well as their **size** (205,683,020, 120,990,384 and 3,312,523 tokens); and target **audience** (medical personal, politicians and children).

Table 2. Distribution of verbs of sight, hearing, smell, touch and taste per domain-related corpus.

Table 3 shows that the verbs of sight appear most frequently in each of the three domains, followed by the verbs of hearing, smell, touch and taste. This is true for all three corpora except the medical corpus, where no verbs of smell are detected. The obtained results are also supported by the existing literature, which reports that sight verbs have the greatest possibility of expressing metaphorical meaning.

Table 3. Corpus statistics: the total number of lemmas per sensory modality and corpus domain.

	Prcp.	Touch	Smell	Taste	Hearing	Sight
TOTAL	86	9	11	4	19	**43**
MED	23	1	0	1	4	**17**
PARL	73	5	6	3	17	**34**
CH. LIT	81	8	8	4	15	**27**

Furthermore, we have detected three verbs (*ispipavati*, *prigledavati* and *zasmraditi*) that have not occurred in any of the domain-related corpora. There are no clear indications as to why they do not appear in these corpora, but this may be clarified in further research. The full list of verbs not occurring in the corpus is given in Table 4.

Table 4. Corpus statistics: the list of verbs not occurring in each of the corpus domains.

Verbs of prcp.
MED — *blejati, blenuti, buljiti, dirkati, dočuti, ispipati, **ispipavati**, izvidjeti, načuti, namirisati, nanjušiti, naslušati, ogledavati, okusiti, omirisati, onjušiti, opipavati, osladiti, osluhnuti, osluškivati, oslušnuti, osmatrati, ožednjeti, piljiti, pipati, pipkati, pipnuti, počuti, pogledavati, pomirisati, ponjušiti, popipati, posluhnuti, prečuti, prigledati, **prigledavati**, primirisati, prisluhnuti, prisluškivati, pročuti, progledati, pronjuškati, providjeti, proviriti, provirivati, razgledati, razgledavati, razvidjeti, sagledati, sagledavati, saslušati, saslušavati, škiljiti, uviđati, vonjati, zagledati, zagledavati, zapiljiti, **zasmraditi**, zasmrditi*
PARL — *blenuti, **ispipavati**, onjušiti, ožednjeti, piljiti, pipkati, ponjušiti, popipati, **prigledavati**, prisluhnuti, škiljiti, **zasmraditi***
CH. LIT — *ispipavati, opservirati, **prigledavati**, providjeti, sagledavati, **zasmraditi***

The data from Table 5 follow the ratios of the data from Table 3, and show the expected results.

Table 5. Corpus statistic: the total number of perception verb types per sensory modality and corpus domain.

	Prcp	Touch	Smell	Taste	Hearing	Sight
MED	44,547	82	0	90	95	**44,280**
PARL	147,035	16	3	32	10,623	**36,368**
CH. LIT	22,808	139	116	88	5,892	**16,572**

2.2 Corpus Annotation

The design of the syntactic grammar from the first phase allowed us to extract all occurrences of perception verbs found within the three domain-related corpora, and automatically annotate each one regarding its sensory modality. This provided us with the data that served as a foundation for the next stage, in which we manually marked their semantic and syntactic properties.

First, the tag PROT was added if the verb was used in its prototypical meaning and the tag MET if used in its non-prototypical meaning – i.e., in its extended physical or metaphorical meaning (at this stage, we did not differentiate between these two subcategories of non-prototypical meaning). Regarding syntactic annotation, we marked two specific types of information: the type of the verb complement (NP, CP, PP, PAS, GL-PR-SD, GL-PR-PR, NA, ADV or INF) and some additional information about the complement, where applicable, as displayed in Table 6.

Table 6. List of perception-verb complements.

Complement TAG	Type of COMPLEMENT	Additional information about the complement CASE
NP	noun or nominal word	Nominative	Genitive	Dative	Accusative	Vocative	Locative	Instrumental
CP	dependent clause	a conjunction that introduces a dependent clause
PP	prepositional phrase	preposition and case of prepositional phrase
PAS	passive	N – subject
GL-PR-SD	present participle	
GL-PR-PR	past participle	
NA	not available	
ADV	adverb	
INF	infinitive	

3 Analysis and Results

The syntactic analysis of predicate complements of perception verbs has shown that they sometimes express their prototypical physical meaning and are without complements in the sentence. Furthermore, there are five categories of complements, namely noun phrases (NP), prepositional phrases (PP), dependent clauses (CP), adverbs (ADV) and infinitives (INF). As exemplified in Table 7, nouns and noun phrases as complements can be expressed in three different cases: accusative (A), genitive (G) and instrumental (I). Prepositional phrases (PP) as complements of perception verbs can be expressed in 19 different combinations composed of 19 prepositions and 5 cases. A dependent clause as a complement of a perception verb in the Croatian language can be introduced by 12 different conjunctions and by the interrogative complementizer *li*. We annotated an adverb as a complement to verbs of perception in those sentences in which there is no other complement and in which the sentence would no longer be grammatical without that adverb.

In his article, Mihaljević [7] mentions that perception verbs often come with a complement consisting of a combination of infinitive and accusative or infinitive and prepositional phrase. Our corpus has shown that such cases are marginal since we have only detected one example, specifically in the corpus of children's literature.

Table 7. Predicate complements of perception verbs.

Comp	Case	Example
NA		*Čujem! Slušajte! Jedan zastaje za časak,onjuši, okreće glavu...* 'I **hear**! **Listen up**! One stops for a moment, **sniffs**, turns his head…'
NP	A	*još jedamput pipne sjekiru* 'he **touches the ax** one more time'
	G	*ne opažaš nesklada* 'you don't **perceive inconsistency**'
	I	*ako se osladi plodovima sitne krađe* if he **sweetens himself with the fruits** of petty theft
PP	ispred + G	*počne pipati ispred sebe* 'he starts to **grope in front of him**'
	iza + G	*pogledajte iza sebe* 'look **behind you**'
	između + G	*gledaše sažalno između vrba* 'he **looked** pitifully **between the willows**'
	kraj + G	*gledam kraj sebe* 'I **look around me**'
	kroz + A	*je piljila kroz prozor* 'she was **looking out the window**'
	na + A	*on pogleda na sat* 'he **looks at** [his] **watch**'
	niz + A	*zapravo je gledao samo niz cestu* 'in fact, he was only **looking down the road**'
	o + L	*nećeš ni da čuješ o krticama* 'you won't even **hear about moles**'
	oko + G	*Ivo je pipkao oko sebe* 'Ivo **groped around himself**'
	po + L	*počne se pipkati po džepovima* 'he starts to **grope in his pockets**'
	pod + A	*on se sagnu i pogleda pod kauč* 'he bends down and **looks under the couch**'

(*continued*)

Table 7. (*continued*)

Comp	Case	Example
	pred + A	*njegove oči gledahu nepomično pred sebe* 'his eyes **stared** fixedly **in front of him**'
	pred + I	*rukama uzme pipati pred sobom* 'he **groped in front of him** with his hands'
	preko + G	*i drugi gusari pogledaju preko boka* 'the other pirates **look over the side**'
	prema + D	*i pilji prema palači* 'and **looks towards the palace**'
	u + A	*kad sam pogledala u njegove duboke oči* 'when I **looked into his deep eyes**'
	u + L	*Manda pogleda u smjeru* 'Manda **looked in the direction**'
	za + A	*nisam čula za tu zemlju* 'I've never **heard of that country**'
	za + I	*buljio je za malim dječakom* 'he **stared after the little boy**'
CP	da	*on nanjuši da se pijani Ogi* 'he **sniffs that** Ogi is drunk'
	gdje	*uspio je ispipati gdje se nalazi velika skupina* 'he managed to **sense where** the large group was'
	kad	*nije ni opazila kad je prošao Veliki Vjetar* 'she didn't even **notice when** the Great Wind had passed'
	kakav, kakva	*da čuju kakve im glasove nosim* 'to **hear what kind** of voices I bring to them'
	kako	*i ču kako ga doziva* 'and **heard how** he calls him'
	kamo	*Zašto ne gledaš kamo skačeš?* 'Why don't you **watch where** you jump?'
	koji	*kad sam opazio kojim smjerom jedri* 'when I **noticed which way** he was sailing'
	koliko	*kad ste opazili koliko je nalik na oca* 'when you **noticed how much** he looked like his father'
	odakle	*pokuša ispipati odakle je došao* 'try to **find out where** he came **from**'
	što	*možeš omirisati što kuhaju u gornjem ognjištu* 'you can **smell what** they're cooking in the upper fireplace'
	tko	*skriveni motre tko će doći* 'hidden, they **watch who** will come'
	zašto	*hajde da čujemo zašto si ti došao* 'let us **hear why** you have come'
	li	*kako biste vidjeli ima li unutra mjehurića* 'to **see if** there are bubbles inside'
ADV		*Pogleda djevojka dolje* 'The girl looked **down**' *bulji netremice ovamo* 'staring **straight here**'
INF		*Nisi čula govoriti o pošti u boci* 'You haven't heard talking about mail in a bottle'

There are also numerous sentences in which the passive construction is expressed by a perception verb, so in these sentences, we only find the subject in the nominative case along with the perception verb (e.g., *divlja odlučnost se opažala u njemu* 'wild determination could be seen in him'). In addition, our corpus offers evidence of present participles (e.g., *opipavajući je tražio svoj trag* 'groping for his clue') and past participles (*gledani sa Zemlje, liče na sporu* 'seen from Earth, they look like slow') expressed by perception verbs. In these cases, they are serving as adverbial markers in sentences.

In the semantic analysis, we checked in which cases metaphorical meanings were realized, and if there were some specific markers that this decision could be made upon. Considering that this article represents a work in progress, only some verb forms have been verified so far across all three domain-related corpora, namely verbs of sensory modalities for smell, taste and touch (Fig. 1), and detailed data on metaphorical versus physical meaning of one sensory modality verb (*gledati* 'to look') is represented in Figs. 2 and 3.

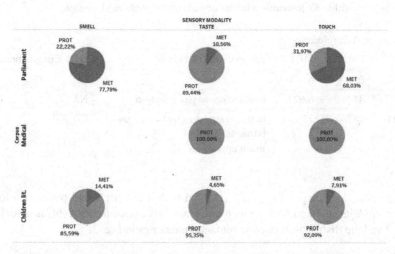

Fig. 1. Distribution of metaphorical *vs.* physical meaning within each sensory modality type of verbs across the corpora.

Unlike the data for the medical corpus, where no verbs of smell are detected, and where we see a uniform pattern of using only the prototypical meaning of the verbs belonging to the categories of taste and touch, distribution is more colorful in the other two corpora. Still, the children's literature corpus gives preference to the use of the physical meaning of the verb for all three sensory modalities, while the Parliamentary corpus follows the same model only for the verbs of taste, and shows dominant usage of metaphorical meaning within the smell and touch sensory modalities.

Since the verb *gledati* 'to look' is especially noted in the literature [5, 6, 8] as having a high possibility of expressing a metaphorical meaning, we will present our findings on it as well. Contrary to our expectations, a preliminary examination of the corpus showed that not all verb forms are highly metaphorical but that the forms used to express the imperative have a metaphorical meaning. The forms *gledaj* (2nd person singular imperative) and *gledajte* (2nd person plural imperative) of the verb *gledati* were separately explored across all three domains. Table 8 shows us that the realization of the metaphorical meaning depends on the corpus domain. There is a high rate of realization of the metaphorical meaning (indirect perception) of these two verb forms in the parliamentary texts and in the corpus of children's literature, there is a greater rate of prototypical, physical meaning (direct perception). The verb forms also differ in the metaphorical meaning itself in different corpora, as well as in the verb complements that come with the perceptual verb. Burić [8] got the same results on the web corpus as we did on the corpus of parliamentary texts. We believe that this is because both corpora have the characteristics of spoken language, language that has had no intervention in content or spelling and grammar, while the corpus of children's literature can be described with quite opposite attributes – i.e., great attention is given to content as well as to spelling and grammar.

Table 8. Semantic analysis of verb forms *gledaj* and *gledajte*.

	gledaj/gledajte			
	PROT	MET	metaphorical meanings	pred. Complements
MED	0	0		
PAR	41	6,674	to listen up, to pay attention	NA
CH. LIT	187	25	to try, to strive, to mind your own business, listen up	CP + da

Distribution per corpus for *gledaj* (marked with a red circle and positioned to the left) and *gledajte* (marked with a green circle and positioned to the right) is visualized in Fig. 2 and the distribution of their semantic meanings in Fig. 3.

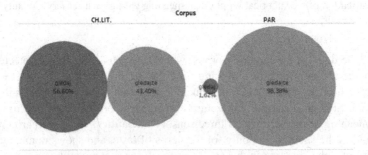

Fig. 2. Distribution of 'gledaj' and 'gledajte' in the children's literature corpus *vs.* the parliamentary corpus.

We see from Fig. 2 that the parliamentary corpus is dominated by the verb *gledajte*, i.e., by the 2nd person plural imperative form of the verb 'to look' with over 98% of occurrences. This is to be expected since speakers in Parliament are more likely to address each other either in the plural form (as if speaking to a group) or more formally with respect (which is expressed as the second person plural) than in the singular person, which would be more expected if their talk was in the less formal environment. On the other hand, the results for children's literature corpus are more evenly divided among the two forms.

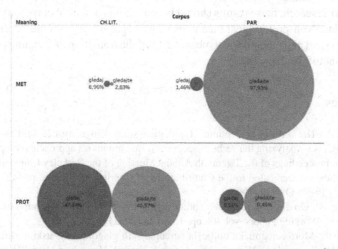

Fig. 3. Distribution of meanings for 'gledaj' and 'gledajte' in the children's literature corpus *vs.* the parliamentary corpus.

If we drill down into these results, we can observe additional differences, more precisely, the difference in the usage of different meanings within each verb form. Results favor more prototypical meaning in the children's literature corpus, and show quite the opposite usage in the parliamentary corpus. This behavior is portrayed in Fig. 3. Again, in this case as well, the explanation for detected results can be found in the type of corpus, but in this case, also in the interlocutor – i.e., the target audience that can understand the conveyed meaning (speakers in the Parliament), and on the other side, an audience that is not yet able to recognize extended physical and metaphorical meanings (children).

4   Concluding Remarks and Future Work

This research shows that, in order to make general conclusions about perception verbs, future research should include many more perception-verb lemmas than have been researched so far. We confirmed Vieberg's theory that some perception verbs are more frequent in usage, and that they are more versatile for polysemous expression. Furthermore, we also showed that the scale of sensory modalities (Sight > Hearing > Touch > Smell > Taste) needs further research because, for example, taste verbs are the least represented in the corpora, but all their lemmas have both meanings – i.e., metaphorical senses as well as a basic, physical meaning. On the other hand, visual perception verbs have the greatest number of lemmas and forms represented in the corpora, but only some of them express non-prototypical or metaphorical meaning. Our research also shows that the selection of the corpus domain strongly influences the results of research on Croatian perception verbs. The same type of verb lemma can, in one corpus domain, have a dominantly physical, prototypical meaning, and in another domain can have a dominantly metaphorical meaning.

In further research, these results should be verified on a neutral corpus, as well as on other domains. Non-prototypical meanings of perception verbs should be divided into extended physical and metaphorical meanings, and the transition of meaning per sensory modalities should be explored.

References

1. Vieberg, A.: The verbs of perception: a typological study. Linguistics **21**(1), 123–162 (1983)
2. Atkins, B.T.S.: Analyzing the verbs of seeing: a frame semantics approach to corpus lexicography. In: Proceedings of the Twentieth Annual Meeting of the Berkeley Linguistics Society: General Session Dedicated to the Contributions of Charles J. Fillmore, pp. 42–56. Oxford University Press, Oxford (1994)
3. Usoniene, A.: On direct/indirect perception with verbs of seeing and seeming in english and Lithuanian. Working Papers, vol. 48, pp. 163–182 (2001)
4. Raffaelli, I.: Morfosemantička obilježja percepcijskih glagola u hrvatskom. In: Botica, S., Nikolić, D., Tomašić, J., Vidović Bolt, I. (eds.) Zbornik Hrvatskog Slavističkog Kongresa, pp. 375–387. Hrvatsko filološko društvo, Zagreb (2017)
5. Whitt, R.J.: Evidentiality and Perception Verbs in English and German. Peter Lang, Oxford & New York (2010)
6. Gisborne, N.: The Event Structure of Perception Verbs. Oxford University Press, Oxford (2010)
7. Mihaljević, M.: The structure of complements of verbs of perception in Croatian. In: Franks, S., Chidambaram, V., Joseph, B. (eds.) A Linguist's Linguist: Studies in South Slavic Linguistics in Honor of E. Wayles Browne, pp. 317– 353. Slavica Publishers, Bloomington (2009)
8. Burić, H.: Kognitivnolingvistički pristup sintaktičko-semantičkomu opisu osjetilnih glagola u hrvatskome jeziku. Disertacija. University of Zagreb, Faculty of Humanities and Social Sciences, Zagreb (2021)
9. Gnjatović, T., Matasović, R.: Evidencijalne strategije u hrvatskom jeziku. In: Birtić, M., Brozović Rončević, D. (eds.) Sintaksa padeža, pp. 89–99. Institut za hrvatski jezik i jezikoslovlje i Filozofski fakultet Sveučilišta Josipa Jurja Strossmayera u Osijeku, Zagreb & Osijek (2010)
10. Tadić, M., Fulgosi, S.: Building the Croatian morphological lexicon. In: Erjavec, T., Vitas, D. (eds.) Proceedings of the 2003 EACL Workshop on Morphological Processing of Slavic Languages, pp. 41–45. ACL, Budapest (2017)

NooJ Grammars for Morphophonemic Continuity and Semantic Discontinuity

Mario Monteleone[(⊠)]

Università degli Studi di Salerno, 84084 Fisciano, SA, Italy
mmonteleone@unisa.it

Abstract. If we give someone just one slap, are we actually slapping him or her? More precisely: how many slaps must we give someone so to mean that we are concretely slapping him or her? These two questions seem quite odd and too much driven by "semantic subtleties", especially if we bear in mind all Lexicon-Grammar (LG) [1] studies on sentence transformations relating predicative nouns to verbs [2–12], that is nouns as *schiaffo* (slap) to verbs as *schiaffeggiare* (to slap). As is well known, these transformations almost never lead to perfect semantic equivalence. This is evident also with the couple *passeggiata* (walk) and *passeggiare* (to walk), in the Italian sentences *Max fa una passeggiata* (Max takes a walk, support verb) vs. *Max passeggia* (Max walks, regular verb). Actually, the previous support verb sentence does not imply the same not–finite verbal action as the regular verb sentence, in which the derivative suffix *-eggi* in *passeggiare* refers to a reiterated and iterative action.

Besides, concerning the lacking of perfect equivalence between these types of sentences, the aforementioned noun *schiaffo* seems to pose additional problems, together with a series of other nouns semantically contiguous to it and that express the action of "hitting someone with a part of the body or with an object, be it itemized or not". In this case, we refer to nouns such as *bastonata* (blow struck with a stick), *botta* (hit), *calcio* (kick), *gomitata* (elbow hit), and similar.

Keywords: NooJ · NooJ Grammars · Morphophonemic Continuity · Semantic Discontinuity

1 Introduction

If we give someone just one slap, are we actually slapping him or her? More precisely: how many slaps must we give someone so to mean that we are concretely slapping him or her? These two questions seem quite odd and too much driven by "semantic subtleties", especially if we bear in mind all Lexicon-Grammar (LG) [1] studies on sentence transformations relating predicative nouns to verbs [2–12], that is nouns as *schiaffo* (slap) to verbs as *schiaffeggiare* (to slap). As is well known, these transformations almost never lead to perfect semantic equivalence. This is evident also with the couple *passeggiata* (walk) and *passeggiare* (to walk), in the Italian sentences *Max fa una passeggiata* (Max takes a walk, support verb) vs. *Max passeggia* (Max walks, regular verb). Actually, the

© The Author(s), under exclusive license to Springer Nature Switzerland AG 2024
A. Bartulović et al. (Eds.): NooJ 2023, CCIS 1816, pp. 139–149, 2024.
https://doi.org/10.1007/978-3-031-56646-2_12

previous support verb sentence does not imply the same not–finite verbal action as the regular verb sentence, in which the derivative suffix *-eggi* in *passeggiare* refers to a reiterated and iterative action. Besides, concerning the lacking of perfect equivalence between these types of sentences, the aforementioned noun *schiaffo* seems to pose additional problems, together with a series of other nouns semantically contiguous to it and that express the action of "hitting someone with a part of the body or with an object, be it itemized or not". In this case, we refer to nouns such as *bastonata* (blow struck with a stick), *botta* (hit), *calcio* (kick), *gomitata* (elbow hit), and similar.

As for this class, at present it includes thirty-nine nouns that, as we will see, do not show semantically linear behaviour in the passage from regular-verb constructions to support-verb ones. We will also assess that, depending on the starting lexical morpheme concerned:

1. When one of these words is used as a predicative noun, the semantic contiguity with the respective support-verb constructions is often quite variable and depends on the presence and quality of specific co-occurring (pre)determiners;
2. In some cases, and always in an unpredictable way, this passage can also produce fixed, frozen or semantically non-compositional sentences;
3. In many cases, the meanings of these non-compositional sentences appear to be well lexicalized, but they assume values quite different from their literal ones.

In the following pages, starting from some nouns of the previously mentioned class, we will verify the quality and nature of the acceptable transformations connecting ordinary-verb sentences to (supposed) support-verb constructions. Subsequently, we will use some sample NooJ grammars to classify and tag coherently the sentences produced.

Hence, this study aims to investigate the typology of formal and semantic relationships existing between ordinary-verb sentences and (supposed) support-verb constructions, describing in detail, where possible, the existing differences with what established and consolidated in LG studies up to today.[1]

---

[1] We list hereby a series of the most relevant studies achieved on verb supports, with both a transformational and a Lexicon-Grammar approach (source: http://infolingu.univ-mlv.fr/Men uPrincipal.html#, section "Bibliographie". See also the paragraph "References" for more titles.

Daladier, Anne:

- 1978. Quelques problèmes d'analyse d'un type de nominalisation et de certains groupes nominaux français Thèse de 3ème cycle, Paris : Université Paris 7.
- 1990. Aspects constructifs des grammaires de Zellig Harris. Langages 25, 57–84. D.
- 1996. Le rôle des verbes supports dans un système de conjugaison nominale et l'existence d'une voix nominale en français. Langages, 30(121), 35–53.
- 1999. Auxiliation des noms d'action. Langages, 33(135), 87–107.

Harris, Zellig Sabbetai:

- 1954. Distributional Structure, Word, 10:2-3, 146-162.
- 1957. Co-Occurrence and Transformation in Linguistic Structure, Language, Vol. 33, No. 3, Part 1, 283-340, Linguistic Society of America.
- 1964. Elementary transformations. In Transformations and discourse analysis papers, 54. Philadelphia: University of Pennsylvania.
- 1988. Language and Information, New York: Columbia University Press.

2   Logical-Linguistic Discrepancies

As already mentioned, we will be dealing with thirty-nine Italian (supposed) predicative nouns[2], which create logical-linguistic discrepancies when they participate in the transitions among ordinary-verb sentences and support-verb ones. These discrepancies do not come from generic "sentence interpretations", and affect specific syntactic-semantic delineations of verb profiles, hence verb logical-linguistic definitions and classifications. Besides, such discrepancies cannot be formally highlighted, since, as we will see, they are not predicted or determined by the maintenance of Morphophonemic Continuity (MC) in the previously mentioned transitions. In fact, they induce clear meaning differences between the two types of sentences, and push towards different syntactic classifications of those verbs selecting all our thirty-nine specific nouns.

In one of the next paragraphs, we will show how MC works. Moreover, we will use the LG analytical methods not only to highlight the discrepancies already mentioned, but also to indicate where and why a supposed support verb must instead be labeled as an ordinary one.

3   What is Morphophonemic Continuity

First, in order to define MC, we must briefly recall the definitions of phoneme and morpheme. As known, a morpheme is a non-segmentable element of the phonological representation of an utterance, the nature of which is determined by a set of distinctive features.[3] In its coding functions, each language has a limited and restricted number of phonemes (about twenty to fifty, depending on the language) which are to be combined,

- 1991. A Theory of Language and Information: a mathematical approach, Oxford: Clarendon.
- 2007. La langue et l'information [Traduction par Amr Helmy Ibrahim & Claire Martinot de Language and Information (1988)], Paris: CRL.

Tesnière, Lucien:

- 1959. Éléments de syntaxe structurale, Paris: Klincksieck.

Vives, Robert

- 1983. Avoir, prendre, perdre: Constructions à verbes supports et extensions aspectuelles, Thèse de 3ème cycle, Paris: Université de Paris III.
- 1985. Lexique-Grammaire et didactique du français langue étrangère. Langue française 68, 48–65.

[2] The list of such nouns is not complete, since all the other "types of blows" that can be inflicted have not yet been examined (for instance *cannonata* (cannonade), *racchettata* (hit given with a racket), *scarpata* (hit given with a shoe), *stivalata* (hit given with a boot), *vangata* (hit given with a spade) and so on). A complete list of these nouns may be very rich, thus requiring a review of all the correlation parameters highlighted in the past for the relationships among ordinary-verb and support-verb constructions.

[3] Easy to attain is the reference literature, both digital and paper, about phonemes specific distinctive features of all the languages of the World. For this reason, we will not list them in these pages.

along the spoken chain, to constitute the signifiers of messages. Besides, morphemes oppose each other punctually, in different points in the spoken chain, to differ messages from each other. This function being its essential function, the phoneme is often defined as the minimal distinctive unit of language. Moreover, a same single phoneme may be concretely realized by different sounds, forming an open class of elements, which oppose this phoneme to all the other phonemes of the same language. These different sounds, which make up the same phoneme, are called variants or allophones. For instance, in the French word *rare*, the phoneme /r/ can be pronounced as a vibrating dental [r] called *r bourguignon*, like a vibrating uvular [r] called *r grasseyé*, or like a vibrating uvular [r] called *r Parisian*. These are three different sounds, or three different variants (here regional and social variants) producing the same phoneme.

As for Italian, we have similar utterance condition, as shown in the following examples:

A ***phoneme*** in a minimal pair (i.e. a pair of two words, which differ only due to one sound):

palla vs. *balla* (Eng. ball – lie)

Three possible allophones of the phoneme /n/:

- *naso* (Eng. Nose) pronounced '*nazo*
- *conca* (Eng. Dip) pronounced '*oːŋka*
- *anfibio* (Fr. Amphibious) pronounced '*aɟːfibjo*

As for ***morphemes***,[4] we can list three types, that is:

- Lexical morphemes, which define the main meaning of a word;
- Grammatical morphemes, which provide the grammatical information of a word, in order to give its correct form in a specific context (gender and number of nouns and adjectives; persons and number of verbs);
- Derivational morphemes, which are added to a lexical morpheme to obtain verbs, nouns, adjectives and other word forms. It regularly precedes the grammatical morpheme, which always appears at the end of words.

We give hereby some examples on how morphemes can form Italian words:

Pass = lexical morpheme*; eggi, at* = derivational morphemes; *o, are, a* = grammatical morphemes, as in: *Pass-o* (noun m.s., Eng. step); *Pass-eggi-are* (verb int., Eng. to stroll); *Pass-eggi-at-a* (noun f.s., Eng. stroll).
Schiaff = lexical morpheme*; eggi* = derivational morpheme (iterative)*; o, are* = grammatical morphemes, as in: *Schiaff-o* (noun m.s., Eng. slap); *Schiaff-eggi-are* (verb t., Eng. to slap).

---

[4] Although the words of all world languages are composed of morphemes, here we will only deal with the compositional morphology of inflectional languages, as are especially Romance ones, such as Italian and French, as well as, although to a lesser extent, English. As is known, agglutinative and polysynthetic languages, from a word formation point of view, make different use of their morphemes. However, we will not delve into these issues in depth, as they would not be relevant to the main theme of this study. Beside, also in this case, a very detailed reference literature, both digital and paper, is easy to attain.

Combining the morphemes of a language,[5] MC makes it possible to transfer the meaning of a word to another, derived from it, adding or removing specific phonemes/ allophones/morphemes in order to both modifying meanings and/or grammatical categories of arrival, as shown by the following Italian examples:

Verbs: *infett-are* vs. *dis-infett-are* (Eng. infect – disinfect). Adjectives: *sett-ic-o* vs. *a-sett-ic-o* (Eng. septic – aseptic). Noun: *calci-o* vs. verb: *s-calci-are* (Eng. kick – to kick up)

4   The Notion of Support Verb in Lexicon-Grammar

Preserving the starting lexical morpheme in the passage from one word to another, MC results to be the basis of the notion of support verb, support verb extension, as well as of predicative nouns/adjectives, as established by the LG of Maurice Gross [2–12]. As known, in all languages, support verbs do not have a predicative function: during sentences production, they neither select any arguments nor change the contextual meaning of such arguments. Their function is only to actualize their nominal/adjectival predicates functions, obtained by nominalization/adjectivation from ordinary verbs, with which they are in a relationship of MC. Besides, as for these actualizations, in general a construction with an ordinary verb (*passeggiare*, to stroll) is synthetic if compared to a construction with a support verb (*fare una passeggiata*, to take a stroll) which is on the contrary analytical.

A list of the most common (not only) Italian support verbs includes *avere* (to have), *essere* (to be), and *fare* (to do, to make):

*Max **adora** Paola* (Max adores Paola) = *Max **ha adorazione** per Paola* (Max has adoration for Paola).
*Questo evento **scoraggia** Paola* (This event discourages Paola) = *Questo evento è **scoraggiante** per Paola* (This event is discouraging for Paola).
*Piero **sogna*** (Peter dreams) = *Piero **fa** dei **sogni*** (Peter has some dreams).

In addition, we speak of support-verb extensions when the support verb used adds semantic/aspectual value to a given sentence, while replacing a more common support verb:

*Max **si scusa** con Paola* (Max apologizes to Paola) = *Max **fa le sue scuse** a Paola* (Max makes his apologies to Paola) = *Max **presenta le sue scuse** a Paola* (Max offers his apologies to Paola).

However regular these actualizations of predicative nouns and adjectives may appear, in the following paragraphs we will verify, instead, how in Italian some sentences obtained by nominalization/adjectivation turn out to produce (non-interpretative) meanings significantly different from that of ordinary-verb sentences. In the presence of specific co-occurrences of words, we will observe that some (apparently) support-verb constructions do not preserve semantic continuity (SC), while preserving morphophonemic one. As will be seen, this is a regular phenomenon, concerning the previously

---

[5] It is worth remembering that, in each and any language, also morphemes combinations are the results of the Saussurean relationship between *Langue* and *Parole*.

mentioned class of nouns (see 1. Introduction), together with specific uses of determiners/predeterminers. This "anomaly" in the transition from ordinary sentences to support-verb constructions seems to suggest that the studies on support verbs, nominalizations and adjectivation, should not be considered accomplished, and that they should probably be reviewed, using a less binary and more "quantum" approach.

5 Morphophonemic Continuity and Meaning Mismatches

The Italian examples that follow will help us to define the semantic mismatches that occur in the interrelationships between sentences with ordinary-verb, support-verb and support-verb extension. As already stated, the ordinary verb *schiaffeggiare* (to slap) includes the derivative suffix *-eggi*, the presence of which expresses an intensive and iterative[6] meaning, that is, that of an action carried out in a repetitive way and without a precise point of conclusion on the axis T of time.[7] Therefore, it ensues that the analytical construction *dare uno schiaffo* (to give one slap) does not have the identical meaning of the infinitive verb, especially because in it, *uno* is not an indefinite article (a), but a numerical pre-determiner (one)[8], aspect that is the concrete source of the meaning mismatch.

A further confirmation to this comes from the fact that simple sentences with verb as *schiaffeggiare* are into perfect paraphrastic equivalence with non-simple synthetic sentences in which mode adverbs occur. For instance, *Lo schiaffeggiò (rapidamente + velocemente + improvvisamente)* (He slapped him (rapidly + quickly + suddenly)), in which the mode adverbs serve to reduce, as far as possible, the duration of the verb action. On the contrary, in the analytical sentence *Gli diede (velocemente + rapidamente + improvvisamente) uno schiaffo*, (He gave him (rapidly + quickly + suddenly) a slap), the mode adverbs serve to define the speed of the action, and not its duration in terms of "number of slaps given". An even supplementary example of meaning mismatch is provided by the support verb extension sentence *prendere qualcuno a schiaffi*[9] (to slap so. repeatedly), which does not have the same meaning as *dare uno schiaffo a qualcuno* (to give so. one slap), while it has a perfect meaning correspondence with the verb *schiaffeggiare*, Hence, the impression is that *dare uno schiaffo a qualcuno* is not a support-verb construction, but a normal dative one. On the contrary, are support-verb

---

[6] The same can be said for many other Italian verbs, such as: *amareggiare* (embitter), *amoreggiare* (flirt), *biancheggiare* (whiten), *corteggiare* (woo), *favoleggiare* (fable), *folleggiare* (fool around), *guerreggiare* (war), *indietreggiare* (retreat), *lampeggiare* (flash), *largheggiare* (widen), *occhieggiare* (ogle), *scarseggiare* (be scarce), *sceneggiare* (dramatise), *signoreggiare* (lord over), or *vaneggiare* (rave). It is also worth stressing that not all verbs including this suffix participate in transformations towards support verb or support verb extension sentences. Only those nominalizable do. Nonetheless, all of them retain an intensive and iterative meaning.

[7] To confirm this, we note that a double conclusion point on the T axis of time is present in the (not simple) sentence *Max schiaffeggia Luca ogni giorno, per dieci minuti* (Max slaps Luca every day, for ten minutes).

[8] This is because the slap given, in the specific case, would not be just any slap, but only one, numerically.

[9] The construction **prendere qualcuno a schiaffo* (singular of *schiaffi*) is not acceptable in Italian.

constructions all those sentences in which the word *schiaffi* (pl. for *schiaffo*) occurs, not preceded by a numeric pre-determiner, as in *dare schiaffi a qualcuno* (to give slaps to so.), which is clearly a nominalisation from *schiaffeggiare*.

Other adverb occurrences tend to strengthen these observations, as shown in the following examples with the quantity adverb *una volta* (once). In fact, its use brings sentences with *schiaffeggiare* and dative verb into perfect correspondence: *Max schiaffeggia Paola una volta* (Max slaps Paola once) = *Max dà a Paola uno schiaffo* (Mac gives Paola one slap) = *Max dà uno schiaffo a Paola* (Max gives one slap to Paola).

It is worth noting that the meaning mismatch just highlighted does not arise only from the occurrence of the suffix *–eggi*. As mentioned, it comes also and above all from the fact that the nominalizations in question concern the already class of nouns expressing the action of "hitting someone with a part of the body, or with an object, be it itemized or not". This seems self-evident since, by definition, infinitive verbs such as *bastonare* (to beat with a cane) or frustare (*to whip*) cannot provide any quantification regarding the actions they refer to. The same may be observed for *accoltellare* (to stab), which is in a meaning mismatch relationship with *dare una coltellata* (to give one stab), while has a perfect correspondence with *prendere a coltellate* (plural, to stab repeatedly). Some more examples are:

- *bastonare* (to club, to beat up) = *prendere a bastonate* (to club repeatedly, to give beatings) ≠ *dare una bastonata* (to cane once, to give one beating)
- *scalciare* (to balk) = *tirare calci* (to give kicks, to kick up) ≠ *prendere a calci* (plural, repeatedly, to give kicks, to kick up) ≠ *dare un calcio* (to give one kick, to kick once).

As can be deduced, in all these cases the occurrence of the numerical pre-determiner *un* + *uno* + *una* plays a crucial role.

6   Semantic Discontinuity

As for the nominalisations we are dealing with, Semantic Discontinuity (SC) becomes more evident when the nouns in the class observed co-occur in their plural forms. In such cases, the numeric pre-determiners play a very important role. For instance, the co-occurrence of the Italian numeric pre-determiners *due* (two) and *quattro* (four) produces ambiguous results, i.e. sentences that are both figurative and support-verb constructions. In fact, starting from *Paola schiaffeggia Luca*, we can have *Paola da (due + quattro) schiaffi a Luca*, which means both "Paola gives (two + four) slaps to Luca" in a literal sense, and "Paola fixes Luca", that is, metaphorically, "Paola violently calms Luca down".[10] In its figurative meaning, the Italian sentence does not quantify *due* and *quattro* as a concrete number of slaps. As mentioned, it is possible to observe this phenomenon

---

[10] The figurative meaning of this sentence and other similar ones is strictly dependent on the type of pre-determiners co-occurring with the noun used. To demonstrate this, it is possible to insert a correlation with the verb *urlare* (to scream) of the sentences *Paola urla contro Max* = *Paola lancia (due+quattro) urla contro Max* (Paola screams at Max = Paola shouts two+four screams at Max). In fact, also in this case, the two nominalization sentences similarly have a figurative sense, meaning *Paola calma Max (E+urlando)* (Paola calms Max down (E+with her screaming)).

systematically, with all the nouns of the class we are dealing with. However, this ambiguity only occurs with *due* and *quattro*. With three and with the numbers from five onwards, these sentences actually behaves as support-verb constructions derived from ordinary-verb sentences.

From a morphophonemic point of view, the nouns here investigated and which express the action of "hitting someone with a part of the body or with an object, be it itemized or not" can be divided into those which are correlated with an ordinary verb and those which are not. Certain diminutives and augmentatives are also to take into consideration. The nouns in correlation with an ordinary verb are: *bacio* (kiss), *bastonata* (beating), *calcio*, (kick), *carezza*, (caress), *colpo*, (blow), *coltellata*, (stab), *frustata*, (whip), *gomitata*, (nudge), *manganellata*, (truncheon), *percossa*, (blow), *pugnalata*, (stab), *randellata* (bludgeon), *schiaffo* (slap), *scossone* (jolt), *spinta, spintone* (push), *stangata* (sting), *stilettata* (jab), *trafittura* (stab), *urto* (bump).

The nouns not in correlation with a verb are:

botta (blow), *cazzotto, cazzottone* (punch, hard punch), *ceffone* (slap), *legnata* (beating with a piece of wood), *manata* (slap), *manrovescio* (backhand), *mazzata* (blow with a club), *pacca* (pat), *pedata* (kick), *pugno* (punch), *revolverata* (revolver shot), *rovescione* (backhand), *sberla* (slap), *sganasso* (smack), *scapaccione, sganascione, sganassone* (hard smack), *scappellotto* (slap), *scoppola* (blow) *stoccata* (jab), *sventola* (slap).

Below, we provide two examples, one for each list. We start from a specific ordinary-verb sentence, to which we apply a nominalisation. We also indicate the possible classifications of both the verbs with which the ensuing nominalisations co-occur, and the types of sentences in which they participate. Although there is MC in all the following these sentences, their morphosyntactic classification and specific meaning mainly depends both on the grammatical number of the occurring nouns itself, and on the eventual correlation with an ordinary verb. To a certain extent, such result seem to suggest that further studies should be carried out on support verbs, also taking into account the morphosyntactic characteristics of certain nouns occurring within specific sentences.

Noun: *manganellata* (truncheon), related to the verb *manganellare* (to truncheon).

- *Max manganella Paolo* (Max truncheons Paul)
- *Max dà + tira una manganellata a Paolo* (Max hits Paul with one truncheon): ordinary-verb dative construction
- *Max dà + tira due/quattro manganellate a Paolo* (Max hits Paul with two/four truncheons): figurative use / ALUs (no concrete count, figurative meaning: to handle someone, to deal with someone, but in a negative way)
- *Max dà + tira (due, tre, quattro, cinque, sei, sette... n−1) manganellate a Paolo* (Max hits Paul with (two, three, four, five, six, seven... n−1) truncheons): support-verb construction
- *Max prende Paolo a manganellate* (Max truncheons Paul repeatedly): support-verb construction
- *Max tira manganellate a Paolo* (Max gives Paul lots of truncheons): support-verb construction

Noun: *sberla* (wallop), no Italian verbe **sberlare* (to wallop).

- *Max dà una sberla à Paolo* (Max gives one wallop to Paul): ordinary-verb dative construction

- *Max dà + tira due/quattro sberle a Paolo* (Max gives two/four wallops to Paul): figurative use/ALUs
- *Max dà + tira (due, tre, quattro, cinque, sei, sette... n−1) sberle a Paolo* (Max gives two, three, four, five, six, seven... n−1 wallops to Paul): both ordinary-verb dative construction and support-verb construction, due to the non-existence of the verb **sberlare*
- *Max prende Paolo a sberle* (Max gives several wallops to Paul): support-verb construction
- *= Max tira sberle a Paolo* (Max gives several wallops to Paul); support-verb construction

7 Some Nooj Grammars on Morphophonemic Continuity and Semantic Discontinuity

The observations previously produced can be inserted as tags in NooJ electronic dictionaries, or as instruction in NooJ grammars [13–16], to annotate texts, remove ambiguity (thus achieving formal semantics classification), or automatically address and process the knowledge extraction from a text. As shown below, to these possible functions, the following grammars add some transformations, as well as some equivalence between support-verb and support-verb extension constructions. Together with tagging instruction, the grammar of Fig. 1 also includes the support-verb extensions *mollare* and *ammollare* (intensive aspectual variants of *to give*):

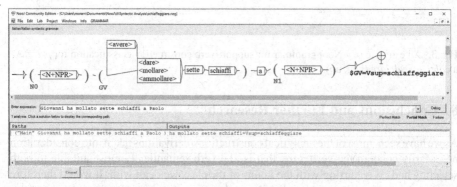

Fig. 1. An example of a Nooj grammar for support-verb construction classification for *schiaffeggiare* (slap).

The grammar in Fig. 2 describes *dare* as an ordinary dative verb, related to *ricevere:*

The grammar in Fig. 3 describes recognizes and tags the sentence *prendere a calci* as a support-verb extension sentence from *scalciare* (kick up, intensive iterative variant of *to kick*):

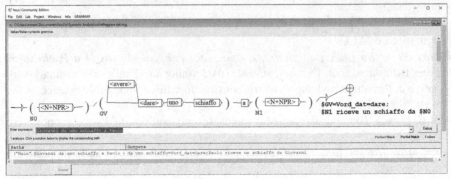

Fig. 2. An example of a Nooj grammar for ordinary dative verb classification *schiaffeggiare* (to slap).

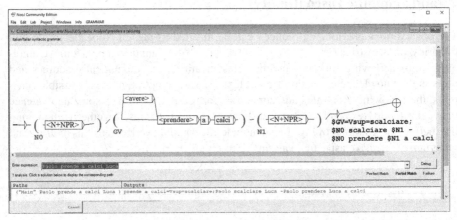

Fig. 3. An example of a Nooj grammar for support-verb construction classification for *prendere a calci + scalciare* (kick up).

8   Conclusions and Further Research

As we have seen, most of the analytical constructions/derivations taken into consideration necessarily concern the verb *dare*, that is, the verb semantically most suitable to both selecting and co-occurring with the nouns of the class we dealt with. It would therefore be extremely necessary to accomplish the analysis we carried out also for the verb *receive* (receive), which as indicated by [18] is closely connected to give, both transformationally and semantically. As for our study, such an analysis will represent a future step, of which here we give a quick hint, underlining that in the passage from *dare* to *ricevere*, the sentences *dare (due + quattro) (manrovesci* (backhands) + *schiaffi + pugnalate* (stabs) + *randellate* (bludgeons) + ...) *a qualcuno* lose their figurative meaning. In fact, *ricevere (due + quattro) (manrovesci + schiaffi + pugnalate + randellate + ...) da qualcuno* (to receive (two + four) (backhands + slaps + stabs + bludgeons + ...) from so.) only have the meaning of being hit more than one single time, i.e. they are only support verb constructions. On the contrary, the sentences *ricevere (un + una + uno) (manrovescio + schiaffo + pugnalata + randellata + ...) da qualcuno* (to receive one (backhand +

slap + stab + bludgeon + ...) from so.) are in perfect correlation with those of *dare* classified as an ordinary dative verb.

However, we very much want to reaffirm that, as is well known, since the 1970s, especially at Maurice Gross's LADL [17], support verbs have been the focus of prestigious and in-depth research, in relation to which the brief considerations expressed in these pages undoubtedly represent a "heretical" position, which, however, was elaborated using classic LG "tools". While deeply respecting all important past research (see footnote 1), we thought it appropriate to raise the problems highlighted, since as we have seen, they are supported by objective observations, involving an elevate number of words, morphosyntactic constructions and sentences.

Without either the idea or the scientific strength to reform unaided LG studies on support verbs, we close our considerations hoping that younger researchers will consider them as a starting point, useful to either confirm or invalidate what we have exposed here, so far.

References

1. Wikipedia page. https://en.wikipedia.org/wiki/Lexicon-grammar. Accessed 13 Sep 2023
2. Gross, M.: Méthodes en syntaxe. Régime des constructions complétives. Hermann, Paris (1975)
3. Gross, M.: Grammaire transformationnelle du français : syntaxe du verbe. Cantilène, Paris (1969)
4. Gross, M.: Sur quelques groupes nominaux complexes. In: Chevalier, J.-C., Gross, M. (eds.) Méthodes en grammaire française, pp. 97–119. Klincksieck, Paris (1976)
5. Gross, M.: Les bases empiriques de la notion de prédicat sémantique. Langages 15(63), pp. 7–52 (1981)
6. Giry-Schneider, J.: Les prédicats nominaux en français : les phrases simples à verbes supports. Librairie Droz, Genève-Paris (1987)
7. Giry-Schneider, J.: L'article zéro dans le lexique-grammaire des noms prédicatifs. Langages 25(102), pp. 23–35 (1991)
8. Gross, M.: Sur la notion harrissienne de transformation et son application au français. Langages **25**(99), 39–56 (1990)
9. Gross, G.: Trois applications de la notion de verbe support. L'Information Grammaticale 59, pp. 16–23 (1993)
10. Gross, G.: Prédicats nominaux et compatibilité aspectuelle. Langages 121, pp. 54–73 (1996)
11. Gross, G.: Verbes supports et conjugaison nominale. Études Francophones 9, pp. 70–92 (1999)
12. Gross, G.: Les verbes supports et la prédication des prédicats nominaux. In: Ibrahim, A. H. (ed.) Supports et prédicats non-verbaux dans les langues du monde. CRL, Paris (2010)
13. Silberztein, M.: NooJ Manual. (2003). www.NooJ-association.org
14. Silberztein, M.: An alternative approach to tagging. In: Kedad, Z., Lammari, N., Métais, E., Meziane, F., Rezgui, Y. (eds.) NLDB 2007. LNCS, vol. 4592, pp. 1–11. Springer, Heidelberg (2007). https://doi.org/10.1007/978-3-540-73351-5_1
15. Silberztein, M.: Les unités linguistiques et leur annotation automatique. Modèles Linguistiques 55, pp. 109–120 (2007)
16. Silberztein, M.: Formalizing Natural Languages: The NooJ Approach. Wiley-ISTE, London (2016)
17. UNISA. https://labgross.unisa.it/LADL. Accessed 19 Sept 2023
18. Vives, R.: Avoir, prendre, perdre : constructions à verbes supports et extensions aspectuelles. Thèse de 3ème cycle. Université de Paris III, Paris (1983)

Corpus Linguistics and Discourse Analysis

Explicit Language in English Song Lyrics: Should We Be Concerned?

Mila Bikić[(✉)] and Valerija Bočkaj

Faculty of Humanities and Social Sciences, University of Zagreb, Zagreb, Croatia
bikic.mila05@gmail.com, vbockaj@gmail.com

Abstract. A casual music fan who pays attention to song lyrics may notice that explicit lyrics and profanity in music vary across genres, genders and periods. In this sense, the explicit language includes but is not limited to verbal insults (i.e., whore, bitch, faggot, the n-word and other racial slurs), linguistic units that are of sexual nature (i.e., dick, coochie, fuck) and other commonly used profane linguistic units (i.e., shitty, bullshit). To examine this, a linguistic analysis was conducted using the linguistic development environment software and corpus processor NooJ. A corpus of 300 English songs was collected, evenly distributed across six genres (pop, rock, R&B, hip-hop, funk and country), with 25 songs by male and 25 by female artists in each. The lyrics were sourced from Spotify's genre charts for October 2022. A syntactic grammar was employed to identify explicit words and phrases, achieving a precision of 0.95, recall of 0.92, and an F-score of 0.93. Hip-hop exhibited the highest frequency of explicit language, with female hip-hop artists using more profanity than their male counterparts. An upward trend in explicit word usage was noted from the 1950s to the 2020s, indicating a shift towards more explicit content in recent decades. The analysis revealed that hip-hop songs and songs from more recent decades tend to feature a higher frequency of explicit language. The study sheds light on the evolving landscape of explicit content in music and the surprising role of gender and race in its usage.

Keywords: Explicit Lyrics · Linguistic Analysis · Male Versus Female

1 Introduction

The utilization of explicit language in song lyrics has long remained a subject of fascination and concern, captivating the attention of scholars, critics and the public alike. Music, as an art form and a medium for artistic expression, possesses the unique capacity to reflect the social and cultural milieu of its time. Lyrics serve as an effective vehicle for artists to convey their thoughts, emotions and perspectives. In this study, we aim to discern not only the frequency of explicit vocabulary within music but also the contextual factors that shape its usage. By examining a wide-ranging corpus of song lyrics encompassing six popular genres, our goal is to explore the complex connection between music, language and societal norms. In the realm of songwriting, the use of explicit language emerges as a provocative choice that both male and female artists have strategically incorporated into their lyricism.

A. Bartulović et al. (Eds.): NooJ 2023, CCIS 1816, pp. 153–164, 2024.
https://doi.org/10.1007/978-3-031-56646-2_13

To discern and analyze these elements, we employed a systematic methodology involving the development of syntactic grammar within the linguistic development tool NooJ. It allows us to process our corpus in real-time by creating finite-state automata that correspond to the Chomsky-Schützenberger hierarchy [1]. This grammar, designed for the recognition and annotation of explicit words and phrases, aimed to identify linguistic units of various natures, including those referring to taboo topics, such as sexual activities and excretion. Considerable emphasis was placed on evaluating units containing the words 'fuck' and 'ass', which can be associated with Chomsky's notions of rule-bound and rule-breaking linguistic creativity [2].

In this paper, we outline our methodological approach for constructing a corpus that underlies our study. Our hypotheses suggest that among the six chosen music genres, hip-hop exhibits the highest frequency of explicit phrases. We expect that in the 2020s, explicit language will be more commonly used in song lyrics, and we suggest that male artists tend to employ such language more frequently than their female counterparts. Our methodology involves creating a comprehensive corpus of English song lyrics, and then analyzing how often certain words or phrases appear across different music genres and decades, accompanied by a quantitative analysis of token distribution across each genre and decade. Furthermore, we employ a specialized English syntactic grammar within the NooJ software to identify and categorize profane linguistic constructs. Our findings provide insights into how explicit language is used, and our discussion explores potential effects on society, especially on young audiences. Finally, we conclude by outlining avenues for future research, seeking to offer a better understanding of explicit language in the context of song lyrics.

2 Corpus

The corpus was assembled through a structured process of manually selecting songs from curated Spotify genre playlists and acquiring their corresponding lyrics from the website Genius (https://genius.com). This approach ensured the deliberate inclusion of a diverse array of musical genres and decades, establishing an all-encompassing dataset. The songs incorporated into the corpus span eight decades, covering the years from 1954 to 2022. It is worth noting that the corpus is exclusively monolingual, focusing solely on English song lyrics. The corpus encapsulates an expansive musical domain consisting of songs from the following genres: pop, rock, hip-hop, RnB, funk and country.

2.1 Composition of Corpus

The corpus consists of a total of 300 songs that have been evenly distributed, with 150 songs performed by male artists and 150 songs performed by female artists. This balanced gender representation recognizes the potential impact of gender on the lyrics. The corpus is organized into 27 separate text files. These include songs from each decade, spanning from the 1950s to the 2020s, providing a historical perspective for the exploration of the evolution of explicit language in song lyrics. Moreover, within each genre, three separate files are established: one comprehensive file encompassing the entire genre and two distinct files for songs performed by male and female performers within that genre.

In addition, there is a combined file that brings together all the songs in the corpus, allowing for comprehensive analyses across different genres and decades.

2.2 Distribution of Tokens in the Corpus

After the corpus had been collected, we examined the distribution of tokens within the corpus to gain a deeper understanding of the linguistic composition of the dataset and evaluate any potential biases.

Token Distribution Across Genres. Tokens within the corpus are distributed across the six music genres as follows:

a. The country genre contains a total of 15,270 tokens, with 8,188 tokens from males and 7,082 tokens from females.
b. The funk genre consists of 15,130 tokens, with 7,369 tokens found in the male corpus and 7,761 tokens in the female corpus.
c. The hip-hop genre consists of an extensive 27,820 tokens, with 14,874 tokens from males and 12,946 tokens from females.
d. The pop genre has 17,505 tokens, with 9,440 tokens from males and 8,065 tokens from females.
e. The RnB genre comprises 16,903 tokens, with 8,088 tokens by males and 8,815 tokens by females.
f. The rock genre has a total of 13,440, with 6,997 tokens from males and 6,443 tokens from females.

It is important to highlight that even though each genre's corpus contains 50 songs, the hip-hop genre stands out with a significant count of 27,820 tokens, whereas the other five genres range from 12,946 to 17,505 tokens each.

Token Distribution by Decades. The songs are further categorized into eight decades corpora to gain insights into how explicit language has evolved over time:

a. 1950s (970 tokens),
b. 1960s (2,371 tokens),
c. 1970s (11,574 tokens),
d. 1980s (5,899 tokens),
e. 1990s (6,192 tokens),
f. 2000s (13,988 tokens),
g. 2010s (29,457 tokens),
h. 2020s (33,298 tokens).

3 Analysis

To analyze the collected corpus, an English syntactic grammar was constructed in the NooJ software. The main branch of this grammar, shown in Fig. 1, consists of the following subgraphs: "Aphrases", "Fphrases", "Verbs" and "Words".

The "Aphrases" graph, shown in Fig. 2, is used to look for common phrases and collocations with the noun 'ass'. It detects collocations such as 'fat ass', 'far up your ass' and 'kiss my ass'.

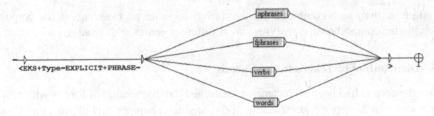

Fig. 1. The main branch of the grammar used to analyze the corpus.

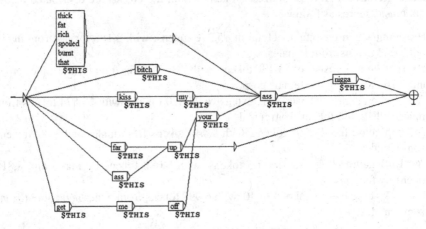

Fig. 2. The "Aphrases" graph.

Figure 3 displays the "Fphrases" graph concerned with the verb 'fuck'. To provide a more precise representation of the contemporary state of explicit lyrics, nouns and verbs were put in angle brackets, which signal NooJ to include inflectional suffixes [1].

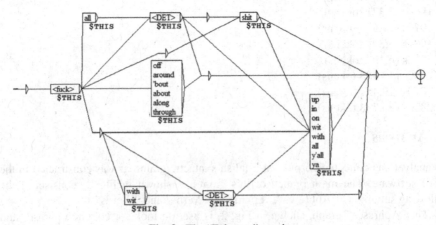

Fig. 3. The "Fphrases" graph.

Figure 4 illustrates the "Verbs" graph, primarily focused on explicit verbs and phrasal verbs, as well as commonly used explicit collocations associated with them. It includes frequently used explicit expressions such as 'give a fuck'. Additionally, verbs of a sexual nature are included.

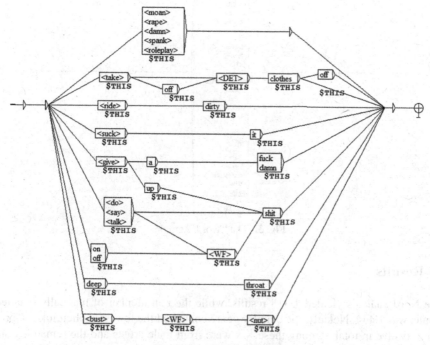

Fig. 4. The "Verbs" graph.

The final graph used to analyze the corpus is the "Words" graph, presented in Fig. 5. It captures tokens that consist of a single word, most of which are written in angle brackets to include their inflectional forms. This list includes nouns that refer to sexual organs, such as 'dick', 'cock' and 'coochie', bodily secretions such as 'cum' and 'piss', insults such as 'faggot', 'asshole' and 'bitch', racial slurs and other explicit words. By splitting the graphs into different categories and creating a capture-all graph, the resulting grammar can capture a vast array of explicit linguistic units in the corpus.

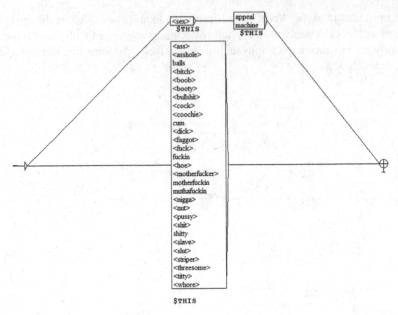

Fig. 5. The "Words" graph.

4 Results

The NooJ analysis yielded 1,313 results, while the real number of manually counted results was 1,444. Notably, the country genre contained the fewest explicit tokens, precisely twelve in total. Among these, six were from male artists and the remaining six were from female artists. In the funk genre, 62 explicit tokens were identified, with 50 performed by male artists and 12 by female artists. The rock genre contributed 68 explicit tokens, primarily by male artists, with 66 tokens, whilst only two stemmed from female artists. The pop genre featured 80 explicit tokens, with 18 by male artists and 63 by female artists. In the RnB genre, 102 tokens were identified, consisting of 63 from male artists and 39 from female artists. In contrast, the hip-hop genre stood out with a substantial 989 explicit tokens, with 371 by male artists and 618 by female artists. The standard score of each of the twelve genre-gender corpora is shown in Fig. 6.

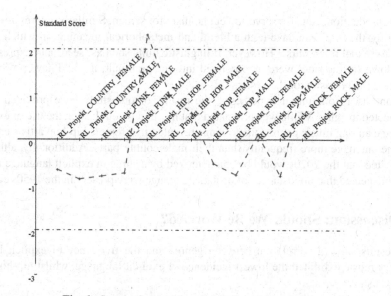

Fig. 6. Standard score of explicit lyrics within corpora.

A subsequent analysis was conducted on the decades corpora, revealing a gradual rise in the frequency of explicit tokens from the 1950s through the 2000s. Nevertheless, a substantial surge was observed in the 2010s, with a total of 451 explicit tokens. This trend continued into the 2020s, where a notable 612 explicit tokens were documented. Figure 7 depicts this progression in the form of a line graph.

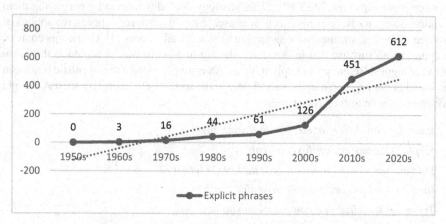

Fig. 7. Explicit tokens over decades.

The results were assessed using the following metrics: a calculated F-score of 0.93, a recall of 0.92 and a precision of 0.95. While the recall metric indicates a satisfactory performance, achieving a higher value would be possible if the system could also recognize sexual innuendos. For instance, the noun 'seed', while typically associated with plant reproduction, can also serve as a euphemism for semen. Similarly, expressions like 'down for the ride' can have both a literal and metaphorical meaning, in which 'ride' refers to sexual intercourse. However, if linguistic units such as 'seed' and expressions like 'down for the ride' were incorporated into the grammar, it could have potentially impacted the precision of the system.

Contrary to our initial hypotheses, the results of our study have provided some unexpected insights. While we anticipated that hip-hop would lead in the use of explicit language among music genres, the findings revealed that female hip-hop artists employ profane language more frequently than their male counterparts. Additionally, although we posited that the 2020s would be characterized by a surge in explicit language use, it was unexpected that no instances of profane language were present in the 1950s corpus.

5 Discussion: Should We Be Worried?

Our results show a correlation between genres and the frequency of explicit lyrics. Country music exhibited the lowest incidence of explicit language, whilst hip-hop had the highest.

5.1 Hip-Hop as the Genre of Misogyny and Black Hardships

Hip-hop, also known as rap, originated in the 1970s in the Bronx, New York. It emerged as a form of cultural and artistic expression among urban African-American youth, and is often regarded as the poetic voice of marginalized youth that addresses issues of race and class. [3].

Misogyny, defined as the hatred or disdain of women, did not become prominent in hip-hop music until the late 1980s. This ideology degrades women by portraying them as possessions, tools, or even objects of abuse. In rap, it reinforces oppressive notions of women as mere instruments for satisfying men's sexual desires [3]. Given this context, it comes as no surprise that in our study, the hip-hop genre was identified as the genre with the highest frequency of explicit lyrics. An example of such misogynistic lyrics can be found in our hip-hop corpus, specifically in the song "Take Shots" by artist A Boogie wit da Hoodie featuring Tory Lanez:

Baby, we can do a trio, me, you and your migo
Sippin' Casamigos, yeah-yeah-yeah
I wanna see you deep throat, girl, that ass is lethal
Bust it then I reload, yeah-yeah-yeah
Tryna see how bad you can get when you're drunk.

These lyrics depict the woman as an object for the artist's sexual pleasure, even implying she can be shared with his "migo" (slang for 'friend'), reducing her and her body to a mere object of desire. Additionally, the reference to her being "drunk" raises concerns about the possibility of non-consensual sexual activity due to her intoxicated state. These topics consist of six prevalent themes in misogynistic rap that Adams and Fuller identify:

a. disparaging remarks about women regarding sexual matters;
b. depictions of violent actions against women, often tied to sexual content;
c. portrayals of women as sources of "trouble" or problems for men;
d. depictions of women as manipulators or "users" of men;
e. references to women as inferior or subordinate to men;
f. depictions of women as expendable and easily disposable entities. [3]

It is important to note that explicit lyrics within our corpus include more than just sexual and misogynistic content. As previously stated, hip-hop articulates the reality of African American youth, which unfortunately involves issues such as substance abuse, violence, racism and crime. The 1980s, a period when the genre gained massive popularity, marked a time of significant hardship for African Americans, who were neglected by the government. The right, led by President Ronald Reagan, disregarded the concerns of black people and the poor. As a result, the living conditions for African Americans deteriorated, leading to rising rates of crime, substance abuse, teenage pregnancies, gang violence, urban violence and the spread of AIDS and other sexually transmitted diseases. [4] Even in contemporary rap, these themes continue to be explored. For example, the posthumously released song "Already Dead" by artist Juice WRLD, who died of an accidental overdose in December 2019, addresses substance abuse, a recurring topic in his musical opus [5]:

> I've been runnin' out of drugs and hope (Yeah, yeah)
>
> I don't even got a plug no more (Yeah, yeah)
>
> Have you ever been so alone? (Yeah, yeah)
>
> That you don't know what to feel no more? (Yeah, yeah)
>
> Ain't no reachin' for the pills no more (Yeah, yeah)
>
> One more and you're on the floor (Yeah, yeah).

5.2 Women's Empowerment Through Assertive Sexuality

Both previously mentioned songs are by male hip-hop artists who, in our research, were found to have a total of 371 explicit tokens in their corpus. Interestingly, their female counterparts had a notably higher count of explicit tokens – 618, to be precise. While female rappers also delve into topics of hardship within black communities, they typically do not write misogynistic lyrics.

Feminist theory posits that narratives portraying black women as unfeminine, with abhorrent sexuality, and as predators dependent on men, serve to justify the oppression of black women and to normalize social inequalities, such as racism, sexism and poverty. Countering these narratives in music fosters the expression of women's desires for sexual satisfaction and pleasure rather than solely catering to their partners' needs. It also challenges patterns of sexual objectification and promotes women's independence by critiquing male dominance and addressing sexual and domestic violence [6]. For example, artist Doja Cat's song "Boss Bitch" can be seen as a feminist anthem, despite containing a total of 33 explicit tokens, according to our grammar. The word 'bitch' is repeated 32 times, primarily due to the recurring chorus line "I'm a bitch, I'm a boss".

Additionally, the lyric "I wear the hat and I wear the pants" symbolizes the female partner's authority in the relationship, as well as her role in the workforce. In artist Cardi B's song "Up", she states:

Niggas out here playin', gotta make 'em understand
If ain't no ring on my finger, you ain't goin' on my 'Gram

This example illustrates female empowerment by highlighting that men should not always take precedence in women's lives unless the relationship is considered serious. While female empowerment can be found in various music genres, due to the nature of hip-hop, which is inherently prone to explicit phrases, female empowerment is taken to an extreme. Herd echoes Skeggs' perspective that female hip-hop artists assert their sexuality as a means of liberating themselves from the moralizing and victimizing narratives that society often imposes on black women. In this way, hip-hop emerges as the only genre that actively responds and protests against such societal views [6].

5.3   Should We Be Concerned?

To our knowledge, there has not been a study specifically exploring the impact of explicit song lyrics on people at large. However, Martino et al. conducted a national longitudinal telephone survey in the United States to examine whether popular music could influence changes in the sexual behavior of American youth. They conducted annual interviews with 1,461 adolescents and their parents over three years. Among the participants, 1,242 consistently reported their sexual behavior and music listening habits across all three-time points. The analysis primarily focused on the effects of degrading sexual lyrics in music, and discovered that listening to such songs was associated with an increase in various sexual activities among adolescents. However, no similar link was observed with lyrics that lacked sexual references or contained non-degrading sexual references. Martino et al. underscored that reducing degrading sexual content in music or limiting exposure to it might help delay the onset of sexual behavior [7].

In conclusion, sexual lyrics can potentially exert a negative influence on youth by encouraging behaviors they may not be ready for. Nonetheless, in the digital age of social media, monitoring adolescents to reduce exposure to such content has become increasingly challenging.

6   Implications and Future Directions

Our study lays the groundwork for subsequent research in this domain, presenting several possible avenues for further exploration:

a. Expand corpus size. To bolster the comprehensiveness of our dataset, we recommend expanding the corpus size by collecting other songs, particularly from genres recognized for their frequent use of explicit language. Moreover, incorporating genres such as jazz, blues or classical music from diverse historical periods would provide a more comprehensive perspective.

b. Crosslinguistic comparative analyses. The comparative analysis of profanities across different languages and cultures presents an intriguing opportunity. Expanding our research to include low-resource languages like Croatian would enable an exploration of how explicit language manifests in various cultural contexts.
c. Comparative analyses. Developing additional corpora focused on different music genres, such as regional folk songs or experimental electronic music, and conducting comparative analyses of linguistic features across these genres could yield valuable insights into the variation of explicit language usage within distinct music styles.
d. Enhanced metadata. Enriching the corpus with additional metadata, such as album information or songwriter identity, can facilitate more nuanced analyses. This would provide valuable insights into the contextual factors influencing explicit language usage.
e. Diverse linguistic features. Broadening the scope of analysis to encompass various linguistic features, including grammatical structures, word frequencies or metaphorical language, would offer a deeper understanding of the multifaceted nature of language within song lyrics.

7 Conclusion

This analysis of explicit language usage in song lyrics has yielded several noteworthy insights that illuminate the dynamic relationship between language, music and cultural evolution. One of the key findings of the research revolves around the substantial variation in the usage of explicit language across six examined music genres. Hip-hop, renowned for its candid and often provocative lyrics, emerged as the genre with the highest frequency of profane language usage, serving as a platform for African-American artists to address issues like racism, poverty, substance abuse, violence and crime.

An intriguing aspect of our findings involves the examination of gender dynamics within the hip-hop genre. Surprisingly, our research revealed that female hip-hop artists tend to incorporate more explicit language compared to their male counterparts within the same genre. This phenomenon aligns with feminist theory, suggesting that female hip-hop artists assert their sexuality as a means of liberation from narratives that portray them as unfeminine. Moreover, hip-hop offers women a platform to critique male dominance and objectification while promoting women's independence.

Furthermore, our analysis offers a historical perspective on the evolution of explicit language in song lyrics. In the 1950s corpus, explicit language was entirely absent, marking a distinct departure from contemporary songwriting. Conversely, we noted a significant increase in the frequency of explicit language in the 2020s corpus. This trend reflects a growing acceptance and prevalence of explicit language in modern song lyrics, mirroring the evolving norms and values of society. The 2020s appear to embrace complete linguistic freedom in music as artists challenge traditional lyrical conventions and push boundaries.

Considering these findings, one might ponder the implications of this upward trend in music. Regrettably, previous research has established a connection between degrading sexual lyrics and increased sexual activities among adolescents. This raises concerns about the potential influence of such content on youth, particularly in today's digital age, where monitoring exposure to explicit content becomes increasingly challenging.

References

1. Silberztein, M., Váradi, T., Tadić, M.: Open Source multi-platform NooJ for NLP. In: Kay, M., C. Boitet (eds.) Proceedings of COLING 2012, pp. 401–408. The COLING2012 Organizing Committee, Mumbai (2012)
2. Chomsky, N.: Syntactic Structures. Mouton, The Hauge (1957)
3. Adams, T., Fuller, D.: The words have changed but the ideology remains the same: misogynistic lyrics in rap music. J. Black Stud. **36**(6), 938–957 (2006)
4. Best, S., Kellner, D.: Rap, Black Rage, and Racial Difference. Enculturation 2(2), (1999)
5. 'I Wanted to Show What Happened': The Tragic Story of Juice WRLD. https://www.thegua rdian.com/tv-and-radio/2021/dec/15/juice-wrld-tragic-story-documentary. Accessed 06 Sept 2023
6. Herd, D.: Conflicting paradigms on gender and sexuality in rap music: a systematic review. Sex .Cult. **19**, 577–589 (2015)
7. Martino, S., Collins, R., Elliott, M., Strachman, A., Kanouse, D., Berry, S.: Exposure to degrading versus non-degrading music lyrics and sexual behavior among youth. Pediatrics **118**(2), e430–e441 (2006)

Immigrant in the Light of Language Production

Barbara Vodanović(✉) (iD)

University of Zadar, Zadar, Croatia
bvodanov@unizd.hr

Abstract. In this paper, we propose to study the semantic development of the term *immigrant* in Croatian based on newspaper articles published in the online version of the Croatian newspaper *Jutrarnji list* from 30 August 2015 to 17 January 2023. Our analysis is based on the approach of the Semantics of Argumentative Possibilities initiated by Galatanu [1], who stated that in the core meaning of every lexical term exists a possibility for deployment of meaning caused by the contextual environment. According to that, the core meaning of the word *immigrant* is calculated based on the lexical definition in the Croatian language. To test the environment of the keyword as the first step in constructing the network of contextual appearances of collocates and other appreciative elements, which can lead us towards the new semantic deployment of the key term, we developed a NooJ syntactic grammar. NooJ located occurrences of the key term and its partial synonyms, enabling us to select our key term's precise meaning. It also showed the immediate collocates of the term. We noticed that the grammar needed some improvement, considering the choice of prepositions in the syntactic grammar branches. However, that is operable, and can be used on larger corpora for further and more thorough analysis.

Keywords: Migrant · Collocates · Discourse Analysis · Corpus Analysis · Digital Humanities · Croatian · NooJ Syntactic Grammar

1 Introduction

Izbjeglica, prognanik, pribjegar odnosno azilant, iseljenik odnosno emigrant, useljenik odnosno imigrant, ili naprosto selilac odnosno migrant – sve to nazivlje pokazuje koliko je fenomen ljudskih seoba odnosno migracija urastao u kolektivni imaginarij i stoga u leksik Hrvata i, dakako, inih naroda ove naše Evrope. Pa znamo li se nositi s time i kako?[1]

Inoslav Bešker, published in *Jutarnji list*, 27 December 2019 (online version 13:51')

As illustrated by the excerpt of journalist Inoslav Bešker, who lists ten different terms, the Croatian language disposes of many terms regarding people's voluntary or

---

[1] 'Refugee, exile, *pribjegar* or asylum seeker, emigrant or *useljenik*, immigrant or simply mover or migrant – all these names show how much the phenomenon of human migrations has grown into the collective imaginary and therefore into the lexicon of Croats and, of course, other peoples of our Europe. So do we know how to deal with it and how?'

© The Author(s), under exclusive license to Springer Nature Switzerland AG 2024
A. Bartulović et al. (Eds.): NooJ 2023, CCIS 1816, pp. 165–175, 2024.
https://doi.org/10.1007/978-3-031-56646-2_14

involuntary migration. They all have a specialized meaning that refers to a specific semantic concept. However, some represent the synonymic pairs *iseljenik – emigrant* or *useljenik – immigrant* and *selilac – migrant*. Nonetheless, the economy of human communication, especially communication through mass media, tends to narrow it down to less specific or more-purpose terms.

We hypothesize that the general "non-marked" term might be migrant. Therefore, this research aims to describe the core meaning of this term and try to define the direction in which the meaning of the term evolves in Croatian. The analysis will be corpus-based, and we will describe the core meaning and its development according to Olga Galatanu's semantic-discursive approach called the Semantics of Argumentative Possibilities.

After this introduction, in Sect. 2, a short overview of the recent research on migrants in Croatia is given, where it is apparent that migrants became the subject of linguistic research just a few years ago. In Sect. 3, we discuss the theoretical background, and present the description of the core meaning of the word *migrant* in Croatian according to Galatanu's theory. Then, in Sect. 4, we explain the methodology of our NooJ syntactic grammar for discourse analysis. The results of the analysis are presented in Sect. 5. Section 6 concludes our findings, and emphasizes some corrections for further NooJ syntactic grammar developments[2] for discourse analysis studies.

2   Research on the Topic of Migrants in Croatia

The subject of recent migrations or persons in the process of migrations in Croatia was primarily discussed in studies on geography [5–8] etc., ethnology [9–12], philosophy [13, 14] or sociology [15–18], and it has become an interest of studies of law and legislation as shown in an analysis conducted by the Croatian Ombudsperson's Office [19].

The Croatian Ombudsperson's Office launched a study of media reporting on migrant asylum seekers from the perspective of its three primary responsibilities: work on combating discrimination, responsibilities for the promotion of human rights (part of work with the public and the media) and the National Preventive Mechanism against Torture, to research into compliance of journalistic reporting on migrants, asylum seekers with the principles of the Code of Honour of Croatian journalists. For the analysis, the Croatian Ombudsperson's Office selected the texts that were published on the most read internet portals in 2013, and determined the readership criterion according to the Gemius readership index from January 2014, and ultimately included eight internet portals where 78 articles from the beginning of March until the end of July 2014 were found. The research was intended for "services that work under various responsibilities of the Office of the Ombudsman (…) and editors of the main internet portals, printed and other media" (cf. *Ured pučke pravobraniteljice*). This article lists several previous relevant studies on migrations in Croatian media [20–23].

The subject became a topic of linguistic studies recently and mainly in the domains of (critical) discourse analysis and narratology in the works of Bezić and Petrović [24], Podboj [25] and Panjić [26], to name but a few. They each approach the topic from

[2] I would like to thank Kristina Kocijan, PhD, Associate Professor at the Department of Information and Communication Sciences of Faculty of Humanities and Social Sciences in Zagreb for her help in developing the syntactic grammar for this study.

different perspectives and primary goals. Thus, Bezić and Petrović [24] are focused on the strategies of nomination and predication in media discourse on migration according to Reisigl and Wodak. Podboj [24] introduces a possible model of narrative analysis based on findings from more extensive empirical research on identity construction in personal narratives of migration. Most recently, in her doctoral thesis, Panjić [26] analyses, according to Fairclough's three-dimensional model, various characteristics of the migration discourse developed in Croatian news media *Jutarnji list, Večernji list, Slobodna Dalmacija* and *Glas Slavonije* during one year, from 1 July 2015 to 30 July 2016.

3   Theoretical Background

Namely, according to Galatanu's [1–4], semantic-discursive theory called the Semantics of Argumentative Possibilities, language stereotypes represent an open set of associations to the core traits of any word form. The core traits are abstract predicates partly similar to Wierzbitcka's semantic primitives [27]. Galatanu states that the argumentative possibilities of the core unfold in blocks of external argumentation, associating the language production with an element of the core stereotype. These stereotypes decline predicates, and associate them with other representations in blocks of argumentative meaning, relatively stable in a given linguistic community at a given moment in its cultural evolution [2, 4]. This association allows the discursive deployment that, strictly speaking, constitutes the argumentative sequences. We can identify this deployment through the list of core modifiers represented by adjectives, nouns and adverbs.

First of all, we have to describe the core meaning of the word *immigrant* in Croatian based on its lexicographic definition and then check the direction of development of the stereotypical meaning based on the syntagmatic deployment of the collocates of the given word in the corpus.

3.1   Core Meaning

The dictionary is, as is well known, a metalinguistic work and a didactic work that defines a norm, and presents the rules for the good and correct use of words.

According to the discursive approach to the meaning set by Ducrot [28, 29] and Ducrot and Anscombre [30], the description of the lexical meaning must be able to account for:

a. the representation of the world perceived and modeled by language;
b. the argumentative potential of words and, in particular, the level of inclusion of this potential in the lexical meaning.

In Croatian, the "neutral" term *migrant*, a predicating person making a migration from one point to another, is not listed in the large *Etymological Dictionary of the Croatian and Serbian language* (latest edition 1971 – 1974) by Petar Skok nor in the form of immigrant/emigrant or migration. This should not surprise us since in Croatian the term *iseljenik* is used for the person who moves from one country to another and *useljenik* for the person who settles in a country. Both derive from the verb *seliti* 'to migrate' without any axiological connotation.

Croatian distinguishes the term 'emigrant', but until recently, there has been a clear notional differentiation between the terms *iseljenik* and *emigrant,* although the two are formally synonymous. An *emigrant* had to move for undesirable political/ideological reasons, cf. *Politički emigrant,* 'the political emigrant' or *ekonomski emigrant,* 'the economic emigrant' who emigrates for economic reasons. Croatian further differentiates the term *izbjeglica* 'refugee' (cf. Verb *izbjeći* 'to get away from something unpleasant, dangerous, not wanting to have a relationship with anyone') for the person who left their country for fear of persecution.

It is interesting to notice that, according to the corpus analysis of the parliamentary debates in the Croatian Parliament (*Sabor*) [31], in the concerned period (2003–2021), the deputies instead opted for other terms adopted in the Croatian linguistic and legislative systems. The most commonly used terms by male and female deputies were the noun and adjective derivatives of the noun *ilegalac* 'illegal' and the derivatives of the verb base *seliti* 'to migrate'. Then there were the derivatives of the term *migrant* followed by the derivatives of the term *azilant* 'asylum seeker'. It is striking that the term *izbjeglica* 'refugee' was not mentioned even once. This awareness of semantical and, thus, terminological differences is appropriate according to the disposition of terms in the Croatian language.

The online base of the Croatian language, *Hrvatski jezični portal* 'Croatian Language Portal' (HJP) [32], differentiates the following terms related to the term *migrant*: one who is included in the migration, one who migrates (cf. "onaj koji je obuhvaćen migracijom, onaj koji migrira"):

a. **imigrant** ('immigrant'), one who settled in a foreign country for long-term or permanent residence (cf. "onaj koji se naselio u stranoj zemlji radi dugotrajnog ili stalnog boravka"); syn. **useljenik**, anth. **emigrant (iseljenik)**
b. **izbjeglica** ('refugee')
   i. one who escaped from their homeland or permanent residence [that refugee] (cf. "onaj koji je izbjegao iz svoje domovine ili iz stalnog prebivališta [taj/ta izbjeglica]"),
   ii. neol. During the Homeland War, a person who fled from other republics of the former Yugoslavia to the Republic of Croatia, syn. Prognanik (cf. "neol. u Domovinskom ratu osoba izbjegla iz drugih republika bivše Jugoslavije u Republiku Hrvatsku, usp. **prognanik**")
c. **azilant** ('asylum seeker'), one who has the right to asylum, who enjoys asylum in a foreign country (cf. "onaj koji ima pravo azila, koji uživa azil u stranoj zemlji").

The Croatian National Bureau of Statistics (DZS), on the other hand, offers some further differentiation regarding the term *migrant* itself, defining it as *osoba koja sudjeluje u procesu prostorne pokretljivosti stanovništva* ('a person who participates in the process of spatial mobility of the population'), and proposes two types of migrant person: *doseljenik* 'one who settles in' and *odseljenik* 'one who moves away'. According to the DZS [33], migration implies the relocation of persons within the country (internal migrations) and the relocation of persons from one country to another (external migrations).

On the other hand, the media discourse is relatively distinctive in the case of these terminological differences. In her doctoral thesis, Panjić [26] analyses migration discourse in the Croatian printed media during the migration crises in 2015 and 2016. Panjić [26, pp. 78–79] sets the comparative list of definitions of the terms migration, migrant and related terms *immigrant*, *emigrant* and *refugee* according to linguistic and legislative resources, showing that differences in the meaning exist, but newspaper authors mostly use different terms in the same discursive context without implying any kind of semantic discrepancy. Some journalists, such as Inoslav Bešker, use the term *migrant* as a hyperonym for the term *refugee*. On the other hand, some authors tend to dissociate the two most used terms using the connective 'i' 'and', creating a syntagmatic expression *immigrants and refugees* (cro. *Migranti* i *izbjeglice*) to emphasize the different semantic values of terms:

"the syntagmatic use of the two terms creates a difference in meaning between them, and thus the term *migrant* is narrowed down to a fundamental general and neutral meaning that presupposes all causes movements, and it is precisely in syntagmatic use that the term *migrant* can receive a negative connotation which is connected with the economic context of people's movements, which opens up space for creating a distinction between 'deserved' and 'justified' versus 'undeserved' and 'unjustified' migration." [26, p. 82]

The first step towards describing the core potential of the term *migrant* is to investigate whether the core meaning changes and, if so, in which direction.

4   Methodology of Data Programming in the NooJ Syntactic Grammar for Discourse Analysis

The first step towards the complete analysis of the semantic deployment of the term *migrant* includes gathering a corpus.

For this preliminary study, we collected the corpus from an online edition of the Croatian newspaper *Jutarnji list* from 30 August 2015 to 17 January 2023. The corpus comprises 35,998 tokens in 71 text files containing at least one occurrence of the keyword 'migrant'.

We then collected the list of possible nouns and adjectives, synonyms to the key term 'migration', and added it to the NooJ Croatian dictionary, which now comprises the following terms:

– added nouns:

- *tražitelj, tražiteljica* 'seeker', *m* and *f*,
- *ilegalac, ilegalka, ilegalnost* 'illegal person' *m* and *f*, 'illegality',
- *azilant, azilantica* 'asylum seeker', *m* and *f*,
- *prognanik, prognanica* 'person in exile', *m* and *f*,
- *prognanstvo, progon, progonstvo, progonjenje* 'exile',
- *prebjeg* 'defector', *m*,
- *došljak, došljakinja* 'newcomer', *m* and *f*.

– added adjectives:[3]

- *raseljen* 'displaced',
- *doseljen, doseljenički* 'immigrated',
- *iseljen, iseljenički* 'expatriate',
- *naseljen, naseljenički* 'populated',
- *novodoseljen* 'newly arrived',
- *odseljen* 'mowed away',
- *preseljen* 'relocated',
- *useljenički* 'immigrated.

The further step was to create a syntactic grammar in NooJ (Fig. 1) to find and annotate noun phrases (NP) that represent different uses of the keyword 'migrant'. The attribute "Type" was added to enhance the search by distinguishing among different terminology used in the corpus. The upper branch recognizes constructions that portray a specific type of migrant (e.g., *somalijski migrant* 'Somali migrant', *ekonomski migrant* 'economic migrant', *ilegalni migrant* 'illegal migrant') by providing an additional adjective (Fig. 1: "Adj" node) that precedes the main noun (Fig. 1: "Migrant" node) with the additional constraint that both an adjective and a noun have to match in case, number and gender.

The second branch recognizes only the main noun (Fig. 1: "Migrant" node) that can also be replaced with two types of syntagma that use the noun 'citizen' either in a masculine (*<državljanin >*) or feminine (*<državljanka >*) gender. In some cases, this noun can be preceded by an adjective such as *strani državljanin* 'foreign citizen' or followed by a proper noun denoting some geographical location (*<N + vl + geo >*) such as *državljanin Francuske* 'citizen of France'.

The analysis of the content of the Internet portals on the subject of migrants made by the Office of the Ombudsman (*Ured pučke pravobraniteljice*) in 2014 has found that in their reporting on migrants, the media most often (80%) use attributes that express the ethnic or national affiliation of individuals, and therefore we have inserted prepositional phrases that are used in the construction of these phrases in our grammar. Thus, both branches can be followed by additional information on the location from which a migrant is coming, such as *ilegalni migrant iz Indije* 'illegal migrant from India' or *ekonomski migrant s područja Bliskog Istoka* 'economic migrant from the area of Middle East'.

---

[3] In the further development of the NooJ syntactic grammar, we should pay attention to the fact that some adjective forms are homonymous to adverbs, ex. *Naseljenički, iseljenički, useljenički* which should be taken in consideration. These parts of speech are lemmatized but we did not take them into account in this study.

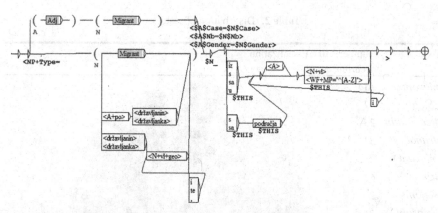

Fig. 1. The "Main" syntactic grammar that recognizes and annotates occurrences of synonymous terms of the word *migrant*.

We noticed that the preposition *u* 'in' that we included in the syntactic grammar resulted in false positives indicating the current placement of the person in transit, which is not relevant to our current analysis.

5 Results

The grammar (Fig. 1) resulted in 618 concordances, giving us an insight into the section of the corpus where it was detected and an annotation about its type (Table 1).

Table 1. An excerpt of concordances.

Corpus	Concordance	Annotation
JutarnjiList_2019_06_06.not	*Migrantima*	< NP + Type = migrant >
JutarnjiList_2019_11_28.not	*alžirski migrant*	< NP + Type = migrant >
JutarnjiList_2015_10_05.not	*Izbjeglice*	< NP + Type = izbjeglica >
JutarnjList_2023_01_17b.not	*marokanski državljanin*	< NP + Type = državljanin >
JutarnjList_2019_12_27.not	*iseljenik iz Afrike*	< NP + Type = iseljenik >

The grammar identified 12 NP types, including the term *migrant* and its lexical synonyms, and the ratio of the distribution of lexical synonyms is given in Table 2.

Table 2. Distribution of results.

Term	Number of occurrences	Visualization
migrant	*484*	
izbjeglica	62	
državljanin	27	
stranac	21	
imigrant	7	
azilant	6	
iseljenik	2	
emigrant	2	
useljenik	2	
pribjegar	1	
prognanik	1	
selilac	1	

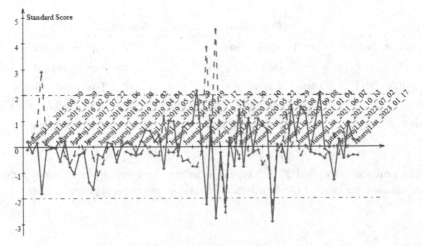

Figure 2 shows the standard score distribution for the term *migrant* (color-coded in red full line) and the use of all the other synonyms we have detected (color-coded in the green dashed line).

Fig. 2. Standard score for the term *migrant* vs *other synonyms*.

We can notice a few outbreaks to the standard deviation. It mainly happened during the second big migrant wave through the Balkan route during the autumn of 2019 when newspapers reported information about statistics of illegal transfers, or commented on the conditions of deaths in the migrant population in transfer. We have noticed that journalists tend to use the term *migrant* regardless of the person's status. As for the state representatives, they tend to use other terms, mostly the term 'foreign citizens' / 'citizens of [name of the country]/ foreigner'. That leads us to the conclusion that the term *migrant* is commonly used as a hyperonym for all the lexemes in the semantic field.

The second most used term, *izbjeglica* 'refugee' tends to be used exclusively for persons fleeing from countries involved in war conflicts such as Syria, Afghanistan and Iraq, or when the author has the intention to specify the status of persons in migration from these counties as it was noticed in the articles from the beginning of the first big migrant wave during 2015 where the ratio is 3 to 12 for the semantically precise term.

Other occasions where the term *migrant* is low in representation or even non-existent is in the news on the number of asylum seekers, or when the article refers to the official statistical data of the status of persons in migration given by authorities, as where the ratio of the term *migrant* is 0 to 3 for other terms.

6 Conclusion

As the core meaning of the recent term *migrant* is based on the non-marked verb *seliti* 'to move from place to place', therefore the Croatian equivalent *selilac* which is possible but poorly functional in media communication (not one case of that term was found in our corpus), the language disposes of other more semantically specific terms which take into consideration the status of the person in transfer (*izbjeglica* 'refugee', *azilant, tražitelj azila* 'asylum seeker') or the direction of its transfer (*useljenik, doseljenik, iseljenik* and its equivalents *immigrant* and *emigrant,* 'immigrant' and 'emigrant').

According to our corpus analysis, the use of the non-marked term *migrant* is appropriate in the context of non-specific news reports or newspaper comments on the transfer condition of the people executing the transfer. Still, it is to avoid it in semantically specific conditions where the terms must describe the particular status of the people in transfer.

The constructed NooJ syntactic grammar has proven to be adequate for the investigation of syntactic deployment of the key term. Nevertheless, we have noticed that some corrections must be made in choosing possible prepositions due to some discrepancies in the findings. In this regard, the present grammar should be taken as a training tool for testing a broader corpus to determine other possible discrepancies and resolve them later on.

The further goal of our research to investigate the direction of development of the stereotypical meaning based on syntagmatic deployment of collocates of the given word in the corpus has to be done in further research where we should consider the choice of collocates and other appreciative expressions. It should be essential to identify them in the immediate and larger context, sentence or paragraph to indicate in which way the axiology of the term is evolving. For that purpose, we should choose a more comprehensive corpus sample.

References

1. Galatanu, O.: Le phénomène sémantico-discursif de déconstruction-reconstruction des topoï dans une sémantique argumentative intégrée. Langue Française **123**, 41–51 (1999)
2. Galatanu, O.: La sémantique des possibles argumentatifs et ses enjeux pour l'analyse de discours. In: Salinero Cascante, M. J., Iñarrea Las Heras, I. (eds.) El texto como encrucijada: estudios franceses y francófonos 2, pp. 213–226. Universidad de La Rioja, Logroño (2003)
3. Galatanu, O.: L'Analyse du Discours dans la perspective de la Sémantique des Possibles Argumentatifs : les mécanismes sémantico-discursifs de construction du sens et de recon-struction de la signification lexicale. In: Garric, N., Longhi, J. (eds.) L'analyse linguistique de corpus discursifs : des théories aux pratiques, des pratiques aux théories, pp. 49–68. Presses universitaires Blaise-Pascal, Clermont-Ferrand (2009)
4. Galatanu, O.: La sémantique des possibles argumentatifs : génération et (re)construction discursive du sens linguistique. Peter Lang, Bruxelles (2018)
5. Mikačić, V.: Spatial Mobility of the Population of Croatia – Internal Migration. Hrvatski geografski glasnik 62(1), pp. 1–21 (2000)
6. Klempić Bogadi, S.: Utjecaj migracije na demografski razvoj riječke aglomeracije. Hrvatski geografski glasnik **70**(1), 43–65 (2008)
7. Klempić Bogadi, S., Podgorelec, S.: Sociodemografske značajke i procesi u hrvatskim obalnim gradovima. Geoadria **14**(2), 221–247 (2009)
8. Svynarets, S., Leibert, T., Mrazova, L., Mikhaylov, R.: Social innovation approaches to support integration of Non-EU-migrants in rural central Europe: lessons learned. Conclusions Drawn. Hrvatski geografski glasnik **84**(2), 37–53 (2022)
9. Čapo Žmegač, J.: Dva lokaliteta, dvije države, dva doma: transmigracija hrvatskih ekonomskih migranata u Münchenu. Narodna umjetnost **40**(2), 117–130 (2003)
10. Čapo, J., Kelemen, P.: Zagreb očima međunarodnih migranata: značenja, potencijali i (re)skaliranja grada. Studia ethnologica Croatica **29**(1), 251–276 (2017)
11. Božić, S., Burić, I.: Migracijski potencijal Hrvatske – mikroanalitički aspekti. Migracijske i etničke teme **21**(1–2), 9–33 (2005)
12. Rajković Iveta, M., Babić, D.: Poljaci u Hrvatskoj: od pripadnika 'stare' nacionalne manjine do suvremenih migranata. Stud. Ethnol. Croat. **30**(1), 169–202 (2018)
13. Bagarić, Ž., Mandić, A.: Istina, mediji i žilet-žica: migranti u hrvatskom medijskom krajoliku. In medias res **8**(15), 2423–2443 (2019)
14. Poljak, M., Hadžić, J., Martinić, M.: Govor mržnje u hrvatskom medijskom prostoru. In medias res **9**(17), 2709–2744 (2020)
15. Peračković, K.: Sociološki pristup u istraživanju procesa povratnih migracija. Društvena istraživanja: časopis za opća društvena pitanja vol. 15 no. 3(83), pp. 475–498 (2006)
16. Kuti, S., Božić, S.: Analitičke dimenzije za istraživanje transnacionalnih aktivnosti: primjer kineskih migranata u Hrvatskoj. Revija za sociologiju **41**(3), 315–340 (2011)
17. Čačić-Kumpes, J., Gregurović, S., Kumpes, J.: Migracija, integracija i stavovi prema imigrantima u Hrvatskoj. Revija za sociologiju **42**(3), 305–336 (2012)
18. Mrakovčić, M., Gregurović, M.: Neprijatelj pred vratima? Ili kako studenti prava iz četiriju najvećih hrvatskih gradova doživljavaju azilante i migrante s Bliskog istoka. Sociologija i prostor **58**(3), 291–328 (2020)
19. Analiza sadržaja: Pisanje internetskih portala o temi migranata, tražitelja azila i azilanata u 2013. godini. Ured pučke pravobraniteljice, kolovoz (2014). http://ombudsman.hr/images/Analiza_izvjestavanja_UPP.pdf. Accessed 29 June 2023
20. Kanižaj, I.: Manjine – između javnosti i stvarnosti: nacionalne manjine u novinama 2001. – 2005. Sveučilišna knjižara, Zagreb (2006)

21. Ciboci, L., Kanižaj, I.: Nacionalne manjine u hrvatskim medijima 2001. – 2011. In: Romić, M. (ed.) Izolacija ili integracija – kako mediji pristupaju uključivanju manjina u javnu sferu?, p. 147–179. Udruga Babe, Zagreb (2011)

22. Car, V.: Javni medijski servisi – čuvari demokracije. In: Romić, M. (ed.) Izolacija ili integracija – kako mediji pristupaju uključivanju manjina u javnu sferu?, pp. 41–62. Udruga Babe, Zagreb (2011)

23. Župarić-Iljić, D.: Percepcija tražitelja azila u javnosti i medijski prikazi problematike azila u Hrvatskoj. In: Župarić-Iljić, D. (ed.) Prvih deset godina razvoja sustava azila u Hrvatskoj (s osvrtom na sustave azila u regiji), pp. 201–220. Institut za migracije i narodnosti (IMIN), Zagreb (2013)

24. Bezić, M., Petrović, I.: Diskursne strategije u medijskom prikazu migranata. Zbornik radova Filozofskog fakulteta u Splitu **12**, 81–98 (2019)

25. Podboj, M.: Narativna analiza kao metoda uvida u diskursnu konstrukciju identiteta. Suvremena lingvistika **90**, 239–264 (2020)

26. Panjić, S.: Analiza diskursa o migracijama u hrvatskim dnevnim novinama. Disertacija. Sveučilište Josipa Jurja Strosmayera u Osjeku, Filozofski fakultet, Osijek (2022)

27. Wierzbicka, A.: Semantics Primes and Universals. Oxford University Press, Oxford (1996)

28. Ducrot, O.: Le dire et le dit. Minuit, Paris (1980)

29. Ducrot, O.: Les Echelles argumentatives. Minuit, Paris (1980)

30. Ducrot, O., Anscombre, J-Cl.: L'argumentation dans la langue. Mardaga, Bruxelles, (1983)

31. Kocijan, K., Šojat, K.: Who is guilty and who is responsible in the Croatian parliament: a linguistic approach. In: Misuraca, M., Scepi, G., Spano, M. (eds.) Proceedings of the 16th International Conference on Statistical Analysis of Textual Data, pp. 503–510. Vadistat Press, Naples (2022)

32. HJP. https://hjp.znanje.hr/index.php?show=baza. Accessed 18 Aug 2023

33. DZS, htps://web.dzs.hr/Hrv/DBHomepages/Stanovnistvo/Migracije/metodologija.htm, last accessed 2023/08/18

Semantic Analysis of Migrants'
Self-entrepreneurship Ecosystem Narratives

Cecilia Olivieri[✉], Lorenzo Maggio Laquidara, and Agathe Semlali

X23 – Science in Society, Treviglio, Italy
{cecilia.olivieri,lorenzo.maggio,agathe.semlali}@x-23.org

Abstract. NooJ represents a powerful tool for discourse analysis, and promises great developments in the interpretation of articulate concepts across texts. In spite of the software's ability to integrate syntactic operations in text parsing, social scientists seldom use NooJ for large discourse analysis procedures, leaving NooJ-powered discourse analysis protocols largely underdeveloped. This study chiefly aims to establish an early discourse analysis canon for NooJ analysts to use in social science research, in particular, sociolinguistics. We identified migrant self-entrepreneurship as a subject of study, and investigated its conceptual development across seven separate interviews with aspiring migrant entrepreneurs. Our data collection primarily consisted of semi-structured interviews, which we conducted in anticipation of NooJ-powered co-occurrence analysis. This article offers insights into research best practices we recommend researchers to employ when conducting co-occurrence analysis, with special regard to congruence patterns, overlapping expressions, divergence patterns and low occurrences. In conclusion, this study comes as a demonstration that NooJ is a perfect fit for a form of scientific text interpretation that goes beyond well-established thematic analysis techniques in terms of representational insightfulness and analytical depth. Importantly, NooJ-powered discourse analysis makes it possible to aid qualitative methods with quantitative assessments, ushering promising developments in computational sociolinguistics. We see this publication as a possible first step for NooJ-powered analysis to new sociolinguistic pursuits and for its affiliated scientific community to study social phenomena with novel depth.

Keywords: Migrant Self-Entrepreneurship · Discourse Analysis · Lexical Grammars · Ecosystem Analysis · Self-Narratives

1 Introduction

The depiction of migrants in mainstream media often exhibits biases, portraying them as a vulnerable social group that burdens host countries via financial, material and labor costs. Such narratives, at best, highlight the need for socio-economic integration based on migrants' specific needs and challenging living conditions and are often referred to as "miserabilistic narratives" [1]; these narratives risk reinforcing the dichotomy and myth of "otherness" between locals and migrants, while also biasing public perceptions of migrants [2].

© The Author(s), under exclusive license to Springer Nature Switzerland AG 2024
A. Bartulović et al. (Eds.): NooJ 2023, CCIS 1816, pp. 176–187, 2024.
https://doi.org/10.1007/978-3-031-56646-2_15

Contrary to these narratives, migrant communities exhibit diverse characteristics in terms of demographic composition (i.e., generation, socioeconomic status, place of origin, economic background, gender, migration purpose and education) [3]. These factors intersect and form complex ecosystems. Migrants worldwide face economic integration challenges, especially in developed countries; entrepreneurship has become one of the main opportunities to try to overcome them, and now represents an important feature for international migration to foster economic and social mobility among migrants [4]. Migrant entrepreneurs are self-employed individuals, they are either immigrants in the respective countries or descendants of immigrants [5]. European scholars and practitioners alike call to reinvent the public approach to migration, conflicted between an economistic agenda favoring the clustering of migrants in low-skilled jobs and a solidarity and human-rights-based approach by identifying human capital as a "structural resource for the economic and social development of European societies" [6]. Consequently, gathering primary evidence directly from migrant communities becomes an invaluable tool for understanding the European migrant self-entrepreneurship ecosystem, not only for migrants themselves but also for locals who share a common interest in defining their identities and the spaces they inhabit [7].

Moreover, migrants occupy a unique and advantageous position that enables them to unlock insights into their personal migration experiences [6], their communities and their engagement with the entrepreneurial ecosystem, offering the most authentic perspective possible. To do so, we developed an innovative methodology to better delve into the narratives of the migrants. The objective of the research is, hence, to develop a discourse analysis model by means of NooJ in support of the formal description and analysis of the narrative produced by migrants' discourse. Our inquiry protocol intends to study a corpus of interviews collected on the field through "analysis by concepts" [8] and to delve into the methodology so developed. The socio-linguistic analysis considers the authentic meaning of interviews and is more accurate than statistics-based instruments. This methodology strives to make sense of migrants' specific realities, anchoring this perspective in a social constructivism framework [9, 10]. If we consider language as producing meaning, it is, therefore, shaping and shaped by social realities [9]. One's discourse partially reveals one's own understanding of the world in that "words form a web of meaning" [10]. Exploring the complexities of migrant entrepreneurship through this approach enables a deeper understanding of migrant entrepreneurs' realities, perspectives and ecosystem, and empowering their community to act and invest in positive change [9].

2 Methodology

Our primary data collection strategy consisted of semi-structured interviews. During our research program, we conducted interviews from a diverse sample frame [11], which included prospective migrant entrepreneurs, third-sector organization representatives, public officials, policymakers and migration scholars. Although our data collection achieved a sample size of n = 35 interviews, we purposely selected seven interviews for inquiry within this study. This study's sample comprises seven migrant entrepreneurs, prospective or established. Our sample included two women and five male members between the ages of 24 and 50 years old. The sample also controls for countries of origin (i.e., Syria, Senegal, Guinea Bissau, Liberia, Pakistan) and destination (i.e., Italy, France, Sudan, the Netherlands), generation (i.e., first- as opposed to second-generation migrants), education level and socio-economic status (SES). We selected semi-structured interviews as our primary data-gathering strategy in the wake of their ability to stimulate respondents to engage in questions spontaneously [12]. Migrant perspectives have historically risked underrepresentation in academic and policy literature alike [13]. Ethnography-inspired research methods have given increasing space to semi-structured interviews as a way to give migrants access to their own self-narration [2, 14]. We, in turn, propose a form of discourse analysis that deepens text investigation beyond narrative themes.

NooJ is a natural language processor structurally capable of parsing through different levels of linguistic phenomena [15]. We manually transcribed our interviews' audio/video recordings, obtaining seven distinct written texts. Some interviews were conducted in English and some in Italian. We parsed the texts through NooJ's linguistic analysis and manually overviewed the resulting tokens to check for orthographic mistakes and redundancies. Our analysis consisted of two key steps. First, we parsed the texts, selected significant tokens, and clustered them into concepts. Conceptualization was aided by an open coding phase, followed by literature validation and a thorough group discussion about which ideas were reported in each interview. The open coding phase was independent for each interview, which featured its unique set of concepts, albeit some recurring themes were found across most texts. Open coding enables new ideas and concepts to emerge by categorizing data without preconceived codes [16]. We represented each concept as a lexical grammar composed of all the tokens we reputed relevant to a given topic. Figure 1 portrays one of our lexical grammars. Lexical grammar only features regular expressions. Due to low proficiency in Italian and English and the influence of their mother tongues, our research subjects often contradicted syntactic and orthographic rules. They also attributed unique meanings to expressions they are not entirely familiar with, sometimes combining words that often do not occur together. Syntactic indications would not be able to capture those orthographic errors, even if coupled with semantic tags. Manually correcting orthographic mistakes would overcome this limitation but also result in a conceptual loss. Once grammars were structured and tested for precision, we compared the occurrence of different concepts via NooJ-mediated co-occurrence analysis. We only conducted co-occurrence analysis at the single-text level, neglecting corpus analysis in the name of sample representativeness and result generalization.

The second stage consisted of studying the co-occurrence of grammars in pairs. Co-occurrence patterns suggest interrelation or at least proximity between two grammars within a specific part of the text. We used the "Locate Pattern" function to create normal distributions of each grammar within the text. NooJ's occurrence diagrams are representations of the frequency with which the regular expressions that compose a given grammar appear in a text. Because two or more grammars might contain drastically different numbers of regular expressions in absolute terms, their distribution is normalized. That is, frequency values are expressed in relation to standardized mean ($= 0$) and standard deviation ($= 1$) parameters. A distribution with such parameters is called a normal distribution. Normalization allows researchers to compare frequency distributions across different grammars, regardless of the amount of expressions they contain. NooJ co-occurrence diagrams discontinuously plot grammar frequency across segments (parts) of the text. Because each part has equal length (where length is defined as the number of words composing a string of text), standardizing a grammar's frequency of occurrence across different parts is very easy. The frequency of occurrence is expressed in terms of a standard score. Standard scores (Z) are the representation of an absolute value across a normal distribution. Normalization transforms absolute values into standard scores via the following equation: $Z = (x - \mu)/\sigma$.

Where x represents the score in absolute terms, the absolute distribution's mean and the real standard deviation, standard scores are the prime instrument for cross-grammar comparison. Starting from the standard score visualization feature in this research, we rely on the study of co-occurrence between concepts as the main source of text comprehension. Based on semantic network analysis theory [1], we assume that, within the standard score representation of two grammars, co-occurring peaks might signify an interrelation of the meaning of the two represented concepts. Our objective is thus to identify this proximity from the graph (peaks concordance), to search within the text for the precise point of co-occurrence/proximity between the tokens belonging to the two grammars (color-matching sequences in text feature) and to verify a potential logical relationship between the two concepts. With a level of statistical sensibility such as = 0.95 (the probability for an event to be statistically significant is P = 0.95), grammar needs to occur with a standard score such as Z-2 Z2. This means that the further a standard score is from zero, the more statically significant is an occurrence value.

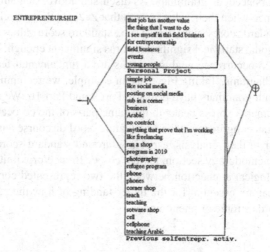

Fig. 1. Lexical grammar: entrepreneurship concept (Interviewee N.4).

We analyzed co-occurrences between "Personal project" grammars (i.e., containing all the regular expressions related to the field of a migrant business idea) and all the other concepts emerging from the text. This process was intended to unveil and reinforce potential hypotheses on how to read, through a certain degree of standardization, interactions between concepts in the text. We conducted our first round of analysis on three interviews, representing our pilot analysis test. We formulated three hypotheses concerning how to interpret analytical results, effectively mapping statistical outputs onto phenomena that we could study using qualitative interpretations of the texts. Then, we tested our key hypotheses on a cohort of four additional interview texts, with the aim of testing our pilot interpretations onto a larger corpus.

3   Analysis

3.1   Hypothesis 1: Diagram Congruency and Overlapping Words

NooJ's co-occurrence analysis chiefly relies on the co-occurrence diagram. As explained above, NooJ fragments a text into parts of equal length. The co-occurrence analysis function plots each grammar's occurrence in all parts of the text across two axes. The *x-axis* enlists all the text's parts, while the *y-axis* measures each occurrence's standard score in relation to its own grammar. Because there is only one standard score per part, occurrence curves are discontinuous, and effectively represent the joining of unique points rather than continuous functions.

Figure 2 portrays the co-occurrence diagram for Interviewee N.3's "Personal project" and "External factors needed" grammars. As discussed above, standard scores indicate statistical significance when their value is such that $Z-2$ $Z2$. We can relax this principle by considering standard scores such that $Z2$ (i.e., standard score values that approach 2) is embedded with some statistical significance or is significant enough. That means that, when performing co-occurrence analysis, peaks are a fundamental feature to observe on co-occurrence diagrams. Taking Fig. 2 as an example, we recommend focusing on the reasons why both grammars have peaks in Part 9 and Part 16. We term a condition in which two grammars express peaks in the same parts of the co-occurrence diagram congruency. Diagram congruency is the first feature NooJ discourse analysis practitioners should look for in their analysis, especially around standard score peaks. Indeed, as reported in the methodology section, textual co-occurrence/proximity within the text might represent a logical connection between the two represented concepts [10]. This connection is, therefore, essential for the understanding of how the subject represents their position towards a topic or phenomenon.

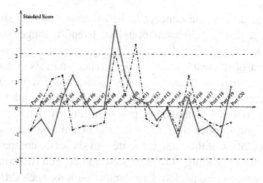

Fig. 2. Co-occurrence diagram: Interviewee N.2 "Personal project" grammar (dots) [Fq = 122] and "External factors needed" [Fq = 109] grammar (continuous line).

As we can observe from Excerpt 1, the two concepts are very close to one another within the text. Furthermore, the two concepts are actually meaningfully connected, expressing a relation of "dependency" from the first concept to the second one. Indeed, Interviewee N.2 talks about specific conditions whenever they mention their project, such as first finding a workplace that allows them to save some resources or getting a driver's license in order to open their own business and find a job respectively. This proximity produces statistically significant co-occurrence.

Excerpt 1. Part 9 and Part 16 from Interviewee N.2 text, represented in Fig. 2.

Part 9: Finding a workplace that allows him to save some resources in advance
La seconda cosa è trovare un posto di lavoro perché non puoi lavorare in un posto prendendo tanti soldi senza iniziare a lavorare, dove prendi qualche soldino. Se inizio a lavorare poi posso fare un mio obiettivo

Part 16: Getting a driver's license
Aspetto ancora. Non c'è tempo per andare fuori dall'Italia. [...]. Rimango qua. Ancora, se trovo la patente sono italiano e basta

---

It is, however, important to remember that grammar design can contribute to diagram congruences. Overlapping words describe regular expressions that are present in more than one grammar. When two or more grammars contain a shared pool of words, the extent of their co-occurrence increases significantly. Obviously, this produces a confusing effect on co-occurrence visualization, which should reflect the extent to which two concepts interact within a discourse rather than meaning similarities among them. On the other hand, two concepts featuring common words normally indicate that they are related. Overlapping words can be seen as a sign of mutual relevance, which represents valuable information for discourse analysis. Therefore, we do not recommend avoiding or removing overlapping words. However, we do advise future analysts to take note of the proportion of two grammars' total expression counts that overlap. Another observed strategy to overcome this graphical bias is disambiguation. By disambiguation, we mean the process of anchoring the single token to its precise in-text meaning by including adjacent words into unique strings [17] in line with Gross's lexicon-grammar framework [18]. This allows one concept to be associated with a single sequence of expressions within the text (e.g., grammars in Fig. 1 reports longer strings of words in addition to single tokens).

A second element of interest for the co-occurrence analysis concerns the value of the standard score. As mentioned above, the standard score represents the text-level distribution of a concept (represented through lexical grammars) calculated on the basis of the normalized distribution of that concept's occurrence within a portion of the text. However, normalization implies that, regardless of whether a grammar contains five tokens or 50, the calculation of the standard score will show two compatible graphs. This aspect can lead to a biased reading of the relationship between two concepts (observing the co-occurrence between two peaks). Grammars that have such different weights do not necessarily engender representative significant relationships between coincidental peaks. The statistical significance (standard score) is relevant but should always be considered in relation to the "weight" of the compared grammars in order not to enforce a structural mistake. Furthermore, we should add how occurrence is not proportional to meaning/substantial significance. Some words may appear a few times along the text yet be very meaningful. The standard score, then, needs to be considered as a simple graphical representation that allows us to detect where, within the text, a concept occurs more compared with other parts. Therefore, we recommend studying dynamics, which we define as the set of frequency variations among the different nodes of a graph rather than the absolute values.

There were cases where the co-occurrence between two concepts, identified by a standard score diagram congruence, turned out to be unreliable. This is the case in the comparison between "Mental Health" and "Education" in Interviewee N.7 interview. From the visual representation, the two graphs co-occur in the same part (part 13), as shown in Fig. 3; however, looking back at the text, the tokens from both grammars are rather distanced from each other (in this specific case, a reason could be the substantial difference in tokens between the two grammars). This condition confronted us with the need to continuously validate co-occurrence from the text (via the feature of coloring text portions) and not take it for granted.

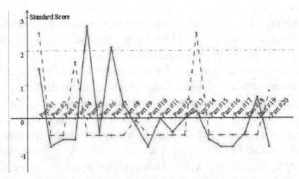

Fig. 3. Co-occurrence diagram: Interviewee N.7's "Education" grammar (continuous line) [Fq = 125] and "Mental health" grammar (dashes): [Fq = 23].

3.2 Hypothesis 2: Alternating Peaks

The pattern, denominated as alternating peaks, reveals a dialectic procedure with consecutive peaks between two graphs from two separate grammars that form a tight logical chain, and indicate an interconnection, correlation or relationship of some kind between two concepts. Alternating peaks usually follow each other but do not co-occur in the exact same part. The following insights from alternating peaks visualization were commonly found. However, consistent relationships are not necessarily given. Alternating peaks might indicate the existence of a logical relationship between two concepts (i.e., the most relevant and sought-after logic precursor of a signifier standing behind), revealing a causal relationship (e.g., cause, effect, opposition or similarity) between the two chosen grammars. If this is the case, such a type of alternating pattern can either generate new insights with regard to the text or can confirm a hypothesis: alternating structures can suggest that a concept serves as an introduction or a conclusion for another one, for instance. Indeed, Fig. 4 represents the said relation: alternating peaks from part 1 to 7, starting with the graph of the grammar "Incubation", encapsulating the graph of "Personal project" peaking in part 4. When discussing his personal project, Interviewee N.3 introduces at the beginning how the incubation program helps in developing an entrepreneurial mindset before discussing the training program's modalities again.

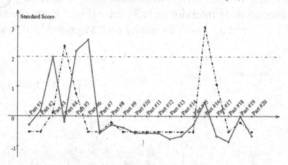

Fig. 4. Co-occurrence diagram: Interviewee N.3's "Personal project" grammar (dots) [Fq = 33] and "Incubation" grammar (continuous line) [Fq = 181].

Furthermore, alternating peaks can also mirror each other throughout the whole evolution of the graphs through parallel or complementary structures. This type of alternating peaks suggests that the two grammars work together dialectically throughout the whole text. However, the causal relationships linking the two grammars cannot be identified from the graphs solely; a syntactic analysis should be performed for this purpose. One needs to read back the text to identify if the interconnection is due to the overall meaning of the text or because of the interview dynamics. Moreover, the way NooJ partitions the text may misrepresent the frequency in the trend of the alternance of peaks. Indeed, to be identified as alternating, peaks need to be close in the graphs' representation [usually two parts]; however, in some large texts, two parts may be a very broad paragraph, so concepts might not be situated together.

Our conclusion is that the alternating peaks hypothesis is, therefore, productive and insightful only when a very close reading of the text is used to confirm any interconnections between concepts. Indeed, the resulting visualization stands as "a starting point or guide for further close readings" [10].

3.3 Hypothesis 3: Low Standard Score, High Consistency

Low statistical significance does not imply low subject significance. On the contrary, a concept can be very analytically relevant even if its statistical significance is consistently low across the text. Figure 5 provides a good case to illustrate this principle. Interviewee N.3's development on their personal project across the text is represented by the black line. Between Part 6 and Part 15 (i.e., the majority of the interview), "Personal project" has a low, statistically insignificant standard score (1Z0). This would suggest for their own personal project to be a concept of minor significance throughout the interview. However, this conclusion is strongly in contrast with the concept's standard score, which is consistent across the entire interview. Such consistency suggests that the concepts figure virtually all throughout the text, and are seldom absent from the discussion. Albeit this observation might appear insignificant from a statistical perspective, it is of particular relevance to qualitative inquiry. In fact, for a topic to be featured all across a long and multivariate interview, with different and large sections, it means that the topic is implied across disparate discourses. In Interviewee N.3's case (Fig. 5), it is found that their own personal project lies in correlation with his migration ("Migratory path") and life choices.

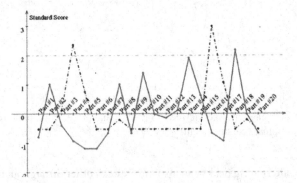

Fig. 5. Co-occurrence diagram: Interviewee N.3's "Personal project" grammar (dots) [Fq = 33] and "Migratory path" grammar (continuous line) [Fq = 110].

We recommend future NooJ analysts to consider standard score and consistency in tandem. That is, integrate considerations on statistical and subject significance. At a deeper level, that means using the statistical description of the observed data and, more specifically, their organization and analysis as a quantitative instrument for qualitative dominant crossover mixed analyses by contextualizing the qualitative findings through a thorough reading of the text.

4   Ethics and Standards in Methodology

We would like to set out some methodological notes about the methodological approach used in our analysis process.

a. Standards: whereas we relied on a repetitive protocol of actions in the conceptualization phase, our team voluntarily opted for an open coding process [16], and adopted
   a continuous dialogue along the way in determining each concept's codification for
   each interview rather than demanding adherence to tightly regulated standards, open
   coding can bring new concepts to come and leads to novel cues of analysis.
b. Extended co-authorship: an inherently diverse research team represents a further trust-
   worthiness tool [16]. Furthermore, we are adopting backchecking text techniques such
   as continuous coding [8] and backtalk with interviewees, which could be instrumental
   in reducing misinterpreted significance and purging unwanted biases in the analysis
   of discourses.

We believe such a model to be beneficial at least for two reasons: first, a mediation mechanism is established by the peer reviewers, i.e., the research subjects themselves; hence, a deeper verification authenticates (authentication coding) each interpretation done by the researchers of the concepts expressed by the subject. The authentication mechanism in coding is dual: from one side, it allows the researcher to have a complete understanding of each signifier included in the text; on the other hand, the subject alone possesses the power of representing a uniform contextualization of each signifier rooted under the hypotheses built by the researcher. Secondly, through the promotion of the subjects of the study as "co-authors" of the same research, we believe we can promote them to a closer stage in the ethical principle of the "benefit given to the human research subjects" that lies at the basis of every research process. It is important to note that the said voluntary choice for (1) substandardization and (2) co-authorship extended to a few representative human subjects of our studies are certainly not naive choices at all, but they belong to technical, de facto, or philosophical standards of science, particularly for analysts who try their hand at finding the meaning of qualitative results via quantitative synthesis. The use of meta-analysis [19], systematic reviews [20], multi-modal analyses and optimization [21] as well as scientific pluralism [20, 22] represent notable examples.

Because of the kind of subjects involved in our studies, which include migrants directly and practitioners of migrants' lives preponderantly, very strong regulations for the protection of human subjects in research were required and observed during all the steps of our investigation.

5   Recommendations

We acknowledge that the analytical tools we rely on, such as semantic network metrics [8] and standard score values, are highly sensitive to frequency (i.e., see Hypotheses 1 and 2), a dimension relevant but not central to our qualitative approach. Indeed, an expression frequency in the text does not necessarily drop obvious suggestions about its substantial significance. Hence, due to NooJ's statistical representations that could incur structural bias, we strongly recommend studying the graph dynamics rather than the absolute values.

We also wish to emphasize another aspect of qualitative analysis. Our analytical protocol produces visual representations that cannot be interpreted without a structural reference to the text. Co-occurrence diagrams, interview rescripts (the questions asked during the interview) and back text reading should be summoned in tandem for a coherent and precise understanding of the meaning extracted from the text (Hypothesis 2 develops in-depth on these considerations). Aside from consolidating this discourse analysis protocol, the investigation process would benefit from an interactive interface allowing the analyst to return to text portions from the diagrams. In the future, we will consider developing such an interactive module opening to inter-operations with other software.

6   Conclusions and Perspectives

After grasping the potential of NooJ functionalities, we envisaged improving our analytical protocol to overcome current limits and unlock insights for socio-linguistic applications. One of the main objectives of this work is to offer a set of cues for novel research pursuits to embrace more complex comparisons and richer visualizations. We anticipated the next steps, such as customizing text partition, considering potential statistical elaboration and side software environments. Furthermore, we advocate for running more than four grammar tests at a time. Such an improvement could enable a more global visualization and distant reading [8] of inter-concept relations across each interview.

The model presented hereby, once refined, will enable us to multidimensionally investigate the content of semi-structured interviews, to formally capture the structure and conceptual connections that characterize the discourse and to validate previously formulated hypotheses about the interpretation of the text while unveiling unintuitive information. Sharpening this methodology would make applications to further relevant social issues and create opportunities for new analytical techniques.

This work represents the first experimental attempt to apply a computational natural language analysis on a qualitatively collected corpus of interviews. We observed how the qualitative aspect was strongly sought and enhanced through our analysis model; on the other hand, we are interested in improving our formal and quantitative operations into mathematical structures to get qualitative dominant crossover mixed analysis. The strength of our methods lies precisely in the harmonious combination of the two approaches "in order to maintain a qualitative sensibility while also daring to zoom out and look at the entire dataset, by refining and validating qualitatively coded concepts through quantitative measures" [8].

References

1. Nikielska-Sekula, K., Desille, A.: Visual Methodology in Migration Studies: New Possibilities, Theoretical, Implications, and Ethical Questions. Springer, Cham (2021)
2. Ryan, L., Umut, E., D'Angelo, A. (eds.): Migrant Capital: Networks, Identities and Strategies. Migration, Diasporas and Citizenship. Palgrave Macmillan, Houndmills (2015)
3. International Organization for Migration: World Migration Report 2020. IOM (2019)
4. Zubair, M., Brzozowski, J.: Entrepreneurs from recent migrant communities and their business sustainability. Sociologia 12(2), 57–72 (2018)

5. Ram, M., Jones, T., Villares-Varela, M.: Migrant entrepreneurship: reflections on research and practice. Int. Small Bus. J. **35**(1), 3–18 (2017)
6. Zanfrini, L. (ed.): The Diversity Value. How to Reinvent the European Approach to Immigration. McGraw-Hill Education, Maidenhead (2015)
7. Buhr, F.: Migrants' mental maps: unpacking inhabitants' practical knowledges in Lisbon. In: Nikielska-Sekula, K., Desille, A. (eds.) Visual Methodology in Migration Studies. IMISCOE Research Series, pp. 51–65. Springer, Cham (2021). https://doi.org/10.1007/978-3-030-676 08-7_3
8. Lindgren, S.: Introducing connected concept analysis: a network approach to big text datasets. Text Talk **36**(3), 341–362 (2016)
9. Parkinson, C., Howorth, C.: The language of social entrepreneurs. Entrep. Reg. Dev. **20**(3), 285–309 (2008)
10. Moser, C., Groenewegen, P., Huysman, M.: Extending social network analysis with discourse analysis: combining relational with interpretive data. In: Özyer, T., Rokne, J., Wagner, G., Reuser, A. (eds.) The Influence of Technology on Social Network Analysis and Mining. Lecture Notes in Social Networks, vol. 6, pp. 547–561. Springer, Vienna (2013). https://doi.org/10.1007/978-3-7091-1346-2_24
11. Babbie, E., Edgerton, J.D.: Fundamentals of Social Research. Cengage, Canada (2023)
12. De Luca, D., Ambrosini, M.: Female immigrant entrepreneurs: more than a family strategy. Int. Migr. **57**(5), 201–215 (2019)
13. Quaranta, I.: The production and transformation of subjectivity: healthcare and migration in the Province of Bologna (Italy). In: Hadolt, B., Hardon, A. (eds.) Emerging Socialities in 21st Century Healthcare, pp. 89–102. University Press, Amsterdam (2017)
14. Facchini, G., Mayda, A., Puglisi, R.: Illegal immigration and media exposure: evidence on individual attitudes. IZA J. Dev. Migr. **7**(14), 1–36 (2017)
15. Silberztein, M.: Formalizing Natural Languages: The NooJ Approach. Wiley-ISTE, London (2016)
16. Bryman, A.: Social Research Methods. Oxford University Press, New York (2012)
17. Della Volpe, M., Esposito, F.: Discursive practices about third mission: a survey from Italian universities' official websites. Qual. High. Educ. **26**(2), 224–239 (2020)
18. Gross, M.: Grammaire transformationnelle du français: syntaxe du verbe. Cantilène, Paris (1969)
19. Gopalakrishnan, S., Ganeshkumar, P.: Systematic reviews and meta-analysis: understanding the best evidence in primary healthcare. J. Family Med. Primary Care **2**(1), 9 (2013)
20. Torgerson, C.: Systematic Reviews. Bloomsbury Publishing (2003)
21. Ledin, P., Machin, D.: Introduction to Multimodal Analysis. Bloomsbury Publishing (2020)
22. Cartwright, N.: The Dappled World: A Study of the Boundaries of Science. School of Economics and Political Science, London (2021)

Natural Language Processing Applications

NooJ Linguistic Resources for Paraphrase Generation of Italian Support Verb Construction

Nicola Cirillo(✉) iD

University of Salerno, Fisciano, SA, Italy
nicirillo@unisa.it

Abstract. Support verb constructions are word combinations composed of a predicative noun/adjective and a semantically bleached verb (e.g., *schiacciare un pisolino* 'to take a nap', *diventare ricco* 'to get rich'). Many support verb constructions can be substituted with a full verb (e.g., *pisolare* 'to nap', *arricchirsi* 'to get rich'). It is argued that this substitution increases readability and facilitates machine translation. However, the substitution of the support verb construction alone does not allow paraphrasing sentences. To ensure grammaticality and preserve (as far as possible) the meaning of the source sentence, it is also necessary to restructure the sentence from both the syntactical and lexical points of view. In this paper, we propose a formal strategy to paraphrase support verb construction with full verbs. It is based on the notion of lexical function. Moreover, we developed a set of Italian linguistic resources for the NooJ software, namely a NooJ dictionary and a NooJ transformational grammar. They perform automatic paraphrase generation of Italian support-verb sentences.

Keywords: Support Verb Construction · Paraphrase Generation · NooJ

1 Introduction

Support verb constructions – SVC [1], also called light verb constructions [2], are complex predicates composed of a support verb and a predicative noun or adjective (e.g., *fare un pisolino* 'to have a nap', *commettere un errore* 'to make a mistake', *tenere un discorso* 'to give a speech'). From the syntactic point of view, the support verb is the head of the expression, and the predicative noun is either its subject, direct object or prepositional complement. Conversely, predicative adjectives are introduced by a copular verb (e.g., *essere chiaro* 'to be clear', *diventare rosso* 'to turn red', *diventare ricco* 'to get rich'). On the contrary, from the semantic perspective, it is the noun/adjective that plays the predicative role, and defines the argument structure of the whole expression, while the verb's function is to convey grammatical information that nouns and adjectives cannot provide by themselves (like tense, person and number); thus it 'supports' the predicative element.

Furthermore, support verbs are categorized into two macro classes: basic support verbs and extensions of support verbs [1]. Basic support verbs comprise high-frequency verbs that do not provide any additional meaning (e.g., *avere* 'to have', *fare* 'to make' and

A. Bartulović et al. (Eds.): NooJ 2023, CCIS 1816, pp. 191–201, 2024.
https://doi.org/10.1007/978-3-031-56646-2_16

dare 'to give'). Conversely, extensions of support verbs are not completely meaningless since they provide aspectual, causative or modal information (e.g., *iniziare una dormita* 'to start a nap', *ripetere un errore* 'to repeat a mistake', *concludere un discorso* 'to end a speech'). Nevertheless, they are still considered support verbs because they do not change the "core meaning" of sentences [3].

One peculiar feature of SVCs is that they can often be substituted with a verb that has the same lexical morpheme as the predicative noun/adjective. For example, in the sentence, *ho fatto una camminata nel parco* 'I took a walk in the park', the SVC *fare una camminata* 'to take a walk' can be substituted with the full verb *camminare* 'to walk'. The co-existence of SVCs and their full-verb counterparts seems to contradict the assumption that languages rarely maintain two competing forms unless they serve distinct purposes [4]. Therefore, several studies investigate which factors differentiate one form from the other [5, 6]. Moreover, the systematic preference for SVCs over full verbs is shown to hinder readability; thus, simplification operations often include the substitution of SVCs with full verbs [7]. SVC paraphrase generation is also useful in the context of machine translation, where SVCs are more difficult to translate than full verbs [8].

In this paper, we propose a paraphrase generation strategy that produces full-verb sentences from support-verb ones. It is based on the notion of Lexical Function – LF [9]. Moreover, as a proof-of-concept, we developed a set of linguistic resources with the NooJ software [10], namely a dictionary and a transformational grammar capable of automatically generating the full-verb paraphrase of simple support-verb sentences.

The remainder of this paper is structured as follows. In Sect. 2, we lay out previous research on SVC paraphrase generation. Section 3 introduces the notion of lexical function, and describes the paraphrase generation strategy we propose. Section 4 illustrates the linguistic resources developed with the NooJ [10] software. They automatically produce the full verb paraphrase of Italian SVC sentences. Finally, in Sect. 5, we outline conclusion, and suggest future research paths.

2 Related Work

The problem of paraphrasing SVCs can be tackled from different perspectives. The simplest approach involves linking SVCs to their full verb counterpart without restructuring the sentence. For instance, Chatzitheodorou [8] developed a NooJ dictionary and a NooJ grammar to substitute Italian SVCs with the corresponding full verbs. His dictionary links predicative nouns and morphologically related full verbs. Similarly, Barancíková and Kettnerová [11] found at least one corresponding verb for 1,421 Czech SVCs by employing word2vec [12]. Barreiro et al. [13] developed a set of linguistic resources for paraphrasing Portuguese SVCs. They also include the nominalization operation that substitutes predicative nouns with morphologically related verbs.

More in-depth studies involve a semantic representation of sentences. They assume that if a support-verb sentence has the same semantic representation as a full-verb one, the former is a paraphrase of the latter. For instance, Fujita et al. [14] propose to paraphrase Japanese SVCs according to the theoretical framework of Lexical Conceptual Structure – LCS [15]. They map SVCs onto the corresponding LCS to match it with the LCSs of full verbs. Finally, they generate surface sentences. Moreover, NLP[YTALY] [16] represents the semantics of Italian sentences through Cognate Semantic Roles [17, 18]. Among other features, it also accounts for SVCs, and produces the same semantic representations, whether the predicate of a sentence is an SVC or the corresponding full verb. However, it does not include a strategy to reconstruct sentences from the semantic representations.

3 Formal Rules for Paraphrase Generation

Our proposal consists of a series of formal rules to transform support-verb sentences into full-verb ones by preserving (as far as possible) the original meaning. For example, from the support-verb sentence *Giovanni da un bacio alla sorella* 'Giovanni gives his sister a kiss', the rules produce the full verb sentence *Giovanni bacia la sorella* 'Giovanni kisses his sister'.

3.1 Lexical Functions

Our starting point is the notion of Lexical Function (LF). LFs are rules meant to describe the relationships between lexical units [9]. For example, the *conversive* LF (Conv), when applied to a lexical unit, produces another unit that has the same meaning, but its arguments are permuted. For instance, *Conv(to give) = to receive*. According to Mel'čuk [19], a support verb corresponds to an LF that is applied to a predicative noun. Three main categories of LFs are strongly related to SVCs: syntactic, aspectual and causative LFs.

Syntactic LFs map the argument structure of the support verb onto the argument structure of the predicative noun, as illustrated in Table 1. For each LF, the table shows the position of the predicative noun and its arguments relative to the syntactic structure of the support verb (the Lexicon-Grammar notation is used).[1]

Table 1. Syntactic lexical functions.

Lexical function	1st argument of V-n	2nd argument of V-n	Predicative noun (V-n)
$Oper_1$	N_0	N_2	N_1
$Oper_2$	N_2	N_0	N_1
$Func_1$	N_1	N_2	N_0
$Func_2$	N_2	N_1	N_0
$Labor_{12}$	N_0	N_1	N_2
$Labor_{21}$	N_1	N_0	N_2
$Func_0$	N_2	N_2	N_0
$Oper_0$	N_2	N_2	N_1

---

[1] In the Lexicon-Grammar notation N_0 is the subject of the verb, N_1 is its first complement (either direct or introduced by a preposition) and N_2 is its second complement.

For example, in the sentence *Mario fornisce assistenza a Pietro* 'Mario gives assistance to Pietro', the support verb *fornire* 'to give' corresponds to the LF $Oper_1$. Therefore, the predicative noun is the direct object of the support verb, the first argument of the predicative noun is the subject of the support verb (i.e., Mario is who/what assists), and the second argument of the predicative noun is its prepositional complement (i.e., Pietro is who/what is assisted).

Furthermore, other LFs account for aspectual and causative extensions of support verbs. Aspectual extensions of support verbs underline a specific phase of the event. Namely, the *Incep* LF focuses on the beginning of the event, the *Fin* LF focuses on its end, and the *Cont* LF focuses on its duration. Causative variants of support verbs add another argument to the structure of the predicate. This argument is the cause of the event. Namely, *Caus* means 'to cause X', *Liqu* means 'to cause non-X', and *Perm* means 'to not cause non-X'.

Syntactic, aspectual and causative LFs, although being the most common, are not the only LFs that are related to support verbs. Some SVCs also convey non-standard meanings (e.g., *coprire di insulti* 'to cover with insults' = *insultare pesantemente* 'to heavily insult'). Finally, it is worth noting that LFs can be used in combination (e.g., $CauseContOper_1$).

3.2 Paraphrase Generation Strategy

The proposed paraphrase generation strategy originates from the LF framework [19] illustrated above. However, we made some modifications to better fit our goals.

a. We consider full verbs (and not predicative nouns/adjectives) to be the arguments of LFs so that $Oper_1(to\ assist) = to\ give\ assistance$.

b. We expand the set of aspectual LFs with the aspects proposed in [20]. Namely, *Reg* [regaining] means that a finished event starts again, and *Rep* [repetition] means that an event is repeated over time. Moreover, we also propose to differentiate LFs that focus on the end of an event. We use *Fin* only when a process ends because its goal has been reached, while we use *Interr* [interrupt] when the process is interrupted without reaching its goal, e.g., $FinOper_1(to\ build) = to\ finish\ the\ building$; $InterrOper_1(to\ build) = to\ stop\ the\ building$.

c. We add another causative LF: *Antic* [anticausative], where the cause is dropped from the argument structure of the lexical unit, like what happens in the causative alternation phenomenon [21]. *Antic* is symmetrical to *Caus*. For instance, $Caus(to\ be\ clear) = to\ clarify$; $AnticOper_2(to\ clarify) = to\ be\ clear$.

Syntactic Lexical Functions. Syntactic LFs determine the argument structure of the full-verb sentence. Therefore, we can use this information to either determine the complement's order or the voice of the full verb. We adopted the latter approach because it keeps the two sentences as similar as possible. For instance, $Oper_1$ and $Labor_{12}$ correspond to the active voice (e.g., *il bambino ha dato la colpa al cane* 'the kid put the blame on the dog' → *il bambino ha incolpato il cane* 'the kid blamed the dog') while $Oper_2$ and $Labor_{21}$ correspond to the passive voice (*il criminale finì in carcere* 'the criminal ended up in prison' → *il criminale fu incarcerato* 'the criminal was imprisoned'). Other syntactic LFs were not addressed due to their scarce representation in our dataset (see Subsect. 4.1).

Aspectual and Causative Lexical Functions. To preserve the aspectual meaning of some support-verb sentences, we add an aspectual verb to the target sentence (see Table 2). Similarly, causative LFs are paraphrased with the addition of causative verbs, except for *Antic*, which does not bring any modification.

Table 2. Aspectual and causative verbs associated with lexical functions.

Lexical Function	Verb added	Example
Incep	*Iniziare* 'to begin'	*trovare alloggio* 'to find lodging' → *iniziare ad alloggiare* 'to begin lodging'
Cont	*continuare* 'to continue'	*rimanere in vita* 'to stay alive' → *continuare a vivere* 'to continue living'
Fin	*Terminare* 'to finish'	*ultimare la costruzione* 'to complete the building' → *terminare di costruire* 'to finish building'
Interr	*Smettere* 'to quit'	*perdere la speranza* 'to lose hope' → *smettere di sperare* 'to quit hoping'
Reg	*riprendere* 'to resume'	*ritrovare la speranza* 'to regain hope' → *riprendere a sperare* 'to resume hoping'
Caus	*Fare* 'to make'	*dare il comando* 'to give command' → *fare comandare* 'to make command'
Perm	*permettere* 'to allow'	*dare accesso* 'to provide access' → *permettere di accedere* 'to allow accessing'
Liqu	*fare smettere* 'to make quit'	*fermare l'aggressione* 'to stop the assault' → *far smettere di aggredire* 'to make quit assaulting'

Other Lexical Functions. SVCs can also convey non-standard LFs [18]. In the examined dataset (see Subsect. 4.1), we found four of them: *Anti* (7 instances), *Able* (3 instances) and *Magn* (2 instances). Moreover, 2 SVCs can be paraphrased by adding the verb *provare* 'to try' to the full verb sentence. They were tagged as *Try*. These non-standard LFs can be paraphrased as follows:

- *Anti* by adding the negative adverb *non* 'not' (e.g., *Mario è in disaccordo con Pino.* 'Mario is in discordance with Pino.' → *Mario **non** concorda con Pino.* 'Mario does not agree with Pino.');
- *Able* by adding the modal verb *potere* 'can' (e.g., *Il tempo è variabile.* 'The weather is changeable.' → *Il tempo può variare.* 'The weather can change.');
- *Magn* by adding the adverb *molto* 'a lot' (e.g., *L'operaio si ammazza di lavoro.* 'The laborer buries himself in work.' → *L'operaio lavora molto.* 'The laborer works a lot.');

- *Try* by adding the verb *provare* 'to try' (e.g., *Il ladro tenta la fuga.* 'The thief tries an escape.' → *Il ladro prova a fuggire.* 'The thief tries to escape.').

Once the relationship between the SVC and the simple verb is established, we produce the full verb sentence in three steps. (1) First, we substitute the SVC with the full verb and add aspectual and/or causative verbs if necessary. (2) Then, we choose the correct verb voice, and inflect the full verb (the tense is taken from the support verb of the source sentence). (3) Finally, we remove or substitute the prepositions based on the syntactic structure of the full verb.

For example, if we know that *IncepOper$_1$*(*comandare* 'to lead') = *assumere il comando* 'to take the lead', the full-verb paraphrase of the sentence (1) is obtained as follows:

Il generale **assumerà il comando** delle truppe.   (1)

'The general will take the lead of the troops.'

*Il generale <iniziare a> <comandare> delle truppe.   (2)

'*The general <to start> <to lead> of the troops.'

*Il generale inizierà a comandare delle truppe.   (3)

'*The general will start leading of the troops.'

Il generale inizierà a comandare di le truppe.   (4)

'The general will start leading of the troops.'

4   NooJ Application

To test the proposed paraphrase generation strategy, we formalized the rules described above with the NooJ software [9]. Namely, we developed a NooJ dictionary and a NooJ transformational grammar. The dictionary describes 131 support verbs, 251 predicative nouns and 38 predicative adjectives, while the grammar formalizes the paraphrase generation rules.

4.1   Data

The approach illustrated in this paper is data-driven. To collect the data, we employed an algorithm designed for SVC extraction. A detailed description of the algorithm is beyond the scope of this paper; however, its functioning can be summarized as follows:

a. It extracts all the sequences of words matching one of two part-of-speech patterns.
   VERB + ?PREP + ?DET + NOUN,
   VERB + ADJ

b. It links all the extracted nouns and adjectives with morphologically related verbs via morphological word embeddings (e.g., the noun *accordo* 'agreement' is linked to the verbs *concordare* 'to agree', *discordare* 'to disagree' and *accordare* 'to grant').

c. It computes the distributional similarity between the extracted word sequences and the corresponding verbs. If a word sequence and the linked verb appear in similar contexts, the sequence is likely to be an SVC.

We ran the algorithm on the Italian corpus *Paisà* [22], then selected the best-ranked 1,000 candidates, and manually filtered them. The final dataset contains 488 SVCs. Each SVC is annotated with the corresponding LFs (see Sect. 3). The result of the annotation is shown in Table 3.

Table 3. Results of the annotation process.

Syntactic LFs	SVCs	Aspectual LFs	SVCs	Causative LFs	SVCs
$Oper_1$	**289**	Incep	**24**	Caus	4
$Oper_2$	89	Cont	10	Liq	0
$Func_1$	1	Fin	2	Perm	2
$Func_2$	0	Interr	3	Antic	**48**
$Labor_{12}$	99	Reg	2	*None*	434
$Labor_{21}$	5	Rep	0		
$Func_0$	0	*None*	447		
$Oper_0$	0				
Other	5				

The most common syntactic LF is $Oper_1$, followed by $Labor_{12}$ and $Oper_2$. Moreover, 5 SVCs correspond to $Labor_{21}$ and only one to $Func_1$. We believe that the distribution of syntactic LFs is influenced by the part-of-speech patterns employed in the extraction algorithm, where the predicative noun follows the support verb (i.e., it is in position N_1).

Less than 10% of the examined SVCs convey an aspectual meaning, *Incep* being the most common. Another interesting figure is the relatively high number of SVCs with the *Antic* LF (10% of the SVCs). In addition, it is always associated with the syntactic LF $Oper_2$. These SVCs often correspond to the result of the process expressed by the full verb (e.g., *il professore chiarisce la lezione* 'the professor clarifies the lecture' → *la lezione è chiara* 'the lecture is clear'). In other instances, the SVC corresponds to the anticausative construction [21] of the full verb (e.g., *il vaso va in frantumi* 'the vase turns into shards' has the same meaning of *il vaso si frantuma* 'the vase *shatters*'). We believe that, at this early stage, it is reasonable enough to paraphrase both cases with the passive voice of the full verb (i.e., *la lezione è chiara* 'the lecture is clear' → la *lezione è chiarita* 'the lecture is clarified'. *Il vaso va in frantumi* 'the vase turns into shards' → il *vaso è frantumato* 'the vase is shattered'). However, further investigation is needed.

4.2 Dictionary

The Nooj dictionary "SvcParaphrase.nod" contains 251 predicative nouns, 38 predicative adjectives and 131 support verbs. Each noun and adjective can have more than one entry in the dictionary based on the support verbs it is associated with. For example, the noun *assedio* 'siege' has at least six entries (see Fig. 1):

a. *Oper$_1$(assediare)* = porre l'assedio 'to lay siege'
b. *IncepOper$_1$(assediare)* = *iniziare l'assedio* 'to begin the siege'
c. *InterrOper$_1$(assediare)* = *rompere l'assedio* 'to break the siege'
d. *Oper$_2$(assediare)* = *subire l'assedio* 'to endure the siege'
e. *AnticOper$_2$(assediare)* = *essere sotto assedio* 'to be under siege'
f. *Labor$_{12}$(assediare)* = *cingere d'assedio* 'to besiege'/*porre sotto assedio* 'to put under siege'.

In the dictionary, predicative nouns and adjectives are treated as inflected forms of the morphologically related verb, enabling the transformational grammar to perform inflection.

```
assedio,assediare,V+FLX=V11+Vn+2arg+tr+Noasp+Nocause+Oper1+vsup="porre"
assedio,assediare,V+FLX=V11+Vn+2arg+tr+Noasp+Nocause+Oper2+vsup="subire"
assedio,assediare,V+FLX=V11+Vn+2arg+tr+Noasp+Nocause+Labor12+vsup="cingere di"+vsup="porre sotto"
assedio,assediare,V+FLX=V11+Vn+2arg+tr+Noasp+Antic+Oper2+vsup="essere sotto"
assedio,assediare,V+FLX=V11+Vn+2arg+tr+Noasp+Incep+Nocause+Oper1+vsup="iniziare"
assedio,assediare,V+FLX=V11+Vn+2arg+tr+Interr+Nocause+vsup="rompere"

chiaro,chiarire,V+FLX=V201+Va+2arg+tr+Noasp+Antic+Oper2+vsup="risultare"+vsup="essere"
chiaro,chiarire,V+FLX=V201+Va+2arg+tr+Incep+Antic+Oper2+vsup="diventare"
chiaro,chiarire,V+FLX=V201+Va+2arg+tr+Noasp+Nocause+Labor12+vsup="rendere"
```

Fig. 1. Excerpt from the "SvcParaphrase.nod" dictionary.

4.3 Grammar

The NooJ transformational grammar "SvcParaphrase.nog" encodes the paraphrase generation rules. It is composed of two main subgraphs, the "Vsup" and the "Vsynt" subgraphs. The "Vsup" subgraph is illustrated in Fig. 2. It recognizes a simple SVC sentence with one, two or three arguments whether the SVC is continuous (e.g., *Il piano prende in considerazione gli ostacoli.* 'The plan takes into account the obstacles.') or discontinuous (e.g., *Il piano prende gli ostacoli in considerazione.* 'The plan takes the obstacles into account.').

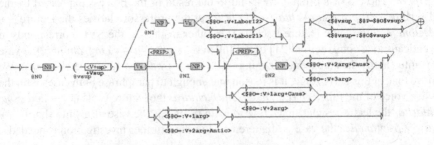

Fig. 2. "Vsup" subgraph.

Conversely, the "Vsynt" subgraph (Fig. 3) produces the full-verb sentence. It decides whether to use the active or passive verb voice, and substitutes or removes the prepositions introducing the second and third argument of the full verb.

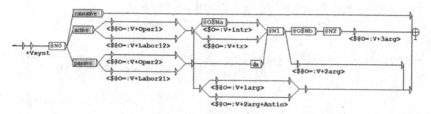

Fig. 3. "Vsynt" subgraph.

At its core, there are the "Active" (Fig. 4) and the "Passive" (Fig. 5) subgraphs. They assemble the predicate by adding aspectual verbs, and inflects it.

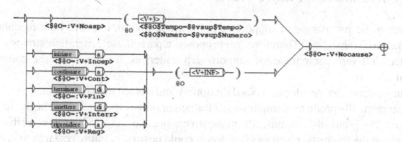

Fig. 4. "Active" subgraph.

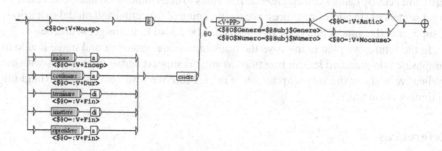

Fig. 5. "Passive" subgraph.

Causative sentences need their subgraph (Fig. 6) because their syntactic structure is more complex. For instance, transitive verbs are directly followed by their object, and have their subject introduced by the preposition *da* 'from'. For example, in the sentence *il re fa comandare le truppe dal capitano* 'the king makes the captain lead the troops', the noun *truppe* 'troops' is the object of the verb *comandare* 'to lead', and immediately follows it, whereas its subject, the noun *captain*, is introduced by the preposition *da* 'from'. Conversely, intransitive verbs are followed by their subject. For example, in the sentence *il cancello fa accedere il contadino ai campi* 'the gate makes the farmer access the fields', the noun *contadino* 'farmer' is the subject of the verb *accedere* 'to access' while the noun *campi* 'fields' is its prepositional complement.

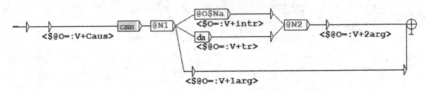

Fig. 6. "Causative" subgraph.

5   Conclusion and Future Work

The automatic paraphrase of support verb constructions can improve both readability and machine translation. Therefore, we proposed a paraphrase generation strategy that produces full-verb paraphrases of support-verb sentences. It is based on the notion of lexical function.

Furthermore, we developed a NooJ dictionary and a NooJ transformational grammar that automatically produces paraphrases of Italian support-verb sentences. The dictionary contains 251 predicative nouns, 38 predicative adjectives and 131 support verbs. We believe that the linguistic resources developed could be used in future research to deepen the knowledge about Italian support verb constructions.

The paper also shows that it is possible to obtain full-verb paraphrases of support-verb sentences by using syntactic lexical functions to determine the syntactic structure of target sentences. In addition, to preserve the meaning of aspectual and modal extensions of support verbs, modal and causative verbs can be added to the target sentence.

In the future, we plan to improve the transformational grammar and make it able to paraphrase non-standard lexical functions as well as support verb constructions with the predicative noun in the subject position (*Func*). Moreover, we also plan to extend the dictionary coverage.

References

1. Gross, M.: Les bases empiriques de la notion de prédicat sémantique. Langages **63**, 7–52 (1981)
2. Jespersen, O.: A Modern English Grammar on Historical Principles, Part VI, Morphology. Allen and Unwin Ltd, London (1965)
3. Gross, M.: Sur la notion harrissienne de transformation et son application au français. Langages **99**, 39–56 (1990)
4. Grice, H.P.: Logic and conversation. In: Cole, P., Morgan, J.L. (eds.) Syntax and Semantics 3: Speech Acts, pp. 41–58. Academic Press, New York (1975)

5. Wierzbicka, A.: Why can you have a drink when you can't *have an eat? Language **58**(4), 753–799 (1982)
6. Leontýna, B.: Le costruzioni italiane a verbo supporto. Un'analisi condotta sul corpus parallelo ceco-italiano. Acta Universitatis Carolinae Philologica **2013**(2), 55–70 (2013)
7. Cortelazzo, M.: Il linguaggio amministrativo. Principi e pratiche di modernizzazione. Carocci editore, Roma (2021)
8. Chatzitheodorou, K.: Paraphrasing of Italian support verb constructions based on lexical and grammatical resources. In: Baptista, J., et al. (eds.) Proceedings of Workshop on Lexical and Grammatical Resources for Language Processing, pp. 1–7. ACL and Dublin City University, Dublin (2014)
9. Mel'čuk, I.: Lexical functions: a tool for the description of lexical relations in the lexicon. In: Wanner, L. (ed.) Lexical Functions in Lexicography and Natural Language Processing, pp. 37–102. Benjamins, Amsterdam & Philadelphia (1996)
10. Silberztein, M.: NooJ Manual (2003). www.nooj-association.org
11. Barancíková, P., Kettnerová, V.: Paraphrases of verbal multiword expressions: the case of Czech light verbs and idioms. In: Markantonatou, S., Ramisch, C., Savary, A., Vincze, V. (eds.) Multiword Expressions at Length and in Depth: Extended Papers from the MWE 2017 Workshop, pp. 36–57. Language Science Press, Valencia (2018)
12. Mikolov, T., Chen, K., Corrado, G., Dean, J.: Efficient estimation of word representations in vector space. In: International Conference on Learning Representations (2013). https://arxiv.org/pdf/1301.3781.pdf
13. Barreiro, A., Mota, C., Baptista, J., Chacoto, L., Carvalho, P.: Linguistic resources for paraphrase generation in Portuguese: a lexicon-grammar approach. Lang. Resour. Eval. **56**(1), 1–35 (2022)
14. Fujita, A., Kentaro Furihata, K., Inui, K., Matsumoto, I., Takeuchi, K.: Paraphrasing of Japanese light-verb constructions based on lexical conceptual structure. In: Proceedings of the Workshop on Multiword Expressions: Integrating Processing (MWE 2004), pp. 9–16. ACL, Barcelona (2004)
15. Mel'čuk, I., Polguère, A.: A formal lexicon in meaning-text theory (or how to do lexica with words). Comput. Linguist. **13**(3–4), 261–275 (1987)
16. Mirto, I.M.: Automatic extraction of semantic roles in support verb constructions. Int. J. Nat. Lang. Comput. (IJNLC) **10**(03), 1–10 (2021)
17. Hurford, J.R., Heasley, B.: Semantics. A Coursebook. Cambridge University Press, Cambridge (1983)
18. Mirto, I.M.: Dream a little dream of me: cognate predicates in English. In: Camugli, C., Constant, M., Dister, A. (eds.) Actes du 26e Colloque international Lexique Grammaire, pp. 121–128. Institut Gaspard Monge, Paris (2007)
19. Mel'čuk, I.: Verbes supports sans peine. Lingvisticae Investigationes **27**(2), 203–217 (2004)
20. Fotopoulou, A., Laporte, E., Nakamura, T.: Where do aspectual variants of light verb constructions belong? In: Cook, P., et al. (eds.) Proceedings of the 17th Workshop on Multiword Expressions (MWE 2021), pp. 2–12. ACL, Online (2021)
21. Vietri, S.: Usi verbali dell'italiano: le frasi anticausative. Carocci editore, Roma (2017)
22. Lyding, V., et al.: The PAISA' corpus of Italian web texts. In: Bildhauer, F., Schäfer, R. (eds.) Proceedings of the 9th Web as Corpus Workshop (WaC-9), pp. 36–43. ACL, Gothenburg (2014)

Spelling Error Detection and Correction for Arabic Using NooJ

Rafik Kassmi[(✉)] [iD], Samir Mbarki, and Abdelaziz Mouloudi

EDPAGS Laboratory, Department of Computer Science, Faculty of Science, Ibn Tofail
University, Kénitra, Morocco
rafik.kassmi@gmail.com

Abstract. This paper presents how we managed to implement a spell checker for
Arabic, benefiting from the power of NooJ and using its functionality, noojapply.
Firstly, we define and describe the types of spelling errors, and give an overview of
the NooJ platform and its command-line tool, noojapply. Then, we present the four
main steps of our spell checker prototype. Actually, we created a local grammar in
NooJ for detecting errors, as well as a morphological and local grammar in NooJ for
generating all possible candidates for corrections. Moreover, we implemented an
improved algorithm to rank these candidates in decreasing order. Then, we created
a web UI to illustrate our work. Finally, we present some tests and evaluations of
our prototype, Al Mudaqiq.

Keywords: Arabic Language · Spell Checker · Spelling Error · NooJ ·
El-DicAr · Morphological Grammar · Local Grammar

1 Introduction

Writing is becoming more and more a part of our daily lives, like texting, emailing,
writing documents or searching for information on the web. And none of us, even the
most gifted, is safe from a typing error for several reasons: unfamiliarity with the word,
fatigue, lack of concentration or simply poor handling of the keyboard.

Arabic has a strong inflective and derivative structure. In addition, it is quite agglutinative, allowing one to add a large number of affixes to each word, widening the number
of possible words [1]. Such richness and complexity can lead to confusion and produce
erroneous texts.

A spell checker is a tool that processes words to identify spelling errors, and helps
correct them [2]. In case it has doubts about the spelling of the word, it suggests possible alternatives. It is a standalone or embedded tool used to efficiently process natural
language in many applications, such as automatic translators, OCR, search engines and
word processors. The spell checker can be interactive or automatic. The interactive spell
checker detects misspelled words, suggests possible corrections for each of them, and
then allows the user to choose the correction. In contrast, the automatic spell checker
automatically replaces the misspelled word with the most likely word without any user
interaction.

A. Bartulović et al. (Eds.): NooJ 2023, CCIS 1816, pp. 202–212, 2024.
https://doi.org/10.1007/978-3-031-56646-2_17

A spell checker is a tool that analyses words to identify spelling errors, and provide corrections [2]. It offers alternative suggestions if it is unsure about the correct word's spelling. Automatic translators, OCR, search engines and word processors, all use it as a standalone or embedded tool to handle natural language effectively. The spell checker can be interactive or automatic. The user can select the corrective choice once the interactive spell checker has identified any misspelled words, and suggested possible corrections for each one. The automated spell checker, in contrast, automatically swaps out the misspelled word with the most likely alternative word without requiring user input.

Today, almost all software packages have spell checkers, although they are not always accurate, at least not for all languages, and especially not for Arabic. Our study aims to create an Arabic spell checker by using the benefits of the NooJ platform and its command-line functionality, noojapply [3].

2 Spelling Types of Errors

The types of spelling errors can be classified into three groups: typographical errors, cognitive errors and phonetic errors [4, 5]. But in some cases, it is even difficult to assign a single category to certain errors.

2.1 Typographical Errors

This category includes all typing errors due to incorrect handling of the keyboard, such as pressing the wrong key or even using a defective keyboard. Thus, the writer commits an error by writing the word even if he knows the spelling. According to Damereau's analysis [6], about 80% of all non-word[1] spelling errors are single errors, and he involves four types of errors: insertion, deletion, substitution and transposition.

Insertion Error. It occurs when the writer adds an extra letter to the word. For example, when typing g مكتتوب [makttūb] for مكتوب [maktūb] 'written', the letter ت [t] is additionally inserted.

Deletion Error. It occurs when the writer forgets one of the letters in the word. For example, when typing مدسة [madsah] for مدرسة [madrasah] 'school', the letter ر [r] is missing.

Substitution Error. It occurs when the writer replaces a correct letter of the word with an erroneous letter. According to Kukich [7], 58% of all substitution errors involve adjacent keys on the typewriter. For example, when typing حديفة [ḥadifah] for حديقة [ḥadiqah] 'garden', the letter ق [q] is mistakenly substituted with ف [f].

Transposition or Permutation Error. It occurs when the writer swaps the letters of the word. For example, when typing برح [barḥ] for بحر [baḥr] 'see', the position of the letter ح [ḥ] is swapped with the letter ر [r].

---

[1] Nonexistent word in the language.

2.2 Cognitive Errors

This category includes errors that occurred when the writer did not know the correct spelling of the word, forgot it, or misconceived it. For example, typing لاكن [lākin] for لكن [lakin] 'but' adds the letter ا [ā].

2.3 Phonetic Errors

One of the most common causes of spelling errors is mispronunciation. Thus, a mispronounced word necessarily leads to a phonetic spelling error. Therefore, this category covers errors that occur when the writer replaces the word with a similar-sounding word. For example, when typing عضيم ['aḍim] for عظيم ['aẓim] 'great', the letter ض [ḍ] is mistakenly replaced with ظ [ẓ].

3 Overview of NooJ and Noojapply

NooJ is a linguistic development platform used for the formalization of natural languages. It provides tools for building, testing and maintaining extensively formatted descriptions of natural languages, as well as for developing automatic natural language processing (NLP) applications such as machine translation, text mining, automatic semantic annotation, spell and syntax checking, named entity recognition, etc.

NooJ builds dictionaries and an organized set of graphs representing grammars. These linguistic resources are applicable to texts in order to locate morphological (inflection and derivation), lexicological (spelling variations), syntactic and semantic patterns. It can be used to perform various statistical analyses in corpus linguistics and digital humanities, as well as to teach linguistics and linguistic computing to students [7].

The strength of NooJ, moreover, is that it provides most of its functions through a command-line program called "noojapply.exe", which can be called either from a basic shell script or from external applications via a system command. Therefore, the user first creates dictionaries and all kinds of grammars on the NooJ platform, and then applies them to texts directly with noojapply.

4 Proposed Approach

Our proposed spell checker consists of four main steps (see Fig. 1). The first step is to detect all non-words in a given text using the El-DicAr dictionary and our morphological grammar in NooJ. The second step consists of generating corrections or suggestions for candidates using morphological and local grammars in NooJ. The third step is to rank the candidates in descending order of the most likely corrected word. And finally, it selects the best candidate as the correction.

Fig. 1. Main steps of our spell checker.

4.1 Detecting Errors

Our error detection method relies on a dictionary lookup approach that is limited to isolated non-words, and we choose to utilize the El-DicAr dictionary [8]. Available for free on the official NooJ website [9], it is a morpho-syntactic analyzer designed to recognize named entities as well as a lemma-based dictionary of the standard Arabic language. We combined a morphological grammar that could identify Arabic agglutination [8, 10] with a local grammar that exclusively retrieved unknown words, i.e., words that are not present in the dictionary.

Consider the sentence below (Fig. 2): كضف باحث بريطاني عن هذا في دراشة متيرة 'A British researcher revealed this in an exciting study' When we apply our local grammar to this sentence, we find three misspelled words: كضف [kaḍafa], دراشة [diraša] and متيرة, [mutira].

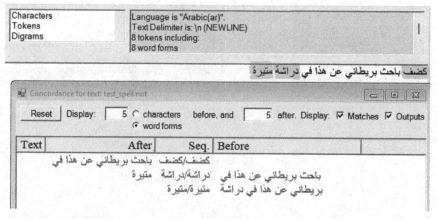

Fig. 2. The three misspelled words identified by the NooJ concordance tool.

4.2 Generating Corrections

In this stage, we made an effort to produce every one of the potential correct candidates that emerged from word-transformations of the misspelled words. To accomplish this, we will need to make:

a. **List of neighboring letters.** Neighbor letters can be adjacent letters, typographical letters that look similar or phonetic letters that sound similar. We compiled a list of all neighbors of Arabic letters based on this concept (see Fig. 3).

Letters	Neighbors					
ء	ؤ	ئ	ا	إ	أ	آ
ئ	ء	ؤ	ا	إ	أ	آ
إ	ﻻ	ئ	ا	إ	أ	
ا	ﻻ	ا	إ	أ	آ	
ا	ت	ل	إ	أ	آ	ى
ؤ	ء	ر	ئ	إ	أ	آ
آ	ﻻ	ا	إ	أ	ؤ	

Fig. 3. An excerpt from the list of neighboring letters.

b. **Morphological grammar.** Based on the neighboring letter list, we have developed a morphological grammar (see Fig. 4), which carries out the four edition operations: add missing letters, replace wrong letters, delete excess letters, or swap two letters. Additionally, we have included special tags to distinguish between the four editing operations' types in order to improve readability and the results' interpretation.

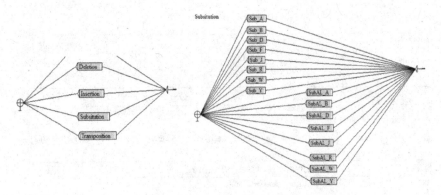

Fig. 4. Morphological grammar.

c. **Local grammar.** Next, based on the morphological grammar and its special tags, we developed a local grammar (see Fig. 5). As a consequence, we have provided the suggested corrections and the various types of editing operations that may be used for each misspelled word.

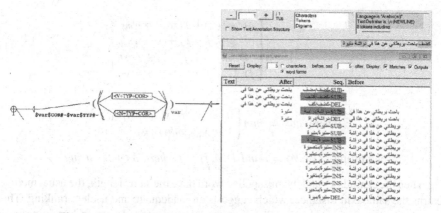

Fig. 5. The local grammar and results in the NooJ concordance tool.

4.3 Ranking Candidates

The classification phase of the candidate list follows the creation of all possible corrections for a misspelled word. The goal is to arrange this list of possibilities in decreasing
order of the most likely corrected word.

The Levenshtein distance [9, 11, 12], often known as the edit distance, is one of the
most well-known metrical procedures in the world of spell-checking. We have chosen to
use this method to rank candidates. As was previously demonstrated, Damereau found
four basic spelling errors. Based on his results, Levenshtein [13] only took into consideration three editing operations – insertion, deletion and substitution – to set up the edit
distance. Thus, the edit distance calculates the number of basic editing operations that
need to be performed to transform a misspelled word into a correct word (a dictionary
word).

Since then, a variety of edit distance versions have been made available according to
the authorized operations and application domains. The longest common subsequence
(LCS) distance, which has applications in computational linguistics, bioinformatics and
revision control systems, allows insertion and deletion but not substitution. The main
use of the Hamming distance, which only applies to strings of the same length since it
only allows substitution, is in block codes (coding theory). The Jaro distance only allows
transposition, and has uses in statistics and computer science. The Damerau-Levenshtein
distance, which allows the four editing operations of insertion, deletion, substitution and
transposition of two adjacent letters, was also chosen.

Calculation Process. Consider the following two strings: $X = x_1 x_2 \ldots x_m$ of length m
and $Y = y_1 y_2 \ldots y_n$ of length n. Recursively computing the distance between various X
and Y substrings is the method for determining the edit distance between two strings:

$$D(i,j) = D(X_1^i, Y_1^j)$$

$$D(i,j) = min \begin{cases} D_{ins}(i-1,j) + 1 - w_{ins} \\ D_{del}(i,j-1) + 1 - w_{del} \\ D_{sub}(i-1,j-1) + cost \\ D_{tr}(i-2,j-2) + 1 - w_{tr} \end{cases} \quad (1)$$

$$\text{where } cost = min \begin{cases} 0 & if \ x_{i-1} = y_{j-1} \\ 1 - w_{sub} & otherwise \end{cases}$$

admitting $D(i, \emptyset) = i$ and $D(\emptyset, j) = j$ where $\emptyset$ empty string

When the candidates and the misspelled word have the same length, the usual method returns the same edit distance, which suggests an inadequate and useless ranking. This prompts us to transform this baseline version into a weighted version by giving each editing operation a specific weight. See Eq. (1).

Applying this revised algorithm to our example متيرة كضف باحث بريطاني عن هذا في دراشة'A British researcher revealed this in an exciting study.'), the candidates are ordered as follows (see Table 1):

Table 1. Candidate ranking.

Misspelled word	Candidates	Weight
كضف [kaḍafa]	كثف	95.33%
	مضف	95.33%
	كف	77.50%

Misspelled word	Candidates	Weight
دراشة [diraša]	دراسة	97.20%
	دراة	88.75%

Misspelled word	Candidates	Weight
متيرة [mutira]	مثيرة	97.20%
	منيرة	97.20%
	متسرة	97.20%
	متصيرة	96.88%
	متطيرة	96.88%
	متيسرة	96.88%
	متسيرة	96.88%
	متغيرة	96.88%
	متخيرة	96.88%
	متحيرة	96.88%
	ميرة	88.75%

We can see that our algorithm has been enhanced to give the correct suggestion a high score.

4.4 Correcting

The best candidate with the highest score and corresponding corrected word is chosen to complete the spellcheck process. Unlike an interactive spell checker that lets the user select the correct word, an automated spell checker will automatically replace a misspelled word with the best candidate. In our case, we have chosen to use an interactive spell checker.

5 Application

After the grammars were created and evaluated on the NooJ platform, we applied them to a Web application we had developed according to the flowchart shown in Fig. 6. We utilized the noojapply tool at this stage, which, as was previously mentioned, enables us to take advantage of the majority of NooJ's functionality.

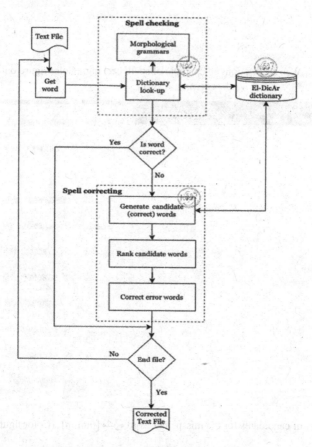

Fig. 6. Flowchart for spell-checking and correcting.

Let us consider the previous example again: كضف باحث بريطاني عن هذا في دراشة متيرة 'A British researcher revealed this in an exciting study', Our spellchecker displays the three misspelled words in this sentence: كضف [kaḍafa], دراشة [diraša] and متيرة [mutira] (see Figs. 7 and 8 words in red). The user may choose the correct word by simply clicking on a misspelled word to display a list of candidates, and so on, until all errors are fixed.

Fig. 7. Web application: an example of spellchecking. (Color figure online)

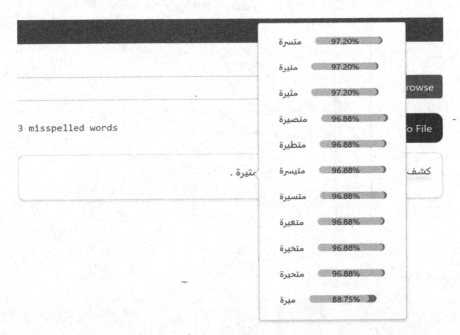

Fig. 8. List of candidates for the misspelled word متيرة [mutira]. (Color figure online)

6 Tests and Evaluation

This section presents the results of evaluations carried out on Arabic articles that were chosen based on four topics: media, economics, sports and society. We need to evaluate our prototype using the standard metrics of precision (2), recall (3) and F-measure (4) in order to validate it (see Tables 2 and 3).

$$Precision = \frac{Number\ of\ errors\ correctly\ detected}{Number\ of\ detections} \quad (2)$$

$$Recall = \frac{Number\ of\ errors\ correctly\ detected}{Number\ of\ introduced\ errors} \quad (3)$$

$$F\text{-}measure = 2*\frac{Precision*Recall}{(Precision+Recall)} \quad (4)$$

Table 2. Experience with our prototype (Al Mudaqiq).

	Text 1	Text 2	Text 3	Text 4
Number of words	165	310	262	238
Number of errors correctly detected	10	18	15	14
Number of detections	13	24	17	16
Number of introduced errors	10	18	16	14
Precision	76.92%	75%	88.24%	87.50%
Recall	100%	100%	93.75%	100%
F-measure	86.96%	85.71%	90.91%	93.33%

Table 3. Experience with Word 2019.

	Text 1	Text 2	Text 3	Text 4
Number of words	165	310	262	238
Number of errors correctly detected	10	16	15	12
Number of detections	14	26	18	15
Number of introduced errors	10	18	16	14
Precision	71.43%	61.54%	83.33%	80%
Recall	100%	88.89%	93.75%	85.71%
F-measure	83.33%	72.73%	88.24%	82.76%

The overall evaluation reveals that our Arabic spell checker, Al Mudaqiq, outperforms Word 2019 in terms of accuracy. In comparison to Word 2019, we acquired an average F-measure of 89.23% for our prototype.

7 Conclusion and Perspectives

In this paper, we demonstrated how we had used NooJ (and noojapply) to develop an Arabic spell checker. After giving an overview of NooJ and its command-line utility, noojapply, we started by defining and describing various types of spelling errors. We have contributed by presenting the four main steps of our spell checker, which include the development of a NooJ local grammar for error detection. In order to generate all possible candidates for corrections, we constructed a morphological and local grammar in NooJ. Then, in order to classify these candidates, we created an improved algorithm. Then, to illustrate our work, a web interface was developed. Finally, we have created a comparison table of tests done on different topics in Arabic articles between our prototype and Word 2019.

Regarding perspectives, our goal is to improve grammar error detection to take real words into account as well as context-dependent and context-sensitive errors, which refer to errors involving textual and linguistic context as well as missed spaces between words.

We also aim to improve our ranking algorithm to be more precise, to avoid having candidates with the same weight, and finally, to improve and enrich the presentation layer of the results.

References

1. Silberztein, M.: La formalisation des langues: l'approche de NooJ. ISTE Editions, London (2015)
2. Olani, G., Midekso, D.: Design and implementation of morphology based spell checker. Int. J. Sci. Technol. Res. **3**, 1–8 (2014)
3. Silberztein, M.: NooJ Manual (2003). www.nooj-association.org
4. Kukich, K.: Techniques for automatically correcting words in text. ACM Comput. Surv. **24**(4), 377–439 (1992)
5. Haddad, B., Yaseen, M.: Detection and correction of non-words in Arabic: a hybrid approach. Int. J. Comput. Process. Oriental Lang. (IJCPOL) **20**(4), 237–257 (2007)
6. Damerau, F.J.: A technique for computer detection and correction of spelling errors. Commun. ACM **5**(3), 171–176 (1964)
7. Silberztein, M., Tutin, A.: NooJ, un outil TAL pour l'enseignement des langues. Application pour l'étude de la morphologie lexicale en FLE. Apprentissage des langues et systèmes d'information et de communication (ALSIC) **8**(1), 123–134 (2005)
8. Mesfar, S.: Analyse morpho-syntaxique automatique et reconnaissance des entités nommées en arabe standard. Thèse de doctorat. Franche-Comte University, Besançon (2008)
9. Bacha, K., Zrigui, M.: Contribution to the achievement of a spell checker for Arabic. Res. Comput. Sci. **117**, 161–172 (2016)
10. Kassmi, R., Mourchid, M., Mouloudi, A., Mbarki, S.: Processing agglutination with a morpho-syntactic graph in NooJ. In: Mbarki, S., Mourchid, M., Silberztein, M. (eds.) NooJ 2017. CCIS, vol. 811, pp. 40–51. Springer, Cham (2018). https://doi.org/10.1007/978-3-319-73420-0_4
11. Gueddah, H., Yousfi, A., Belkasmi, M.: Introduction of the weight edition errors in the Levenshtein distance. Int. J. Adv. Res. Artif. Intell. **1**(5), 30–32 (2012)
12. Gueddah, H., Yousfi, A.: The impact of Arabic inter-character proximity and similarity on spell-checking. In: Proceeding of the 8th International Conference on Intelligent Systems: Theories and Applications (SITA), Rabat, pp. 244–246. IEEE (2013)
13. Levenshtein, V.: Binary codes capable of correcting deletions, insertions and reversals. Soviet Physics – Doklady **10**(8), 707–710 (1966)

Automatic Translation of Continuous and Fixed Arabic Frozen Expressions Using the NooJ Platform

Asmaa Kourtin[1]([✉]) and Samir Mbarki[2]

[1] Computer Science Research Laboratory, Faculty of Science, Ibn Tofail University, Kenitra, Morocco
asmaa.kourtin@yahoo.fr
[2] EDPAGS Laboratory, Faculty of Science, Ibn Tofail University, Kenitra, Morocco

Abstract. Translating frozen expressions between languages is a challenging task due to the intricate linguistic and pragmatic aspects involved. It necessitates translators to possess a thorough understanding of both the target and source languages, as languages are deeply intertwined with their respective cultures. Factors such as religion, geography, ideologies and social classes further complicate the comprehension and translation of frozen expressions. This study focuses on the automatic translator development for continuous and fixed Arabic frozen expressions, intending to translate them into French and English using the NooJ platform. The research process starts by enhancing the existing lexicon-grammar tables with French and English translations of each expression. Subsequently, these enhanced tables are converted into dictionaries using the NooJ platform's dictionary generation program developed in [2]. Finally, the efficacy of this translator is evaluated through extensive testing on diverse texts and corpora.

Keywords: Lexicon-Grammar Tables · Natural Language Processing (NLP) · Frozen Expressions · Automatic Translation · Modern Arabic · NooJ Platform · NooJ Dictionary · Syntactic Grammar · Transformational Grammar

1 Introduction

Research on frozen or idiomatic expressions has gained significant attention in recent years, leading to extensive studies across different languages. These expressions cannot be understood by simply combining the meanings of their components, resulting in challenges for comprehension and translation. Thus, translating these expressions from one language to another poses a significant challenge for translators due to the linguistic and pragmatic specificities involved. It requires translators to possess a solid understanding of both languages and cultures, as inherently tied to their respective cultures. Factors such as religion, ideologies and social classes further complicate understanding and translation of the frozen expressions.

Our main objective is to develop an automatic translator specifically designed for continuous and fixed Arabic frozen expressions, enabling their translation into French

A. Bartulović et al. (Eds.): NooJ 2023, CCIS 1816, pp. 213–224, 2024.
https://doi.org/10.1007/978-3-031-56646-2_18

and English through the utilization of the NooJ platform. The initial phase entails enhancing our lexicon-grammar tables established in [1] by incorporating French and English translations for each frozen expression. These enriched tables are subsequently converted into dictionaries using the NooJ platform's dictionary generation program developed in [2]. To further advance the capability of the translator, we construct corresponding syntactic grammars [3] that facilitate the detection of these expressions within texts and corpora. Additionally, we incorporate transformational grammars to enable the translation of these frozen expressions from Arabic to French and English. The final step of this study involves thorough testing of the translator's effectiveness across a variety of texts and corpora. This evaluation aims to assess the accuracy and efficiency of this translator.

This paper is structured as follows. We begin by reviewing existing works on frozen expressions and their translation in Sect. 2. Section 3 explains the methodology of our work. In Sect. 4, we will implement our proposed lexicon-grammar tables by generating their dictionaries and developing their syntactic grammars to detect these expressions in texts and corpora as well as transformational grammars for the automatic translation process. Finally, Sect. 5 gives an evaluation and discussion of the benefits of our work and its perspectives.

2 Related Works

In recent years, there has been a notable increase in research focused on frozen or idiomatic expressions and their automatic translation. This growing interest has captivated the attention of numerous researchers across different languages. The significance of frozen or idiomatic expressions lies in their unique linguistic characteristics and the challenges they pose for translation.

Gross [4] conducted a study on frozen expressions in the French language, wherein he categorized them into two types. The first type comprises sentences with a single fixed nominal group that can appear in any syntactic position. The second type encompasses sentences with multiple fixed groups, which can occur in various positions within the sentence. Baptista [5] directed his attention to examining the syntactic characteristics that can effectively differentiate compound nouns from ordinary noun phrases. Furthermore, he elucidated how this methodology can be extended to identify compound adverbs as well. Baptista et al. [6] undertook the task of constructing an electronic dictionary specifically for European Portuguese frozen expressions. Their primary emphasis was on addressing the challenges associated with accurately describing the formal variations of these expressions in view of NLP.

In the context of the Arabic language, numerous researchers have dedicated their efforts to studying frozen expressions and their translation, with particular attention given to their translation into French. Alqahtni [7] analyzed idiomatic expressions extracted from the Saudi newspaper "Al Riyadh". The study primarily centered on examining the structure and contextual usage of a sample of these expressions. Boulaalam [8] conducted a study focusing on the category of verbal sentences within Arabic frozen expressions and their corresponding translations in French. In [9], Minko Mi Nseme conducted a comprehensive theoretical investigation of Arabic frozen expressions. The study involved classifying the morphosyntactic structures of these expressions, analyzing their constituent elements and evaluating the level of syntactic-semantic frozenness. The ultimate goal was to develop a lexical database to capture the intricacies of these expressions. Ali [10] dedicated his research to the frozen expressions derived from the Qur'an translation into French. The primary focus was on identifying the challenges and issues that arise during the process of translating these expressions. Abdelmaksoud [11] conducted a study on idioms found in the Qur'an, with a particular focus on analyzing their French translation and examining the process of frozenness that defines these expressions. Asmaa Kourtin et al. [1] conducted a comprehensive study on continuous and fixed frozen expressions in modern Arabic. The focus of their research was to analyze these expressions and develop lexicon-grammar tables for them.

3 Methodology

Frozen expressions have gained prominence due to their semantic and structural stability, making them essential in conveying clear and precise meanings while avoiding ambiguity. These expressions greatly enrich the language, providing a wide range of possibilities to express various meanings. In contemporary linguistics, the study of meaning extends beyond the analysis of individual words and their lexical meanings. It encompasses the examination of syntactic meaning, including the exploration of frozen expressions. As a result, dictionaries dedicated to these expressions have been developed, highlighting the growing interest in understanding them.

Automatic translation is not a new idea; it began decades ago, precisely in 1949, with the American Weaver Warren, and it has been the target of several scientific research projects. The translation of frozen expressions poses both linguistic and extralinguistic problems. The meaning of these particular expressions and their metaphorical aspect makes their translation a real challenge for translators. A literal translation of a frozen expression may not convey the intended meaning unless there is an equivalent cultural or pragmatic reference in the target language. Translating frozen expressions requires careful consideration of the cultural and contextual nuances to ensure a comprehensible and accurate translation.

Our main objective is to develop an automatic translator specifically designed for continuous and fixed Arabic frozen expressions, enabling their translation into French and English through the utilization of the NooJ platform. For that, we start by enhancing the lexicon-grammar tables "EFA1" for nominal expressions and "EFA2" for verbal expressions, created in [1] by incorporating French and English translations for each frozen expression.

These translations are based on two strategies: adaptation and semantic interpretation. Adapting the source expression allows for finding an equivalent expression in the target language that captures the intended meaning while considering cultural and linguistic differences or by analyzing the underlying meaning of the expression and conveying it through alternative linguistic constructs in the target language. These approaches enable us to overcome the challenges posed by frozen expressions and provide accurate and meaningful translations.

Figure 1 shows an excerpt from the updated lexicon-grammar table "EFA1" for nominal frozen expressions where the columns contain the syntactic-semantic features.

We added to the existing table the features "FR" and "ENG", where "FR" represents the French translation of the frozen expression and "ENG" depicts its English translation. For instance, the frozen expression ابتسامة صفراء [ibtissamaton safraâ]means 'a fake smile' in English and 'sourire peu sincère' in French. This expression is a noun phrase having the structure "C0C1" where "C0" is ابتسامة [ibtissamaton]and "C1" is صفراء [safraâ].

<Opt>Exemple	<OPT>ExpFig	ENG	FR	C0Det1C1ConjDet2C2	C0Prép1C1Prép2 C2	C0Det1C1Prép2	C0Det1C1Prép2C2	C0Det1C1Det2C2	C0C1Det2C2	C0Prép1Det1C1	C0Prép1C1	C0Det1C1	C0C1	C0W	C2=Adj	C2=NplObl	C1=Adj	C1=NPlObl	C1=DuelObl	C0=Adv	C0=Adj	C0=NPlObl	C0=N	C2	Det2	Prép2	Conj	C1	Det1	Prép1	N	Det0
ورث هذا القوم البيت أبا عن جد.	أبا عن جد	inherited from fore	de père en fils	-	-	-	-	-	-	-	+	-	-	-	-	-	-	-	-	-	-	-	+	<E>	-	<E>	<E>	جد	-	عن	أبا	-
استقبلني بابتسامة صفراء.	ابتسامة صفراء	a fake smile	Sourire peu sincè	-	-	-	-	-	-	-	-	-	+	-	-	-	+	-	-	-	-	-	+	<E>	-	<E>	<E>	صفراء	-	<E>	ابتسامة	-
الحرب أبغض الحلال بين الدول.	أبغض الحلال	permissible and str	licite et fort déco	-	-	-	-	-	-	-	-	+	-	-	-	-	-	-	-	-	+	-	+	<E>	-	<E>	<E>	حلال	+	<E>	أبغض	-
كانت مبادرة السلام وسيلة لاجتياز حائط الخوف.	اجتياز حائط الخوف	surpass the fear	surpasser la peu	-	-	-	-	-	+	-	-	-	-	-	-	-	-	-	-	-	-	-	+	خوف	+	<E>	<E>	حائط	-	<E>	اجتياز	-
اتخذت الحكومة إجراءات للقضاء على البطالة.	إجراءات	measures	des mesures	-	-	-	-	-	-	-	-	-	-	+	-	-	-	-	-	-	-	+	+	<E>	-	<E>	<E>	<E>	-	<E>	إجراءات	-
الخلافات بين الطرفين تهدد بإجهاض المفاوضات.	إجهاض	to abort	pour faire avorte	-	-	-	-	-	-	-	-	-	-	+	-	-	-	-	-	-	-	-	+	<E>	-	<E>	<E>	<E>	-	<E>	إجهاض	-
سيطرت على المنطقة أجواء عاصفة بعد التهديد.	أجواء عاصفة	stormy weather	temps orageux	-	-	-	-	-	-	-	-	-	+	-	-	-	+	-	-	-	-	+	+	<E>	-	<E>	<E>	عاصفة	-	<E>	أجواء	-
دارت مناقشات بين الوفدين في أجواء ودية.	أجواء ودية	Friendly Atmosphe	une ambiance co	-	-	-	-	-	-	-	-	-	+	-	-	-	+	-	-	-	-	+	+	<E>	-	<E>	<E>	ودية	-	<E>	أجواء	-
تمكنت القوات من إحباط محاولة التهريب.	إحباط ...	frustration	frustration	-	-	-	-	-	-	-	-	-	-	+	-	-	-	-	-	-	-	-	+	<E>	-	<E>	<E>	<E>	-	<E>	إحباط	-
قصور الثقافة تعمل على احتضان المواهب الشابة.	احتضان	embrace	embrassant	-	-	-	-	-	-	-	-	-	-	+	-	-	-	-	-	-	-	-	+	<E>	-	<E>	<E>	<E>	-	<E>	احتضان	-
نريد من وسائل الإعلام أن تكون موضوعية، لا تنجح	إحراق البخور	hypocrisy	hypocrisie	-	-	-	-	-	-	-	-	+	-	-	-	-	-	-	-	-	-	-	+	<E>	-	<E>	<E>	بخور	+	<E>	احراق	-

Fig. 1. Excerpt of the updated lexicon-grammar table "EFA1".

Figure 2 shows an excerpt from the updated lexicon-grammar table "EFA2" for verbal frozen expressions where the columns contain the syntactic-semantic features. For instance, the frozen expression اختل عقل [ikhtalla 'a9lo]means 'lose one's mind' in English and 'perdre la boule' in French. This expression is a verbal phrase having the structure "VC0W" where "V" is اختل [ikhtalla]and "C0" is عقل ['a9lo].

<Opt>Sens	<OPT>ExpFig	ENG	FR	VC1Conj1V1C2	VDet1C1C2	AdvOVDet0C0V1Det1C1	VDet0C0Adv1C1W	VDet0C0Prép1Det1C1	VDet0C0Prép1C1W	VPrép1C1	VDet0C0	VC0W	VN0W	N2NHum	N2Hum	N1pc	N1NHum	N1Hum	N0pc	N0NHum	N0Hum	C2	Det2	C1	Det1	V1	Adv1	Con	Pré	C0	Det0	V	Adv0
أصبح الأمر صعبا، لا يمكن معالجته	اتسع الخرق على الراتق	"the rent is beyon	"le loyer est irrépa	-	-	-	-	+	-	-	-	-	-	-	-	-	-	+	-	+	-	<E>	-	راتق	+	<E>	<E>	<E>	على	خرق	+	اتسع	<E>
للمبالغة في الشعور بالحيرة، و العجز عن حسـ	احتار دليل ...	"very confused"	"très confus"	-	-	-	-	-	-	-	-	+	-	-	-	-	-	+	-	+	-	<E>	-	<E>	-	<E>	<E>	<E>	<E>	دليل	-	احتار	<E>
أصابه الجنون و الهوس، و ضعف تفكيره	اختل عقل ...	"lose one's mind"	"perdre la boule"	-	-	-	-	-	-	-	-	+	-	-	-	-	-	+	+	-	-	<E>	-	<E>	-	<E>	<E>	<E>	<E>	عقل	-	اختل	<E>
للتعبير عن التشوش الحاصل مع عدم القدرة	اختلط الحابل بالنابل	"things got mixed	"les choses se son	-	-	-	-	+	-	-	-	-	-	-	-	-	-	+	-	-	+	<E>	-	نابل	+	<E>	<E>	<E>	ب	حابل	+	اختلط	<E>
مثل يضرب في حال وجود شيئين أو شخصين	إذا حضر الماء بطل التيمم	"if the water is av	"si l'eau est dispor	-	-	+	-	-	-	-	-	-	-	-	-	-	+	-	-	+	-	<E>	-	تيمم	+	بطل	<E>	<E>	<E>	ماء	+	حضر	إذا
كناية عن الخوف الشديد و الإضطراب	ارتعدت فرائص ...	"tremble with fea	"se trembler de pe	-	-	-	-	-	-	-	-	+	-	-	-	-	-	+	+	-	-	<E>	-	<E>	-	<E>	<E>	<E>	<E>	فرائص	-	ارتعدت	<E>
له معنيان : 1. بدأ العرض المسرحي. 2. بداية	ارتفع الستار	"curtain-up"	"le rideau s'est lev	-	-	-	-	-	-	-	+	-	-	-	-	-	+	-	-	+	-	<E>	-	<E>	-	<E>	<E>	<E>	<E>	ستار	+	ارتفع	<E>
بث و استقر و استقام و تهيأ، و أكثر استعماله	استتب الأمر	"calm is restored"	"le calme s'est éta	-	-	-	-	-	-	-	+	-	-	-	-	-	-	-	-	+	-	<E>	-	<E>	-	<E>	<E>	<E>	<E>	أمر	+	استتب	<E>
بث و استقر و استقام و تهيأ، و أكثر استعماله	استتب الأمن	"security settled"	"la paix revient"	-	-	-	-	-	-	-	+	-	-	-	-	-	-	-	-	+	-	<E>	-	<E>	-	<E>	<E>	<E>	<E>	أمن	+	استتب	<E>
بث و استقر و استقام و تهيأ، و أكثر استعماله	استتب النظام	"order was restor	"l'ordre a été réta	-	+	-	-	-	-	-	+	-	-	-	-	-	-	-	-	+	-	<E>	-	<E>	-	<E>	<E>	<E>	<E>	نظام	+	استتب	<E>
للتعبير عن الكثرة و شدة الإنتشار لشيء خطير	استفحل	"get out of contro	"atteindre les pro	-	-	-	-	-	-	-	-	-	+	-	-	-	-	-	-	+	-	<E>	-	<E>	-	<E>	<E>	<E>	<E>	<E>	-	استفحل	<E>

Fig. 2. Excerpt of the updated lexicon-grammar table "EFA2".

4 Implementation and Tests

To implement the lexicon-grammar tables "EFA1" and "EFA2" for continuous and fixed Arabic frozen expressions in the NooJ platform, we create the dictionaries "EFA1.dic" and "EFA2.dic" by running our program that automatically generates the NooJ dictionaries from the lexicon-grammar tables [2].

The generated dictionaries contain all the grammatical, syntactic and semantic characteristics of the entries coded in the lexicon-grammar tables. For each entry, we have added the specific property "FXC" for frozen expressions, which means that the lexical entry should not be treated as an ambiguous linguistic unit [3] and the code "EFA1" or "EFA2" that represents the name of the class "EFA1" or "EFA2" to reference the lexicon-grammar table from which the entry is taken (see Figs. 3 and 4).

```
# NooJ V5
# Dictionary
#
# Language is: ar
#
# Alphabetical order is not required.
#
#.Use inflectional & derivational paradigms' description files (.nof), e.g.:
# Special Command: #use paradigms.nof
#
# Special Features: +NW (non-word) +FXC (frozen expression component) +UNAMB (unambiguous lexical entry)
#                   +FLX= (inflectional paradigm) +DRV= (derivational paradigm)
#
# Special Characters: '\' '"' ' ' ',' '+' '-' '#'

أبا,N+EFA1+FXC+Prép1=عن+C1=جد+C0=N+C0Prép1C1+FR="de père en fils"+ENG="inherited from forefathers"
ابتسامة,N+EFA1+FXC+C1=صفرا+C0=N+C1=Adj+C0C1+FR="sourire peu sincère"+ENG="a fake smile"+ENG="insincere smile"
ابقى,N+EFA1+FXC+Det1+C1=حلال+C0=N+C0=Adj+C0Det1C1+FR="licite et fort déconseillé par la morale islamique"+ENG="..
اجتناز,N+EFA1+FXC+C1=طلحا+Det2+C2=خوف+C0=N+C0C1Det2C2+FR="surpasser la peur"+ENG="surpass the fear"+ENG="get ov
اجراءات,N+EFA1+FXC+C0=N+C0=NP1Ob1+C0W+FR="des mesures"+ENG="measures"+ENG="actions"+ENG="procedures"
اجهاض,N+EFA1+FXC+C0=N+C0W+FR="pour faire avorter"+FR="l'avortement"+ENG="to abort"+ENG="to preempt"
أجوا,N+EFA1+FXC+C1=عاصفة+C0=N+C0=NP1Ob1+C1=Adj+C0C1+FR="temps orageux"+FR="tempéte"+ENG="stormy weather"
أجوا,N+EFA1+FXC+C1=وديه+C0=N+C0=NP1Ob1+C1=Adj+C0C1+FR="une ambiance conviviale"+ENG="friendly atmosphere"
احباط,N+EFA1+FXC+C0=N+C0W+FR="frustration"+FR="déception"+ENG="frustration"+ENG="disappointment"
احتضان,N+EFA1+FXC+C0=N+C0W+FR="embrassant"+ENG="embrace"
احتكار,N+EFA1+FXC+Det1+C1=فجور+C0=N+C0Det1C1+FR="hypocrisie" +ENG="hypocrisy"
أحلام,N+EFA1+FXC+Det1+C1=عصافير+C0=N+C0=NP1Ob1+C1=NP1Ob1+C0Det1C1+FR="les rêves des moineaux"+ENG="the dreams of
```

Fig. 3. Excerpt from the generated dictionary "EFA1.dic".

```
# NooJ V5
# Dictionary
#
# Language is: ar
#
# Alphabetical order is not required.
#
# Use inflectional & derivational paradigms' description files (.nof), e.g.:
# Special Command: #use paradigms.nof
#
# Special Features: +NW (non-word) +FXC (frozen expression component) +UNAMB (unambiguous lexical entry)
#        -          +FLX= (inflectional paradigm) +DRV= (derivational paradigm)
#
# Special Characters: '\' '"' ' ' ',' '+' '-' '#'

التمس,V+EFA2+FXC+Det0+C0=خرق+Prép1=على+Det1+C1=ازل+NONHum+N1Hum+VDet0C0Prép1Det1C1+FR="le loyer est irréparable
احتار,V+EFA2+FXC+C0=دليل+NONHum+N1Hum+VC0W+FR="très confus"+ENG="very confused"
اختل,V+EFA2+FXC+C0=عقل+NOpc+N1Hum+VC0W+FR="perdre la boule"+ENG="lose one's mind"
اختلط,V+EFA2+FXC+Det0+C0=حبل+Prép1=+Det1+C1=ابل+NOHum+N1Hum+VDet0C0Prép1Det1C1+FR="les choses se sont mélang
حضر,V+EFA2+FXC+Adv0=إذا+Det0+C0=لب+V1=همم+Det1+C1=ميه+NONHum+N1Hum+Adv0VDet0C0V1Det1C1+FR="si l'eau est disp
ارتعدت,V+EFA2+FXC+C0=الم+NOpc+N1Hum+VC0W+FR="se trembler de peur"+ENG="tremble with fear"
ارتفع,V+EFA2+FXC+Det0+C0=ستار+NONHum+N1NHum+VC0W+FR="le rideau s'est levé"+ENG="curtain-up"
استتب,V+EFA2+FXC+Det0+C0=امر+NONHum+VC0W+FR="le calme s'est établi"+ENG="calm is restored"
استتب,V+EFA2+FXC+Det0+C0=امن+NONHum+VC0W+FR="la paix revient"+ENG="security settled"
استتب,V+EFA2+FXC+Det0+C0=نظام+NONHum+VC0W+FR="l'ordre a été rétabli"+ENG="order was restored"
استفحل,V+EFA2+FXC+NONHum+VNOW+FR="atteindre les proportions alarmantes"+ENG="get out of control"
استقال,V+EFA2+FXC+NOHum+VNOW+FR="démissionner"+ENG="to resign"
استقرت,V+EFA2+FXC+Det0+C0=ارض+Adv1=تحت+C1=قدر+NONHum+N1pc+N2Hum+VDet0C0Adv1C1+FR="être rassuré"+ENG="is reassu
```

Fig. 4. Excerpt from the generated dictionary "EFA2.dic".

The creation of NooJ dictionaries is not sufficient in the process of integrating lexicon-grammar tables into the NooJ platform. Additionally, the development of syntactic grammar, which must have the same name as the dictionary and be located in the same directory is essential in this process [3, 12]. For that, we have created a syntactic grammar "EFA1.nog" for the class "EFA1" for recognition of all the nominal frozen expressions contained in this table and a syntactic grammar "EFA2.nog" for the class "EFA2" allowing us to recognize all the verbal frozen expressions contained in this table.

As shown in Figs. 5 and 6, each syntactic grammar takes into account all the grammatical, syntactic and semantic characteristics contained in its associated dictionary, such as conditions on the subject, the sentence's structure, etc.

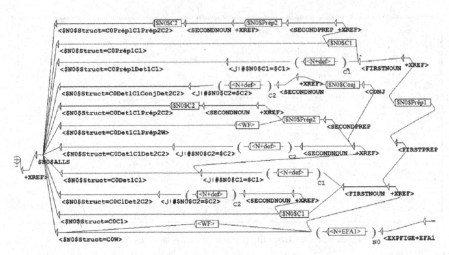

Fig. 5. The syntactic grammar "EFA1.nog" for the lexicon-grammar table "EFA1".

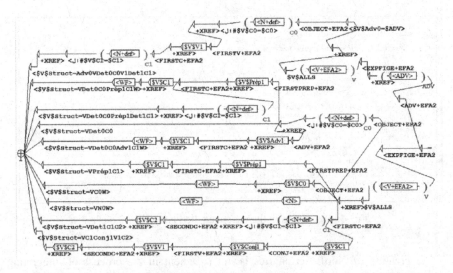

Fig. 6. The syntactic grammar "EFA2.nog" for the lexicon-grammar table "EFA2".

To evaluate our generated dictionaries "EFA1.dic" and "EFA2.dic" (see Figs. 3 and 4) and the syntactic grammars "EFA1.nog" and "EFA2.nog" (see Figs. 5 and 6), we analyzed a few sentences containing continuous and fixed frozen expressions of the lexicon-grammar tables "EFA1" and "EFA2".

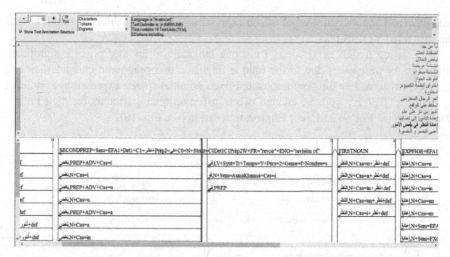

Fig. 7. The annotations of the sentence إعادة النظر في بعض الأمور

The Fig. 7 shows the annotations of the Arabic sentence إعادة النظر في بعض الأمور 'revision of few things', generated by the constructed grammar "EFA1.nog". The grammar was able to recognize and annotate the continuous and fixed nominal frozen expression النظر في بعض إعادة 'revision of' having the structure "C0Det1C1Prép2W".

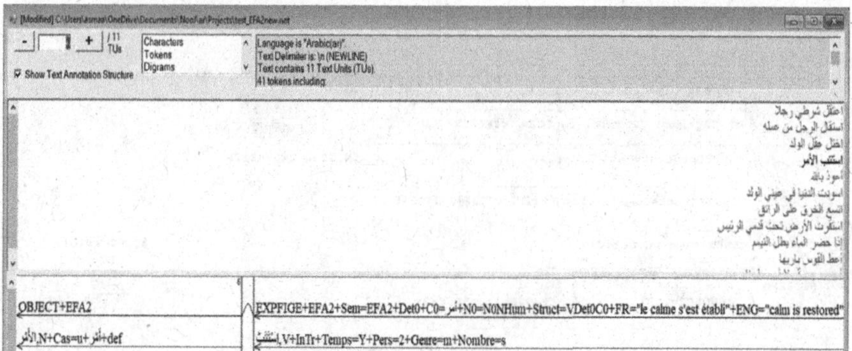

Fig. 8. The annotations of the sentence استتب الأمر

Figure 8 shows some annotations of Arabic sentences containing continuous and fixed verbal frozen expressions such as استتب الأمر 'Calm is restored.', generated by the constructed grammar "EFA2.nog". We see in this figure that the grammar was able to

220   A. Kourtin and S. Mbarki

recognize and annotate the verbal frozen expression استتب الأمر 'Calm is restored' having the structure "VDet0C0".

Translating frozen expressions from one language to another poses a significant challenge for translators due to the unique linguistic and pragmatic characteristics of these expressions. For the continuous and fixed nominal frozen expressions contained in the class "EFA1", we have created two transformational grammars for their French translation (see Fig. 9) and their English translation (see Fig. 10).

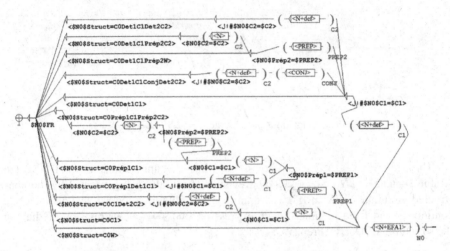

Fig. 9. Excerpt of the French translation grammar for "EFA1" class.

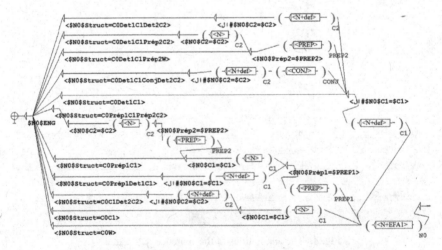

Fig. 10. Excerpt of the English translation grammar for "EFA1" class.

These grammars allow the translation of each nominal expression from Arabic to French and English. First, we have to recognize the frozen expression using the syntactic and semantic features coded in the "EFA1.dic" dictionary, and then we produce its translation.

To evaluate our two grammars mentioned in Figs. 9 and 10, we analyzed a few sentences containing continuous and fixed nominal frozen expressions of the lexicon-grammar table "EFA1". Figure 11 illustrates the results obtained from the translation of the sentence اختراق أنظمة الكمبيوتر in English, which means 'computer hacking', and its translation in French, which is 'piratage'.

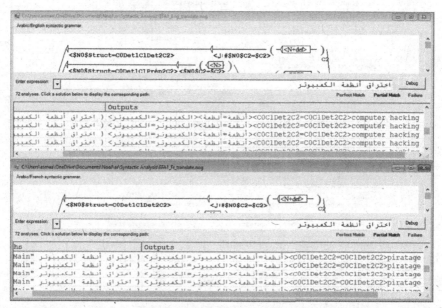

Fig. 11. Excerpt from the translations of the sentence اختراق أنظمة الكمبيوتر in English and French.

For the continuous and fixed verbal frozen expressions contained in the class "EFA2", we have created a transformational grammar for their French translation (see Fig. 12) and another one for their English translation (see Fig. 13). These grammars allow us to translate each verbal expression from Arabic to French and English languages. First, we have to recognize the frozen expression using the syntactic and semantic features coded in the "EFA2.dic" dictionary, and then we produce its translation.

To evaluate our two grammars mentioned in Figs. 12 and 13, we analyzed a few sentences containing continuous and fixed verbal frozen expressions from the lexicon-grammar table "EFA2". Figure 14 illustrates the results obtained from the translation of the sentence استتب الأمر in French, which means 'le calme s'est établi', and its translation in English, which is 'calm is restored'.

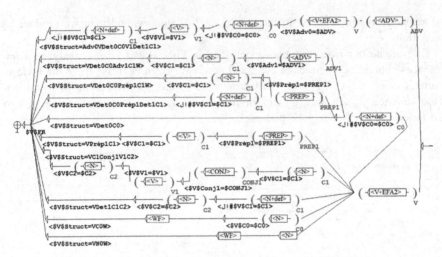

Fig. 12. Excerpt of the French translation grammar for "EFA2" class.

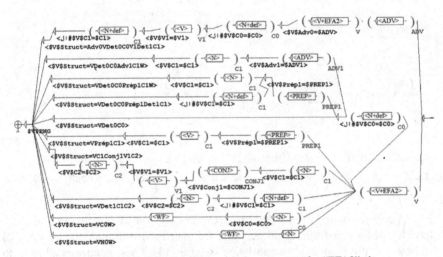

Fig. 13. Excerpt of the English translation grammar for "EFA2" class.

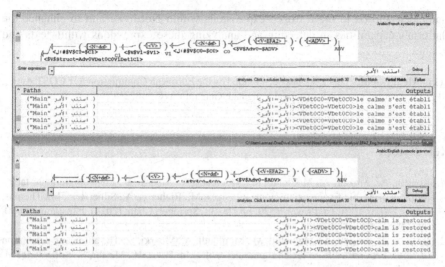

Fig. 14. Excerpt from the translations of the sentence اسْتتب الأمر in French and English.

5 Conclusion and Perspectives

The Arabic language continues to face challenges due to the scarcity of linguistic resources, particularly concerning frozen expressions. Consequently, conducting research on contemporary Arabic frozen expressions and developing lexicon-grammar tables for them would greatly enhance these resources and facilitate the utilization and updates of linguistic data. By studying Arabic frozen expressions and creating lexicon-grammar tables, the language community can benefit from a comprehensive reference that provides detailed information on their structure, meaning and usage. This would simplify the handling of linguistic data and its subsequent modifications, contributing to more efficient and accurate analysis and translation of Arabic texts.

This paper focuses on the comprehensive examination of continuous and fixed Arabic frozen expressions, with the primary objective of updating their lexicon-grammar tables to incorporate translation features. Dictionaries were also generated for these expressions, and syntactic grammars were created to seamlessly integrate them into the NooJ platform. The integration of these resources into the NooJ platform enables users to effectively analyze, process and translate Arabic texts while considering the unique characteristics and nuances of frozen expressions. Overall, this research contributes to advancing the study of Arabic frozen expressions, and provides valuable tools for linguistic analysis and translation, particularly within the NooJ platform.

As perspectives, we plan to expand upon this work by developing lexicon-grammar tables for additional categories of frozen expressions in Arabic and incorporating translation features for these categories as well. This expansion would involve studying and documenting a wider range of frozen expressions, including idioms, proverbs and other fixed expressions commonly used in the language. Furthermore, we intend to convert these comprehensive lexicon-grammar tables into NooJ dictionaries, enabling seamless integration of these resources into the NooJ platform. By building specific syntactic grammars tailored to these frozen expressions within NooJ, we aim to enhance the platform's capabilities in detecting and analyzing these expressions within texts and corpora.

Acknowledgement. This work has been funded by the European Commission ICT COST Action Multi-task, Multilingual, Multi-modal Language Generation (CA18231).

References

1. Kourtin, A., Amzali, A., Mourchid, M., Mouloudi, A., Mbarki, S.: Lexicon-grammar tables for modern Arabic frozen expressions. In: Bigey, M., Richeton, A., Silberztein, M., Thomas, I. (eds.) NooJ 2021. CCIS, vol. 1520, pp. 28–38. Springer, Cham (2021). https://doi.org/10.1007/978-3-030-92861-2_3

2. Kourtin, A., Amzali, A., Mourchid, M., Mouloudi, A., Mbarki, S.: The automatic generation of NooJ dictionaries from lexicon-grammar tables. In: Fehri, H., Mesfar, S., Silberztein, M. (eds.) NooJ 2019. CCIS, vol. 1153, pp. 65–76. Springer, Cham (2020). https://doi.org/10.1007/978-3-030-38833-1_6

3. Silberztein, M.: La formalisation des langues: l'approche de NooJ. ISTE Editions, London (2015)

4. Gross, M.: Les phrases figées en français. L'Information Grammaticale **59**, 36–41 (1993)

5. Baptista, J.: Compositional vs. frozen sequences. J. Appl. Linguist. Special Issue on Lexicon-Grammar 81–92 (2004)

6. Baptista, J., Correia, A., Fernandes, G.: Frozen sentences of Portuguese: formal descriptions for NLP. In: Proceedings of the Workshop on Multiword Expressions: Integrating Processing, pp. 72–79. ACL, Barcelona (2004)

7. Alqahtni Hijab, M.: The structure and context of idiomatic expressions in the Saudi press. Ph.D. thesis. University of Leeds, Leeds (2014)

8. Boulaalam, A.: التعابير المسكوكة والترجمة : دراسة معجمية دلالية. Ph.D. thesis. Sidi Mohamed Ben Abdellah University, Fez (2017)

9. Minko-Mi-Nseme, S.A.: Modélisation des expressions figées en arabe en vue de la constitution d'une base de données lexicale. Thèse de doctorat. Université Lyon 2, Lyon (2003)

10. Ali, M.S.: La traduction des expressions figées: langue et culture. Traduire **235**, 103–123 (2016)

11. Abdelmaksoud, M.: Les expressions idiomatiques dans le Coran et leur traduction française: étude analytique contrastive de l'arabe vers le français dans trois interprétations françaises du sens du Coran. Thèse de doctorat. Mansoura University, Mansoura (2018)

12. Silberztein, M.: Complex annotations with NooJ. In: Blanco, X., Silberztein, M. (eds.) Proceedings of the 2007 International NooJ Conference, pp. 214–227. Cambridge Scholars Publishing, Cambridge (2008)

The Automatic Translation of Arabic Psychological Verbs Using the NooJ Platform

Asmaa Amzali[✉] and Mohammed Mourchid

Science Research Laboratory, Faculty of Science, Ibn Tofail University, Kenitra, Morocco
asmamzali@hotmail.fr, {asmaa.amzali,mohammed.mourchid}@uit.ac.ma

Abstract. In this paper, we are going to conduct a comprehensive study of the inflectional morphology of psychological verbs in both English and Arabic. The focus is also on clarifying the points of convergence and divergence between the inflectional systems of both languages. Moreover, we propose a methodology to develop an Arabic psychological verb translator. Then, we created an automatic translation system based on a carefully curated dictionary containing approximately 400 verb entries. Those entries were generated from our lexicon-grammar table of Arabic psychological verbs. Finally, we finish by testing the efficiency of this translator on texts and corpora.

Keywords: Natural Language Processing · NooJ · Arabic Psychological Verbs · Automatic Translation

1 Introduction

Nowadays, natural language processing (NLP) has emerged as a pivotal research area within data science. It is used in many applications that make our lives easier, such as question-answering systems, text classification, text extraction, sentiment analysis, machine translation, etc. Automatic translation is the process of translating text or speech from one language to another, revolutionizing global communication and breaking down language barriers. It has played a crucial role in various fields, such as business, education, travel, diplomacy, etc. It enables seamless communication across different cultures and nations. It allows us to bridge the gap between languages, facilitating understanding and collaboration. Also, it fosters collaboration in a multilingual world by enabling individuals and organizations to work together across languages, breaking down barriers and leveraging the collective intelligence of a multilingual world.

One language that presents unique challenges for NLP, especially in the realm of machine translation, is Arabic. As one of the world's most widely spoken languages, Arabic is characterized by its rich inflection, complex morphological and syntactical structures, setting it apart from more extensively studied languages like English. Consequently, the translation of Arabic psychological verbs becomes particularly challenging, mainly for these reasons:

a. The verbs have intricate inflection patterns based on the subject, tense, mood and aspect.

A. Bartulović et al. (Eds.): NooJ 2023, CCIS 1816, pp. 225–235, 2024.
https://doi.org/10.1007/978-3-031-56646-2_19

b. The inflections often lack the precise meaning in other languages, making the translation process more challenging (see Fig. 1).
c. The absence of equivalent psychological verbs in English further complicates the translation process.
d. Arabic and English have different linguistic features that make direct translations difficult.

Fig. 1. The translation of Google.

For this reason, this study embarks on a descriptive and systematic comparative analysis, focusing on the inflectional categories of psychological verbs. The objective of this work is to realize an automatic translation of Arabic psychological verbs using the NooJ platform.

This paper is structured in five sections. In Sect. 2, we provide the previous related works. In Sect. 3, an overview of the inflection of Arabic psychological verbs is presented. This section describes the inflectional morphology of psychological verbs in both English and Arabic. In Sect. 4, the methodology used to translate Arabic psychological verbs into English is explained. In Sect. 5, the implementation of the translation system using the NooJ platform is shown. Finally, we close our paper with a conclusion and some perspectives.

2 Related Works

Several studies have been conducted on automatic translation from Arabic to English using various tools. However, there is a lack of research specifically addressing the translation of Arabic psychological verbs. To bridge this gap, we will build upon existing theoretical studies to develop an automatic translation system for psychological verbs.

In a prior work by Medjdoub [1], the author describes the inflectional morphology of verbs in both English and Arabic, and conducts a comparative analysis of the two languages. The focus of this systematic descriptive-comparative study is on the inflectional categories of verbs. The study reveals that the inflectional morphology of Arabic verbs is more extensive and diverse than English verbs. The findings of this study have implications in various fields, such as foreign language teaching and learning, translation, electronic dictionaries, natural language processing, and more.

In [2], Almanna et al. undertook a project that focused on handling tense and aspect configurations in the English translation of Arabic sentences using neural machine translation (NMT) systems. Cheikhrouhou [3] developed a machine translation system for Arabic using the NooJ platform, which takes into account the temporal specificities of both Arabic and French languages. The system was developed based on a comparative study of the temporal systems in both languages and their corresponding tenses. Issa [4] created a machine translation from English to Arabic based on a transfer approach.

3 Overview of the Arabic Psychological Verb Inflection

Psychological verbs play an important role in language as they are used to express emotions, thoughts, perceptions and mental states, such as غَضِب [ghadiba] 'to blow up', أَحَبُّ [ahabba] 'to love', فَكَّر [fakkara] 'to think'. To do this, we will examine the inflectional morphology of psychological verbs in Arabic and English, two languages with different linguistic characteristics. The inflectional morphology of a verb refers to how it changes to convey diverse grammatical features such as tense, aspect, person and agreement. This analysis will shed light on the differences and similarities in how these languages deal with psychological verb inflection.

3.1 Arabic and English Psychological Verb Inflectional Morphology

The verb, as a grammatical category, occupies a crucial position within a sentence, serving as the syntactic and semantic core of the sentence. It provides a pragmatic anchor through morphological features. One of the main functions of a conjugated verb is to establish the temporal framework of action. Consequently, the verb conveys information about designated realities, which can be classified into three types: mood, tense and aspect [1].

In the case of Arabic psychological verbs, they exhibit inflection patterns that convey essential grammatical information. These include tense, aspect, mood, person, voice, transitivity and agreement.

Tense and Aspect. In Arabic, the inflection of psychological verbs for tense and aspect is a complex process. These verbs can convey a wide range of temporal and situational information through their different forms. For English, psychological verbs have a simple inflection system.

Arabic psychological verbs are inflected for different tenses, including past, present and future. Each tense indicates when an action will take place. For example,

- past tense: e.g., أَحَبُّ [ahabba] 'he loved'
- present tense: e.g., يُحِبُّ [yohibbog] 'he loves'
- future tense: e.g., سوف يُحِبُّ/سَيُحِبُّ [sawfa yohibbo/sayohibbo] 'he will love'.

In English, psychological verbs are inflected for tense, specifically past and present. For example, 'loved' is the past tense, and 'love' and 'loves' represent the present tense.

Arabic psychological verbs use aspects to express the nature of actions. There are two main aspects:

a. Perfect aspect refers to actions completed in the past. It is formed by adding specific suffixes to the base form of the verb, such as و-، -ا، -تن، -تما، -نا، -ت، etc. For example, أَحَبَّ [ahabba]'he loved'.

b. Imperfect aspect refers to ongoing or unfinished actions in the present. It is formed by adding both a prefix and a suffix to the verb. For instance, يُحبّانِ [yo-hibbani]'you love'.

Person and Gender. Arabic verbs are inflected according to the person of the subject. This means that the verb form changes depending on whether the subject is in the first, second or third person. For example, يُحبّ [yohibbo]'he loves' is for men, while تُحِبّينَ [tuhubbina]'you love' is for women.

Arabic verbs are sensitive to the gender and number of the subject. The verb form changes when referring to a masculine or feminine subject, and when the subject is singular or plural. For instance, يُحبّ [yohibbo]means 'he loves', and is used for the third person masculine singular pronoun, while تُحبّ [tuhibbo]means 'she loves', and is used for the third person feminine singular pronoun.

Also, the verbs are inflected for number depending on whether they express perfective or imperfective actions. Both a pronominal prefix and a pronominal suffix are used to mark imperfect verbs for numbers, e.g.,

- singular: يَعْشَق [yaa'chaqo]'he adores'
- dual: يَعْشَقَان [yaa'chaqani]'you adore'
- plural: يَعْشَقُونَ [yaa'chaqouna]'you adore'

Mood. In Arabic, the moods can be categorized as follows:

a. indicative (الخبري, elkhabarii)used to express factual statements or ask questions;

b. imperative (الأمر, elamr)used for commands and orders, marked by a pronominal suffix, e.g., اعْشَق [aa'chaq]'adore';

c. subjunctive (المنصوب, elmansoub)used to express wishes, desires or possibilities, marked by a vowel (فتحة, fetha)as in لتحبَّ [litohibba]'may you love';

d. jussive (المجزوم, elmadjzoum)used in a pausal form with sound verbs to express prohibitions or negative commands, as in إن يحزنْ [yahzan]'he should not grieve' or لم يعشقْ [lam yaa'chaq]'he should not adore'.

Voice. In Arabic, there are two voices: active and passive. The passive voice is indicated by a vowel change (mutation) in the verb, e.g.,

- active voice: عَشَقَ [a'chaqa]'he loved'
- passive voice: عُشِقَ [o'uchiqa]'he was loved'

In English, there are also two voices (active and passive). The passive voice is formed by using an auxiliary verb ('be' or 'get') and the past participle of the main verb. In the passive voice, the agent can be omitted. It is worth noting that not all verbs in English have passive forms, only transitive verbs with an appropriate lexical meaning.

Agreement. In Arabic, verbal phrases display agreement only in gender, e.g.,

- يحزن الأولاد على وفات صديقهم [yahzanu elawladu a'la wafati sadikihim]'The boys grieve over their friend's death.'
- تحزن الفتيات على وفات صديقهم [tahzanu elfatayatu a'la wafaati sadikihim]'The girls grieve over their friend's death.'

The verb يحزن [yahzanu]agrees with the masculine plural subject الأولاد [elawladu]'boys', while the verb تحزن [tahzanu]agrees with the feminine plural subject [elfatayatu] 'girls'.

3.2 Comparison Between the Arabic and English Psychological Verb Inflectional Systems

When considering the inflectional systems for psychological verbs, there are some similarities and differences between Arabic and English. In general, while both Arabic and English have inflectional forms for psychological verbs, Arabic is more complex and exhibits a wider range of inflectional patterns and changes.

Convergence. Verbs in both languages exhibit inflection in common categories: aspect, number, tense, voice and agreement. Verb inflectional morphology in Arabic and English displays syncretism, such as:

a. The suffix -ed is used with the simple past and past participle forms in English.
b. In Arabic, the imperfect second-person masculine singular (أنت تعشق, anta taa'chaqu)and third-person feminine singular (هي تعشق, hiya taa'cahqu)are represented by the same morphological form.

Divergence. Verbs are inflected differently in the two languages. In English, inflection involves the addition of a suffix -ed, such as 'crave – craved', or vowel and consonant changes. In Arabic, inflection involves both prefixation and suffixation.

The passive voice is indicated differently. In English, it is indicated by a free morpheme and the past participle form of the verb. In Arabic, it is indicated by diacritics.

Arabic follows a concatenative structure.

Transitivity is an inflectional category for Arabic verbs.

4   Methodology

To translate Arabic psychological verbs, we create a process of automatic translation using the NooJ platform [5]. By proposing an architecture of automatic translation systems, we have developed a translation module using NooJ that involves several steps. The first is the creation of the lexicon grammar tables and dictionaries, followed by the development of grammar for translation. Here is an overview of our methodology (see Fig. 2).

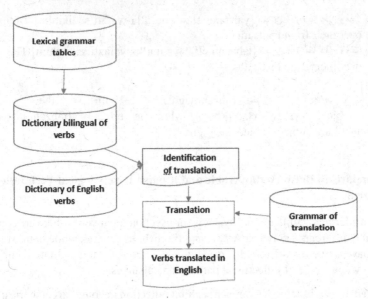

Fig. 2. Proposed architecture of automatic translation system.

In our previous work [6–8], we created the lexicon grammar table [9] for Arabic psychological verbs [10, 11]. In this paper, we have extended our tables by adding the translated English of each verb (see Fig. 3).

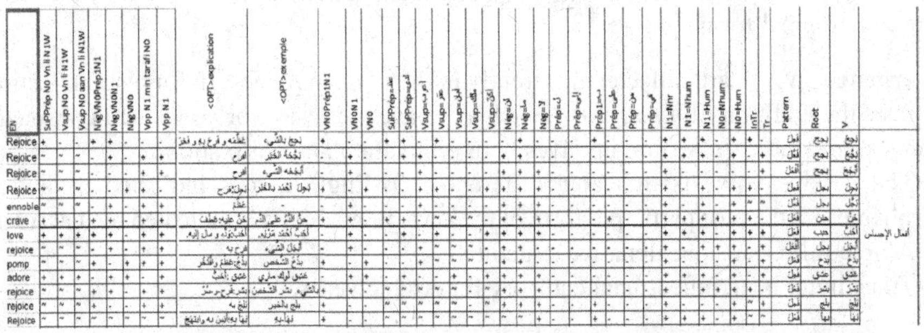

Fig. 3. Excerpt of our lexicon-grammar table of Arabic psychological verbs.

To implement this table in the NooJ platform, we generate its corresponding dictionary using an automatic program designed to create NooJ dictionaries from the lexicon-grammar tables developed in [9].

5   Implementation of the Translation System in the NooJ Platform

Our translation system enables us to translate Arabic psychological verbs into the English language while preserving the verb inflections. To achieve this, we use a bilingual dictionary of psychological verbs (see Fig. 4) and another dictionary of English psychological verbs (see Fig. 5), which includes their inflections with various personal pronouns and tenses. To facilitate this process, we employ the inflectional grammars "Verbe.nof" and "Sample.nof" developed by Silberztein.

```
# NooJ V5
# Dictionary
#
# Language is: ar
#
# Alphabetical order is not required.
#
# Use inflectional & derivational paradigms' description files (.nof), e.g.:
# Special Command: #use paradigms.nof
#
# Special Features: +NW (non-word) +FXC (frozen expression component) +UNAMB (unambiguous lexical entry)
#                   +FLX= (inflectional paradigm) +DRV= (derivational paradigm)
#
# Special Characters: '\' '"' ' ' ',' '+' '-' '#'
#use qualitatif.nof
#use ex2.nof
بهج,V+InTr+بهج+فعل+N0=Hum+N1=Hum+N1=Nhum+Prép1=ب+Vsup=عبر+SupPrep=لدى+SupPrep=عند+Neg=ما+VN0Prép1N1+VppPrép1N1+FLX=V_jaraha+DRV=D_faâala:FLXDRV+EN="rejoice"
بهج,V+بهج+فعّل+N0=Hum+N1=Hum+N1=Nhum+VN0N1+VppN1MinTarafiN0+NégVN0Prép1N1+SuPPrépN0VnliN1W+Neg=ما+Neg=لن+SupPrep=لدى+Vsup=أعرب+FLX=V_darrasa+DRV=D_faââala:FLXDR+EN="rejoice"
حن,V+InTr+فعل+حنن+N0=Hum+N0=Nhum+N1=Hum+N1=Nhum+Prép1=على+VN0N1+VN0Prép1N1+Vsup=عبر+SupPrep=لدى+FLX=V_habba+DRV=D_habba:FLXDRV+EN="crave"
حن,V+InTr+فعل+حنن+N0=Hum+N1=Hum+N1=Nhum+Prép1=إلى+VN0+VN0Prép1N1+Vsup=عبر+SupPrep=لدى+Vsup=عبر+SupPrep=عند+SupPrep=لدى+Neg=لا+Neg=ما+Neg=لن+FLX=V_habba+DRV=D_habba:FLXDRV+EN="crave"
حن,V+InTr+فعل+حنن+N0=Hum+N1=Hum+N1=Nhum+Prép1=ل+VN0+VN0Prép1N1+Vsup=عبر+SupPrep=لدى+Vsup=عبر+SupPrep=عند+SupPrep=لدى+Neg=لا+Neg=ما+Neg=لن+FLX=V_habba+DRV=D_habba:FLXDRV+EN="crave"
أحب,V+InTr+Tr+أفعل+حبب+N0=Hum+N1=Hum+N1=Nhum+VN0N1+VN0Prep1N1+VppN1+VppN1MinTarafiN0+SuPPrepN0VnliN1W+VsupN0VnliN1W+VsupN0aanVnliN1W+Vsup=عبر+SupPrep=عند+Vsup=أكن+SupPrep=لدى+Neg=لا+Neg=ما+Neg=لن+FLX=V_ahabba+DRV=D_
عشق,V+Tr+فعل+عشق+N0=Hum+N1=Hum+N1=Nhum+VN0N1+VppN1+VppN1MinTarafiN0+NegVN0N1+SuPPrepN0VnliN1W+VsupN0VnliN1W+VsupN0aanVnliN1W+SupPrep=لدى+Neg=لا+Neg=ما+Neg=لن+Vsup=أبان+FLX=V_jaraha+DRV=D_achiqua:FLXDR+EN="adore"
```

Fig. 4. Excerpt of bilingual dictionary of Arabic-English psychological verbs.

```
Dictionary contains 258 entries

# NooJ V5
# Dictionary
#
# Language is: en
#
# Alphabetical order is not required.
#
# Use inflectional & derivational paradigms' description files (.nof), e.g.:
# Special Command: #use paradigms.nof
#
# Special Features: +NW (non-word) +FXC (frozen expression component) +UNAMB (unambig
#                   +FLX= (inflectional paradigm) +DRV= (derivational paradigm)
#
# Special Characters: '\' '"' ' ' ',' '+' '-' '#'
#

#use _Verbs.nof
#use _Sample.nof

rejoice,V+FLX=LIVE
crave,V+FLX=LIVE
love,V+FLX=LIVE
adore,V+FLX=LIVE
ennoble,V+FLX=LIVE
```

Fig. 5. Excerpt from the dictionary of English psychological verbs.

Then, in this phase, we developed a syntactic grammar capable of analyzing transitive sentences containing Arabic psychological verbs. Figures 6, 7 and 8 present the grammar based on the transitive verb of the complex sentences containing the Arabic psychological verb. Our grammar not only analyzes but also annotates the components of the input sentence, resulting in the generation of an annotated parse tree.

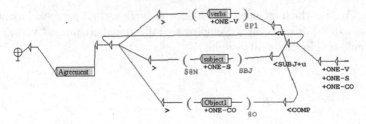

Fig. 6. Excerpt of the syntactic grammar.

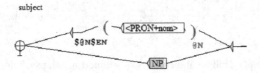

Fig. 7. Subject main structure.

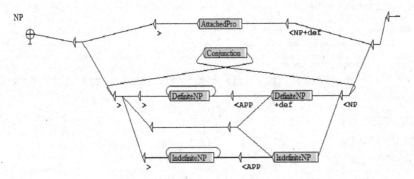

Fig. 8. Subgrammar of noun phrase.

In Fig. 9, we have the main translation, consisting of a total of 4 graphs. This grammar incorporates subgraphs that translate Arabic psychological verbs into English by conjugating them in the appropriate tense.

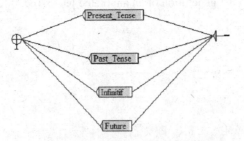

Fig. 9. Excerpt of the grammar of the translation

Figure 10 shows the "Present Tense" graph. This graph presents various pathways that signify the outcomes of verb translation. Within this graph, we carefully consider the information related to the inflection of Arabic psychological verbs. Additionally, we incorporate subject number and gender agreement to provide accurate verb translations (see Fig. 11).

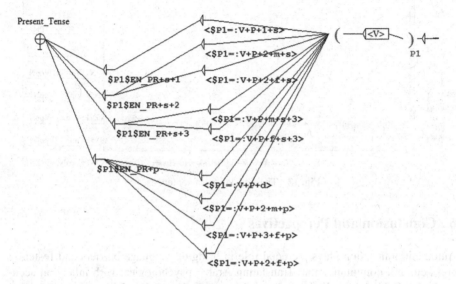

Fig. 10. Subgraph of a subject.

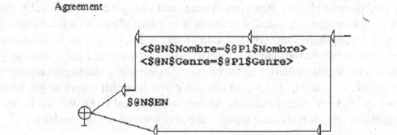

Fig. 11. Graph of agreement.

The application of these grammars in sentences where the verb is conjugated in the simple present or past tense provided the following results (see Fig. 12).

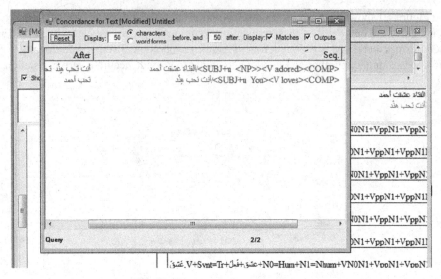

Fig. 12. The translation of sentences.

6 Conclusion and Perspectives

Automatic translation plays a crucial role in bridging language barriers and fostering cross-cultural communication. Translating Arabic psychological verb inflection accurately into English is challenging due to the complexity of verb inflection and structural differences.

In this paper, we studied Arabic psychological verb inflection in both languages, and then compared them to identify their convergences and divergences. Additionally, this study enabled us to create our translation grammar in NooJ based on a bilingual dictionary of Arabic-English psychological verbs and a dictionary of English psychological verbs. Furthermore, our automatic translation enables us to find encouraging results when verbs are translated into English, adhering to the rules of conjugation in the target language.

As perspectives, we aim to develop an automatic translator that covers all grammatical structures within sentences containing Arabic psychological verbs. We also hope to identify additional resources that can enhance the performance of our translator.

Acknowledgement. This work has been funded by the European Commission ICT COST Action Multi-task, Multilingual, Multi-modal Language Generation (CA18231).

References

1. Medjedoub, R.: Verb inflection in English and Arabic: a contrastive analysis study. Milev J. Res. Stud. **8**(1), 414–422 (2022)
2. Almanna, A., Jamoussi, R.: NMT verb rendering: a cognitive approach to informing Arabic-into-English post-editing. Open Linguist. **8**(1), 310–327 (2022)

3. Cheikhrouhou, H.: The automatic translation of French verbal tenses to Arabic using the platform NooJ. In: Mbarki, S., Mourchid, M., Silberztein, M. (eds.) NooJ 2017. CCIS, vol. 811, pp. 156–167. Springer, Cham (2018). https://doi.org/10.1007/978-3-319-73420-0_13

4. Issa, E.S.A.: English-Arabic machine translation: a transfer approach. Ph.D. thesis. Faculty of Arts, Alexandria University, Alexandria (2016)

5. Silberztein, M.: La formalisation des langues: l'approche de NooJ. ISTE Editions, London (2015)

6. Amzali, A., Kourtin, A., Mourchid, M., Mouloudi, A., Mbarki, S.: Syntactic analysis of sentences containing Arabic psychological verbs. In: Bigey, M., Richeton, A., Silberztein, M., Thomas, I. (eds.) NooJ 2021. CCIS, vol. 1520, pp. 51–61. Springer, Cham (2021). https://doi.org/10.1007/978-3-030-92861-2_5

7. Amzali, A., Kourtin, A., Mourchid, M., Mouloudi, A., Mbarki, S.: Lexicon-grammar tables development for Arabic psychological verbs. In: Fehri, H., Mesfar, S., Silberztein, M. (eds.) NooJ 2019. CCIS, vol. 1153, pp. 15–26. Springer, Cham (2020). https://doi.org/10.1007/978-3-030-38833-1_2

8. Amzali, A., Mourchid, M., Mouloudi, A., Mbarki, S.: Arabic psychological verb recognition through NooJ transformational grammars. In: Bekavac, B., Kocijan, K., Silberztein, M., Šojat, K. (eds.) NooJ 2020. CCIS, vol. 1389, pp. 74–84. Springer, Cham (2021). https://doi.org/10.1007/978-3-030-70629-6_7

9. Kourtin, A., Amzali, A., Mourchid, M., Mouloudi, A., Mbarki, S.: The automatic generation of NooJ dictionaries from lexicon-grammar tables. In: Fehri, H., Mesfar, S., Silberztein, M. (eds.) NooJ 2019. CCIS, vol. 1153, pp. 65–76. Springer, Cham (2020). https://doi.org/10.1007/978-3-030-38833-1_6

10. Tolone, E.: Analyse syntaxique à l'aide des tables du Lexique-Grammaire du français. Thèse de doctorat. Université Paris-Est, Paris (2011)

11. El Hannach, M.: Syntaxe des verbes psychologiques en arabe. Thèse de doctorat. Université Paris 7, Paris (1999)

Author Index

A. Bartulović et al. (Eds.): NooJ 2023, CCIS 1816, p. 237, 2024.
https://doi.org/10.1007/978-3-031-56646-2

Printed in the United States
by Baker & Taylor Publisher Services